Houghton Mifflin
Math

 HOUGHTON MIFFLIN BOSTON

Houghton Mifflin Math

Program Authors & Consultants

Authors

Dr. Carole Greenes
Professor of Mathematics Education

Boston University
Boston, MA

Dr. Matt Larson
Curriculum Specialist for Mathematics

Lincoln Public Schools
Lincoln, NE

Dr. Miriam A. Leiva
Distinguished Professor of Mathematics Emerita

University of
North Carolina
Charlotte, NC

Dr. Jean M. Shaw
Professor Emerita of Curriculum and Instruction

University of Mississippi
Oxford, MS

Dr. Lee Stiff
Professor of Mathematics Education

North Carolina State University
Raleigh, NC

Dr. Bruce R. Vogeli
Clifford Brewster Upton
Professor of Mathematics

Teachers College, Columbia University
New York, NY

Dr. Karol Yeatts
Associate Professor

Barry University
Miami, FL

Consultants

Strategic Consultant
Dr. Liping Ma
Senior Scholar

Carnegie Foundation for the Advancement of Technology
Palo Alto, CA

Language and Vocabulary Consultant
Dr. David Chard
Professor of Reading

University of Oregon
Eugene, OR

Reviewers

Grade K

Hilda Kendrick
W E Wilson
Elementary School
Jefferson, IN

Debby Nagel
Assumption
Elementary School
Cincinnati, OH

Jen Payet
Lake Ave. Elementary School
Saratoga Springs, NY

Karen Sue Hinton
Washington Elementary School
Ponca City, OK

Grade 1

Karen Wood
Clay Elementary School
Clay, AL

Paula Rowland
Bixby North Elementary School
Bixby, OK

Stephanie McDaniel
B. Everett Jordan
Elementary School
Graham, NC

Juan Melgar
Lowrie Elementary School
Elgin, IL

Sharon O'Brien
Echo Mountain School
Phoenix, AZ

Grade 2

Sally Bales
Akron Elementary School
Akron, IN

Rose Marie Bruno
Mawbey Street Elementary
School
Woodbridge, NJ

Kiesha Doster
Berry Elementary School
Detroit, MI

Marci Galazkiewicz
North Elementary School
Waukegan, IL

Ana Gaspar
Lowrie Elementary School
Elgin, IL

Elana Heinoren
Beechfield Elementary School
Baltimore, MD

Kim Terry
Woodland Elementary School
West
Gages Lake, IL

Megan Burton
Valley Elementary School
Pelham, AL

Kristy Ford
Eisenhower Elementary School
Norman, OK

Grade 3

Jenny Chang
North Elementary School
Waukegan, IL

Patricia Heintz
Harry T. Stewart
Elementary School
Corona, NY

Shannon Hopper
White Lick Elementary School
Brownsburg, IN

Allison White
Kingsley Elementary School
Naperville, IL

Amy Simpson
Broadmoore Elementary School
Moore, OK

iii

Reviewers

Grade 4

Barbara O'Hanlon
Maurice & Everett Haines
Elementary School
Medford, NJ

Connie Rapp
Oakland Elementary School
Bloomington, IL

Pam Rettig
Solheim Elementary School
Bismarck, ND

Tracy Smith
Blanche Kelso Bruce Academy
Detroit, MI

Brenda Hancock
Clay Elementary School
Clay, AL

Karen Scroggins
Rock Quarry Elementary School
Tuscaloosa, AL

Lynn Fox
Kendall-Whittier Elementary
School
Tulsa, OK

Grade 5

Jim Archer
Maplewood Elementary School
Indianapolis, IN

Maggie Dunning
Horizon Elementary School
Hanover Park, IL

Mike Intoccia
McNichols Plaza
Scranton, PA

Jennifer LaBelle
Washington Elementary School
Waukegan, IL

Anne McDonald
St. Luke The Evangelist School
Glenside, PA

Ellen O'Rourke
Bower Elementary School
Warrenville, IL

Gary Smith
Thomas H. Ford Elementary
School
Reading, PA

Linda Carlson
Van Buren Elementary School
Oklahoma City, OK

Grade 6

Robin Akers
Sonoran Sky Elementary School
Scottsdale, AZ

Ellen Greenman
Daniel Webster Middle School
Waukegan, IL

Angela McCray
Abbott Middle School
West Bloomfield, MI

Mary Popovich
Horizon Elementary School
Hanover Park, IL

Debbie Taylor
Sonoran Sky Elementary School
Scottsdale, AZ

Across Grades

Jacqueline Lampley
Hewitt Elementary School
Trussville, AL

Rose Smith
Five Points Elementary School
Orrville, AL

Winnie Tepper
Morgan County Schools
Decatur, AL

Classification, Positions, and Patterns

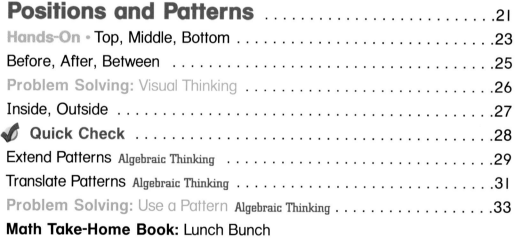

FINISHING THE UNIT

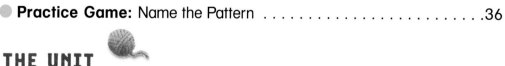

Algebraic Thinking Indicates lessons that include algebra instruction. ● Indicates WEEKLY WR READER® Connection

Getting Started With Numbers

STARTING THE UNIT

FINISHING THE UNIT

Algebraic Thinking Indicates lessons that include algebra instruction.

Geometry, Fractions, and Probability

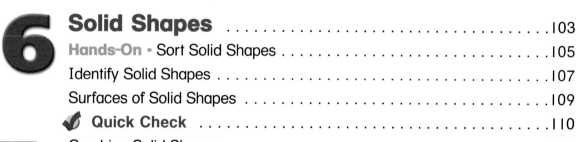

● Indicates **WEEKLY WR READER® Connection**

Numbers Through 12

STARTING THE UNIT

Algebraic Thinking Indicates lessons that include algebra instruction.

Time and Money

STARTING THE UNIT

FINISHING THE UNIT

● Indicates WEEKLY WR READER® Connection

UNIT 5 Time and Money

Measurement

STARTING THE UNIT

Algebraic Thinking Indicates lessons that include algebra instruction.

UNIT 6 Measurement

Addition and Subtraction

STARTING THE UNIT

13 Addition

14 Subtraction

FINISHING THE UNIT

● Indicates **WEEKLY WR READER® Connection**

Greater Numbers

STARTING THE UNIT

FINISHING THE UNIT

BOOK RESOURCES

Algebraic Thinking Indicates lessons that include algebra instruction.   ● Indicates WEEKLY WR READER® Connection

UNIT 8 Greater Numbers

HOUGHTON MIFFLIN MATH

UNIT I

Classification, Positions, and Patterns

From the Read-Aloud Anthology

FIVE CREATURES

by
Emily Jenkins
illustrated by
Tomek Bogacki

Access Prior Knowledge
This story will help you review
• Sorting

MATH at Home

Dear Family,

We are starting a new unit called Classification, Positions, and Patterns. In Chapter 1, we will sort and classify objects by color, size, shape, and kind. In Chapter 2, we will learn words to describe positions and work with patterns.

Love, _____

Vocabulary

sort
To group objects together that are alike in some way.

position words
Words for locations such as top, bottom, up, down, inside, and outside.

inside   **outside**

pattern
Objects or numbers that repeat or grow according to a rule.

A B A B A B

A B C A B C A B C

growing pattern

Vocabulary Activities

- Help your child sort household items such as socks or silverware. Have him or her tell the sorting rule.

- Use position words when playing "I Spy." (I spy something on the middle shelf. It is red. What is it?)

- Let your child make and describe patterns with items such as coins. (penny, penny, dime is an AAB pattern)

Visit *Education Place* at
eduplace.com/parents/mw/
for *e* • WordGame,
e • Glossary **and more.**

Literature to Read Together

- **Gray Rabbit's Odd One Out**
by Alan Baker
(Kingfisher, 1995)

- **More or Less a Mess**
by Sheila Keenan
(Scholastic, 1997)

- **Patterns: What Comes Next?**
by Michele Koomen
(Bridgestone, 2001)

Sorting

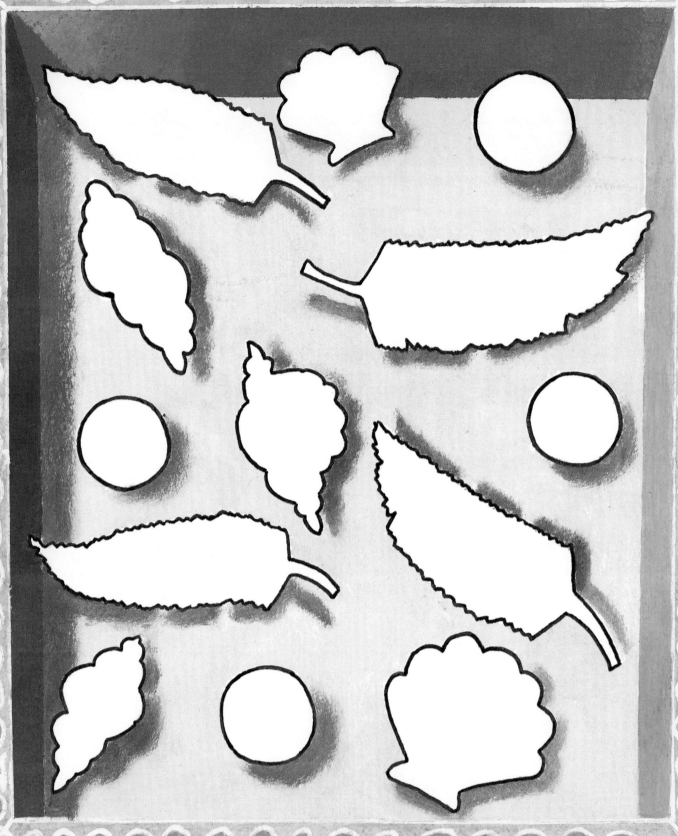

Directions Color the feathers red. Color the shells yellow. Color the marbles blue.

Directions 1–4 Circle the buttons that are alike. Cross out the one that is different.

Directions 1–4 Circle the buttons that are alike.
Cross out the one that is different.

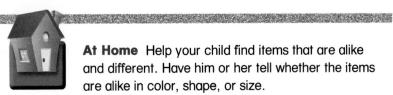

At Home Help your child find items that are alike
and different. Have him or her tell whether the items
are alike in color, shape, or size.

6

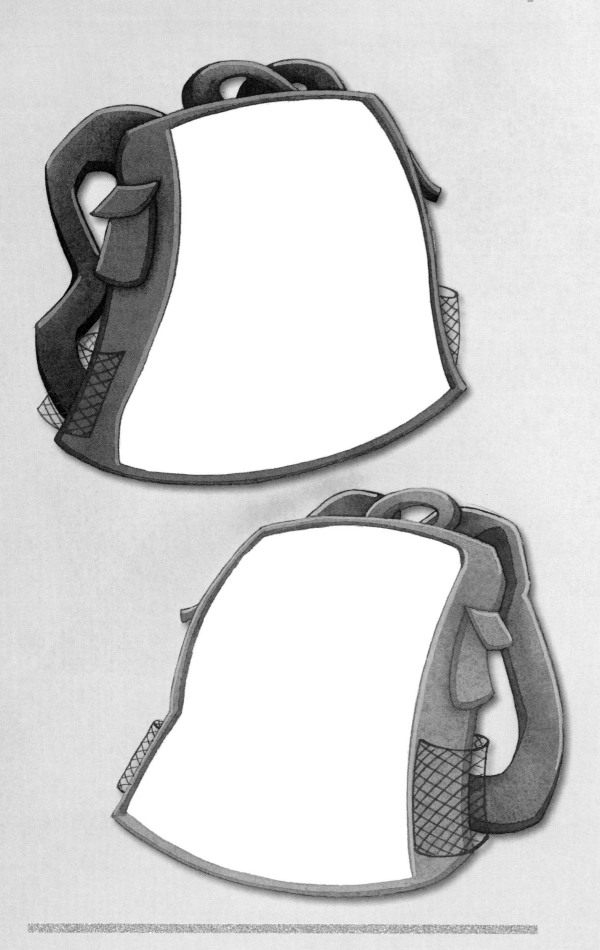

Directions Cut out the pictures. Sort them by color. Glue each picture on the backpack that is the same color.

Chapter 1

7

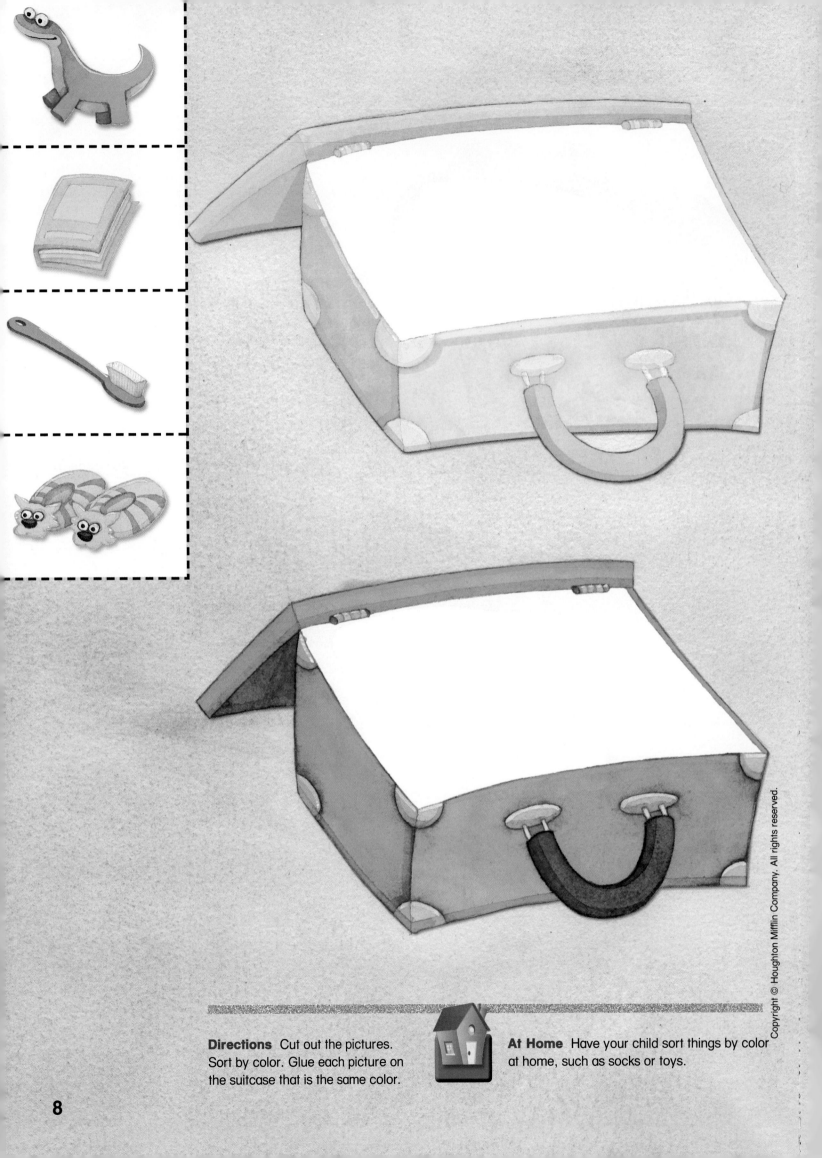

Directions Cut out the pictures. Sort by color. Glue each picture on the suitcase that is the same color.

At Home Have your child sort things by color at home, such as socks or toys.

8

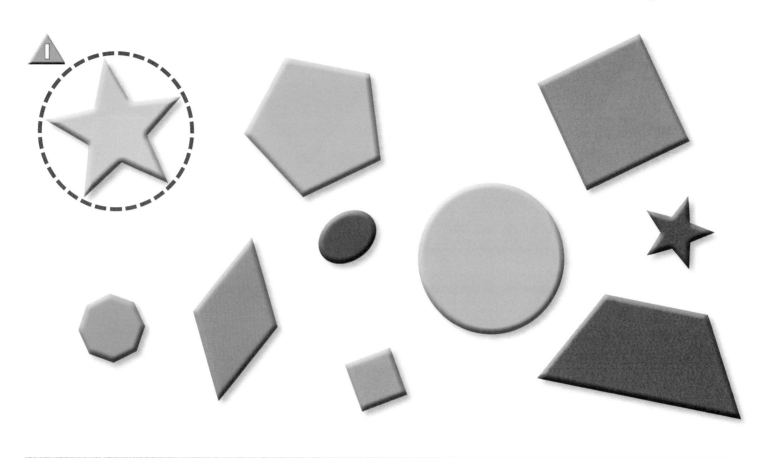

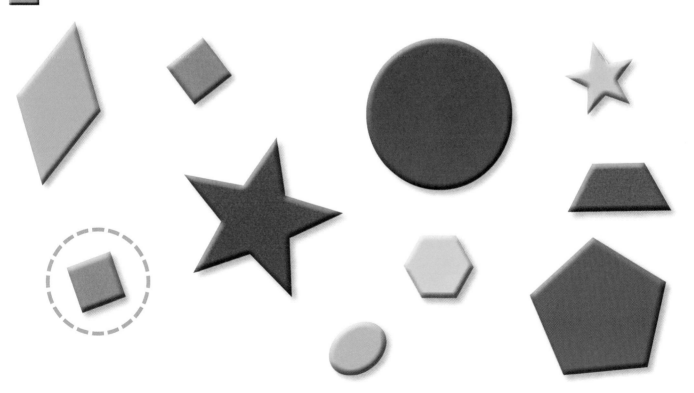

Directions | Circle the big shapes red. 2 Circle the small shapes blue.

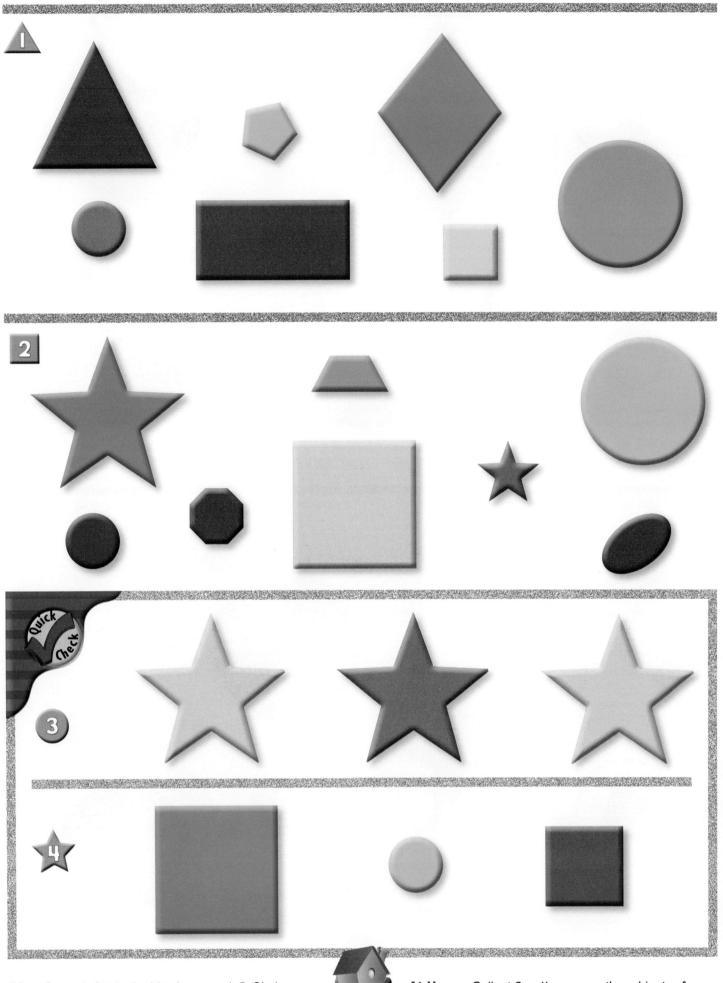

Directions 1 Circle the big shapes red. 2 Circle the small shapes blue. 3 Cross out the one that is different. 4 Circle the ones that are alike.

At Home Collect 3 or 4 cans or other objects of two different sizes. Mix them up. Have your child sort them by size and explain how he or she sorted.

Sort by Shape

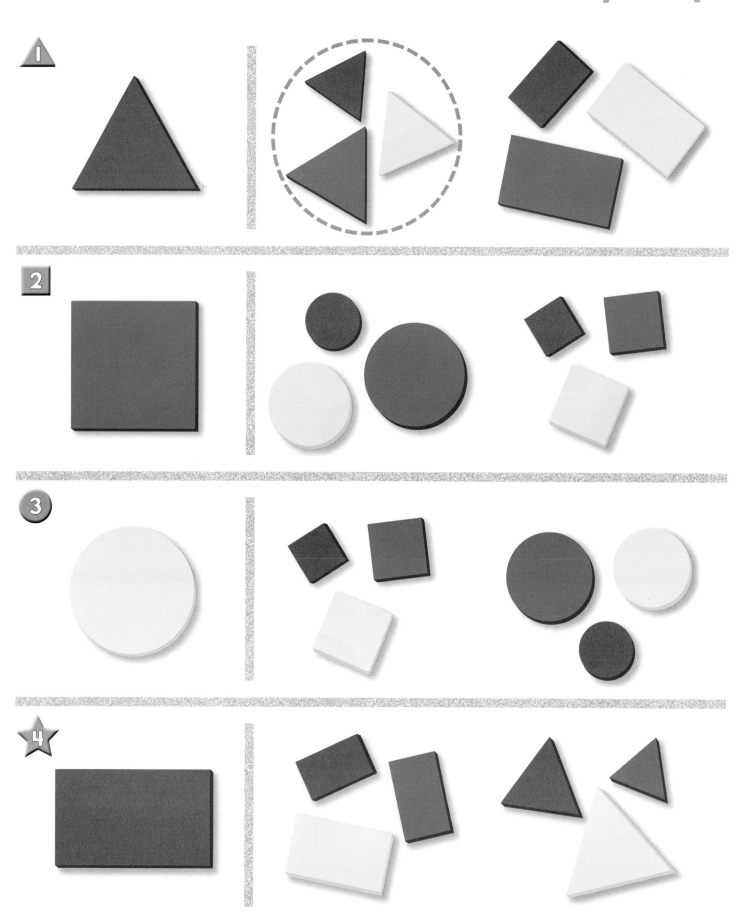

Directions 1–4 Circle the group where the shape belongs.

1

2

Problem Solving ▶ Visual Thinking

3

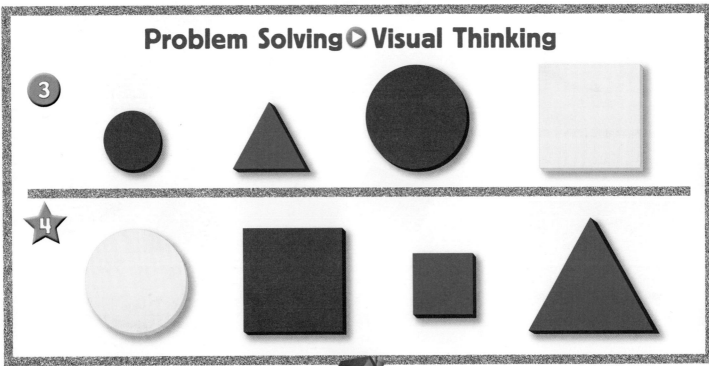

4

Directions 1–2 Circle the group where the shape belongs. 3 Circle the small red shape. 4 Circle the big blue shape.

At Home Collect 3 or 4 circular objects and 3 or 4 rectangular objects. Mix them up and have your child sort them by shape.

1

2

Directions 1 Circle the things that a person can wear. 2 Cross out the things that a person can eat.

Directions I Circle the things that a person can wear on the hands. 2 Cross out the things that a person can draw with.

At Home Give your child several grocery items such as cans, boxes, and bottles to sort by kind.

14

Directions Cut out the pictures. Sort and glue them into two groups. Explain your sorting rule.

Chapter I

15

PET SHOP

Directions Cut out the pictures. Sort and glue them into two groups. Explain your sorting rule.

At Home Give your child 4 or 5 toys to sort into two groups. Have your child explain his or her sorting rule.

16

Name _____

1

2

3

4

Directions Cross out the item that does not belong in a group of: 1 round things; 2 green things; 3 crayons; 4 small things. Explain your reasoning.

1

2

3

4

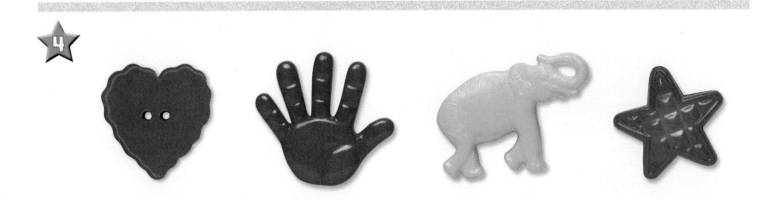

Directions Cross out the item that does not belong in a group of: 1 blocks; 2 thick brushes; 3 big things; 4 blue things. Explain your reasoning.

At Home Gather objects such as 3 spoons and 1 fork, or 3 crackers and 1 slice of bread. Have your child sort the objects by size, shape, or color.

18

Show and Tell

This take-home book will help you review concepts you learned in Chapter 1.

Color the caps to match each group.

Which shells are alike?

2

Where does this animal belong?

4

Where does my bead belong?

How can you sort these objects?
Tell your rule.

How are these objects alike?

6

Which one does not belong in my collection?
Tell why.

8

Name _____

1.

2.

3.

4.

5.

Directions 1–4 Circle the group where the object belongs and tell why. 5 Cross out the one that does not belong and tell why.

PET DAY TODAY

Directions Sort the animals. Use a different color to circle each group. Name each group.

Positions and Patterns

Directions Cover the pictured blocks with cubes. Tell about the positions of the cubes. Place one more cube in the picture. Draw it and tell where it is.

22

Top, Middle, Bottom

Directions Place a yellow cube in the top box, a blue cube in the bottom box, and a red cube in the middle box. Color the boxes to match the colors of the cubes.

Directions Place a red cube on the bottom shelf, a green cube on the top shelf, and a blue cube on the middle shelf. Draw and color the cubes.

At Home Help your child use the words *top*, *middle*, and *bottom* to describe positions of objects around your home.

Name _____

1

2

3

4

Directions 1 Circle the animal that is before the one in red. 2 Circle the animal that is after the dog in red. 3 Circle the animal between the ones in red. 4 Circle the animal that is before the bird in red.

1

2

Problem Solving ▶ Visual Thinking

3

4

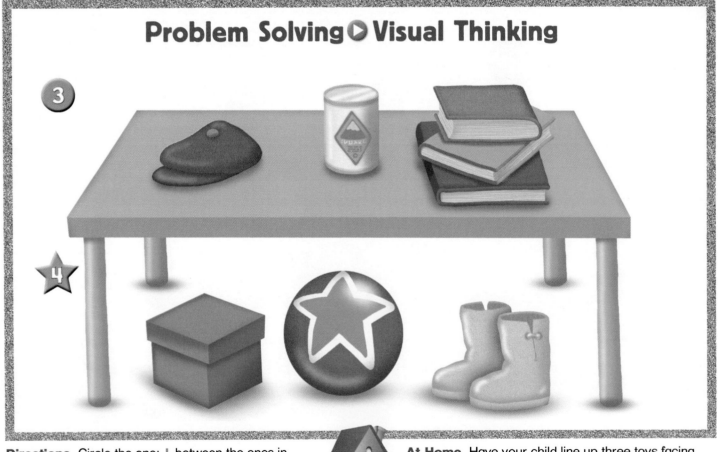

Directions Circle the one: **1** between the ones in green; **2** after the one in green; **3** on top of the table and between the hat and the books; **4** under the table and next to the box.

At Home Have your child line up three toys facing left. Have your child tell which toy comes before, after, and between the others.

26

Directions 1 Draw something red inside the bowl. Draw something blue outside the bowl.
2 Draw something orange inside the box. Draw something green outside the box.

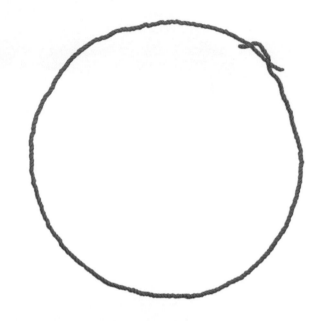

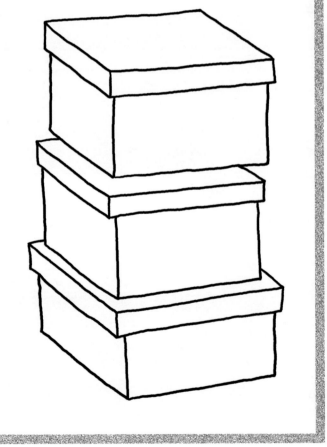

Directions 1 Draw a ball inside the circle. 2 Draw an X outside the circle. 3 Circle the child before the one in yellow. 4 Color the box that is on top.

At Home Have your child name items that are inside and outside drawers, cabinets, and other containers in your home.

Name _____

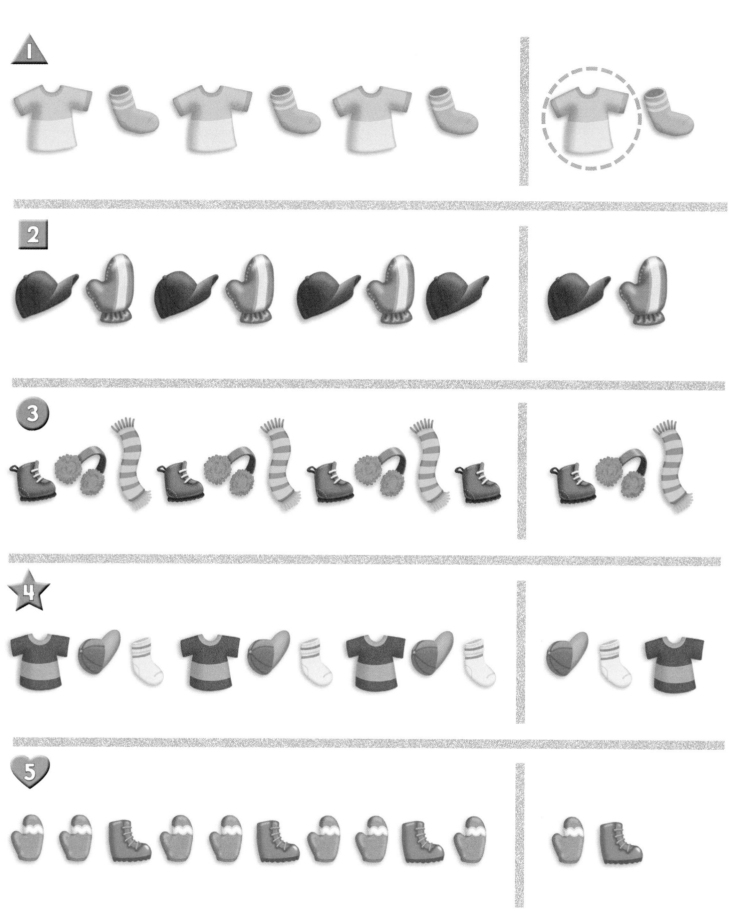

1

2

3

4

5

Directions 1–5 Circle the item that is likely to come next in the pattern.

Directions 1–5 Circle the item that is likely to come next in the pattern.

At Home Let your child use household items to make and extend a pattern, such as knife, fork, knife, fork, knife, fork.

30

Name _____

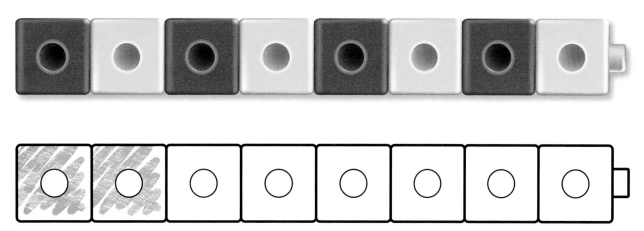

2

3

Directions 1–3 Find the pattern. Show the same pattern using different colors.

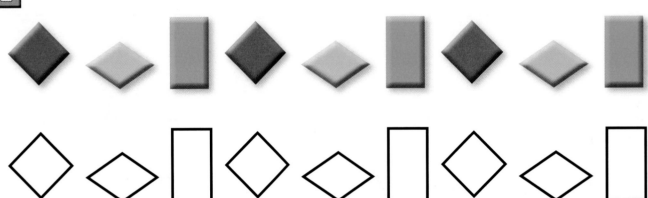

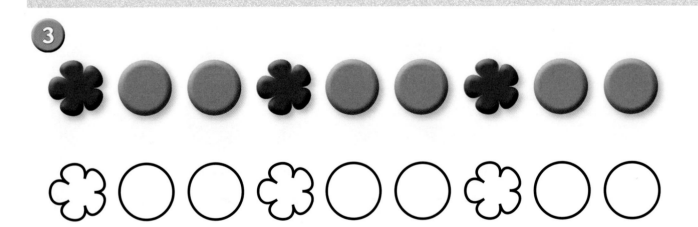

Directions 1–3 Find the pattern. Show the same pattern using different colors.

At Home Have your child tell how each pair of patterns shown above are alike and how they are different.

Use a Pattern

Directions Use pattern blocks to continue the pattern. Draw and color the blocks you used.

Directions Use pattern blocks to continue the pattern. Draw and color the blocks you used.

At Home Have your child explain how each pattern in this lesson grows.

LUNCH BUNCH

This take-home book will help you review concepts you learned in Chapter 2.

1

Which lunch box is before the blue one?

Which lunch box is in the middle?

2

What is inside the lunch box?

4

Color the grapes that are likely to come next.

Show the same pattern using different colors.

Draw the cracker that is likely to come next.

6

Tell how this pattern grows.

8

Name _____

Chapter Review/Test

 1

2

 3

 4

 |

 5

 |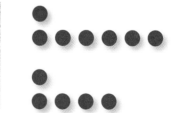

6
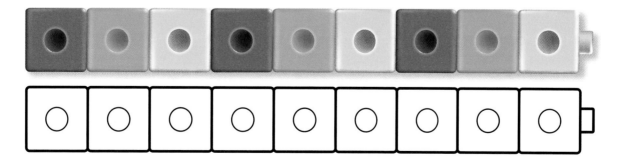

Directions Circle: **1** the bottom book; **2** the shoe outside the box; **3** the duck after the one in blue; **4** the sock that is likely to come next; **5** the dots that are likely to come next. **6** Show the same pattern using different colors.

Chapter 2

35

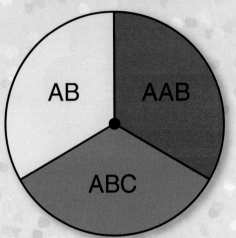

NAME THE PATTERN

What You Need

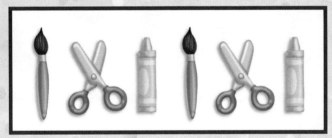

How to Play | Take turns with a partner. **2** Spin the spinner. Place a counter on a space that shows that pattern. **3** Play until all the spaces are covered.

36

Name _____

Unit 1 Test

1

2

3

4

5

Directions Circle the objects that are the same: 1 color; 2 size; 3 shape; 4 kind. 5 Cross out the one that does not belong in a group of things to draw with.

Directions 6 Circle the button in the middle. 7 Circle the animal between the ones in red.
8–9 Draw what is likely to come next. 10 Show the same pattern using different colors.

38

Sort by Two Attributes

Directions Place attribute blocks in the chart where they belong.
Draw and color.

Unit 1

Name _____

Cumulative Review

1

2

3

4

5

Directions Circle: **1** the big shapes; **2** the group where the shape belongs; **3** the boy that is before the girl in green; **4–5** the shape that is likely to come next in the pattern.

Photography Credits: 5–6 © Ken Karp. 17–19 © Ken Karp. 38© Ken Karp. **Illustration Credits:** 2 © Don Stuart. 3–4 © Richard Garland. 7–8 © Peter Grosshauser. 13–14 © Peter Grosshauser. 15–16 © Richard Garland. 19(bml) © Peter Grosshauser. 19(bmr) © Nathan Jarvis. 19(b) © Peter Grosshauser. 20 © Richard Garland. Chapter 1 Story © Richard Garland. 21–22 © Nathan Jarvis. 23–24 © Don Stuart. 25–30 © Nathan Jarvis. 33–34 © Don Stuart. 35–36 © Nathan Jarvis. 37 © Don Stuart. 38 © Nathan Jarvis. 39 © Don Stuart. 40 © Nathan Jarvis. Chapter 2 Story © Don Stuart.

Getting Started
With Numbers

From the Read-Aloud Anthology

A TREE for ME

by Nancy Van Laan

illustrated by
Sheila White Samton

Access Prior Knowledge
This story will help you review
- Counting to 5

ISBN: 0-618-33872-1   Printed in the U.S.A.

MATH at Home

Dear Family,

We are starting a new unit called Getting Started With Numbers.
In Chapter 3, we will compare sets of objects,
and make simple graphs. In Chapter 4 we will
count, read, and write numbers 0 through 5.

Love, _____

Vocabulary

match one to one
A way to compare the
number of objects in
two groups.

graph
Groups of sorted
objects arranged in
rows or columns
to make them
easier to compare.

Sorting Animals

ordinal numbers
Numbers used to indicate position or order.

first **second** **third** **fourth** **fifth**

Vocabulary Activities

• Help your child match sets of objects
  one to one (plates and napkins).

• Give your child a small number of
  objects, such as cans and boxes, to
  arrange to make a simple graph.

• Practice using ordinal numbers
  during daily activities. (We are third in
  line at the store.)

Visit *Education Place* **at**
eduplace.com/parents/mw/
for *e* • WordGame,
e • Glossary **and more.**

Literature to Read Together
• ***Dear Daisy, Get Well Soon***
by Maggie Smith
(Crown Publishers, 2000)

• ***Rooster's Off to See the
  World***
by Eric Carle
(Simon & Schuster, 1972)

• ***More, Fewer, Less***
by Tana Hoban *(Greenwillow, 1998)*

Comparing Sets, Data, and Graphing

Directions Place a different color cube on each different kind of item. Move the cubes to the boxes above. Talk about what you find.

44

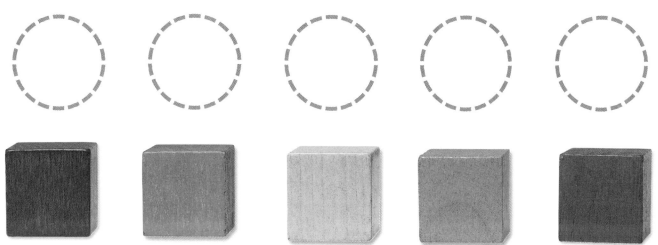

2

3

Directions 1–3 Use counters to show the same number of blocks. Draw the counters.

Directions 1–5 Use counters to show the same number of items. Draw the counters.

At Home Display 1 to 5 items. Have your child make another set with the same number.

46

1

2

3

Directions 1–3 Count the number of items in each set. Circle the set that has more.

Problem Solving ▶ Number Sense

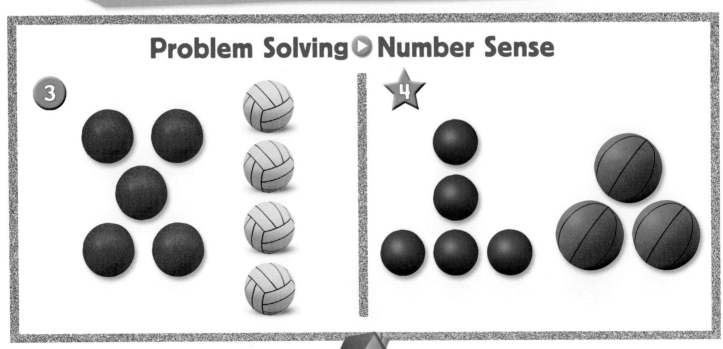

Directions 1–4 Circle the set that has more.

At Home Help your child compare groups of 1 to 5 items, using a different number in each group. Have your child tell you which group has more.

48

1

2

3

Directions 1–3 Match items one to one. Circle the set that has fewer.

Directions 1–2 Match items one to one. Circle the set that has fewer. **3** Draw circles to show the same number. **4** Circle the set with more.

At Home Show your child two groups of dishes, such as four cups and two plates. Have your child tell which group has fewer.

50

Colors of My Blocks

Directions Sort your blocks by color. Place them in the graph. Draw and color the blocks.
Tell about your graph.

Shapes in the Train

Directions Draw and color shapes in the graph for each shape in the train. Tell about your graph.

At Home Place 3 spoons and 4 forks in a pile. Have your child sort and arrange them in 2 rows and draw them to make a pictograph.

52

Which do you like more?

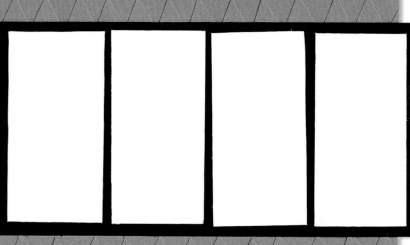

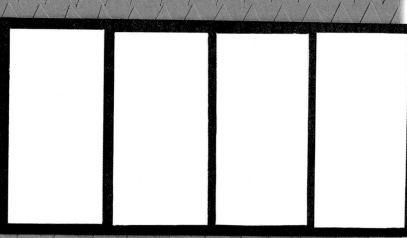

Directions Ask four classmates which of these playgrounds they like more. Color a box for each response. Tell about your graph.

Which do you like the most?

Directions Ask four classmates which playground activity they like the most. Color a box for each response. Tell about your graph.

At Home Have your child explain the graph question and results. Ask your child to tell you what was chosen the most and the fewest.

54

What's in Ben's Sandbox?

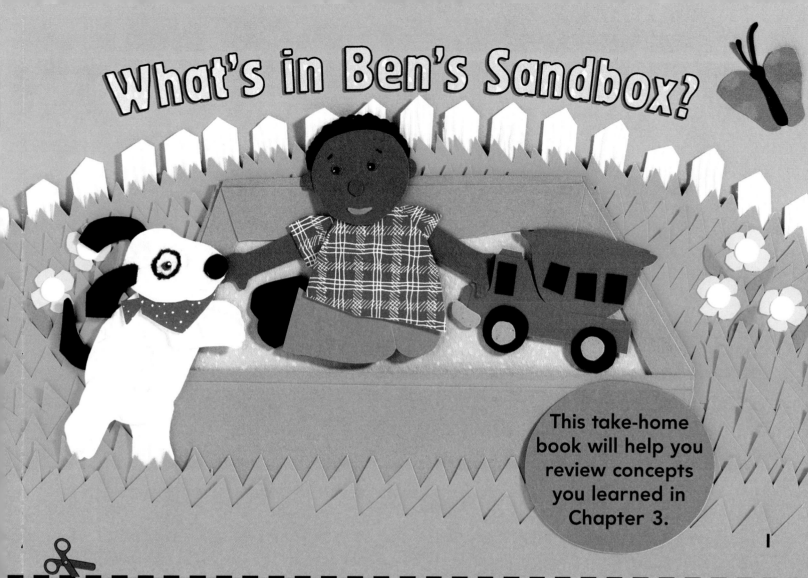

This take-home book will help you review concepts you learned in Chapter 3.

1

Draw a pail for each child.

Draw lines to match one toy to each friend.

2

Are there more children or toys?

4

Are there fewer pails or shovels?

Look! Ben made a graph with his toys.
Does he have more trucks or tools?

How can Ben sort his toys?

6

Is there one toy for each friend?

8

Name _____

Directions I Draw balls to show the same number. 2 Circle the set with more. 3 Circle the set with fewer. 4 Draw blocks in the graph for each block in the picture. Circle the color with the most.

Directions Find two groups of living things in the picture. Count the number in each group. Compare the groups, using the words *more, fewer,* and *same*.

56

Represent and Read Numbers 0-5

Directions Place cubes on the blank spaces. Count and compare the numbers of cubes.
Talk about other numbers of items in the picture.

58

Directions 1–4 Count the children and write the number. 5–7 Write the numbers.

1

2

3

4

5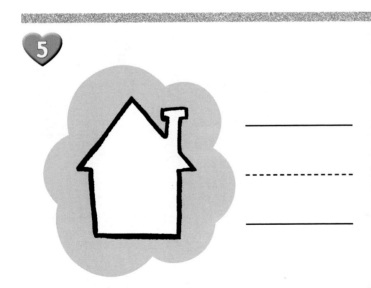

6

Directions 1–6 Count and color the shapes. Write the number.

At Home Have your child look around the room for examples of one and two items. Have your child practice writing the numbers 1 and 2.

Name _____

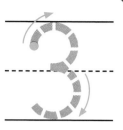

 1

 **2**

 **3**

 **4**

5

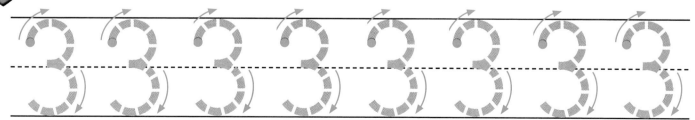

Directions 1–4 Place cubes on the pictures. Count and write the number. 5 Write the number.

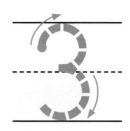

2

3

Directions 1–4 Circle the sets that show 3 blocks. Write the number 3.

At Home Have your child arrange 3 food cans in different ways and count the cans each time to see that there are 3. Have your child practice writing the number 3.

Name _____ **Four**

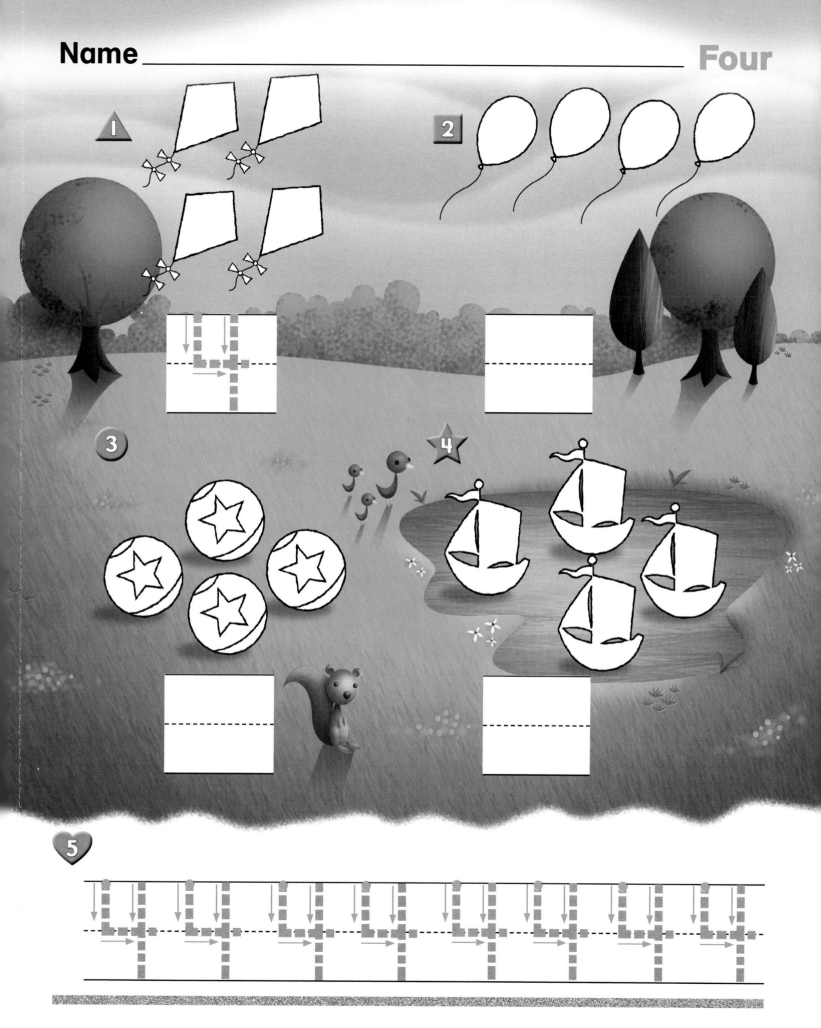

Directions 1–4 Count and color the items. Write the number. 5 Write the number.

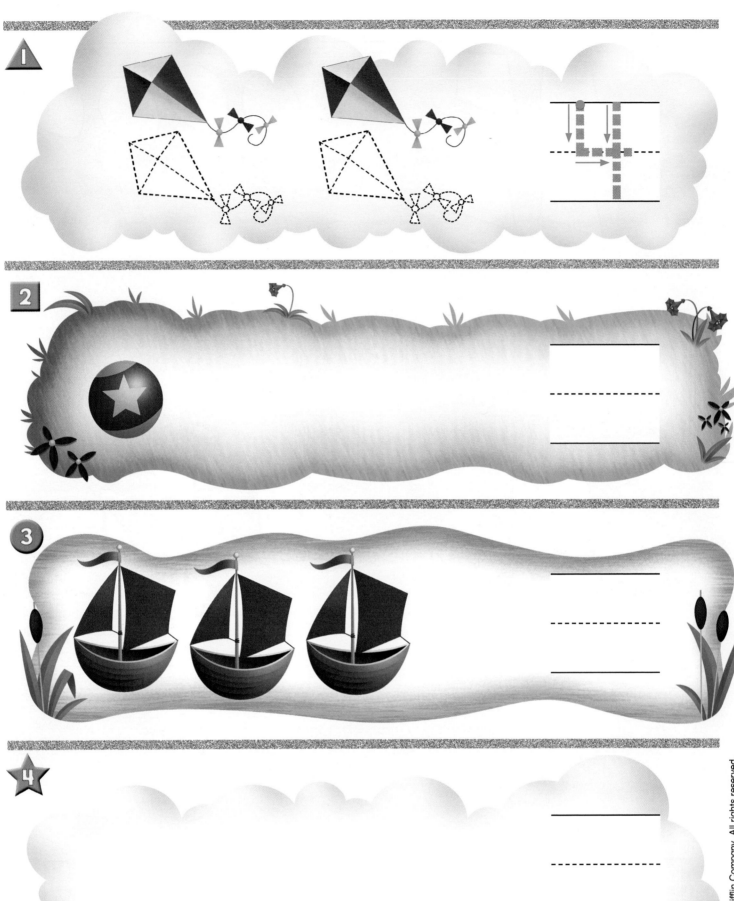

Directions 1–3 Draw more objects to show a set of 4.
4 Draw a set of 4.

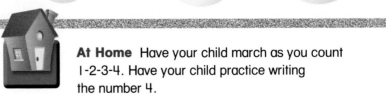

At Home Have your child march as you count
1-2-3-4. Have your child practice writing
the number 4.

1

2

5 5 5 5 5 5 5 5

Directions I Look at the groups of items. Circle the groups that show 5. 2 Write the number.

1

2

5

3

4

Directions 1–4 Count and color. Write the number.

At Home Have your child make sets of 5 items such as pennies, buttons, or paper clips. Have your child practice writing the number 5.

66

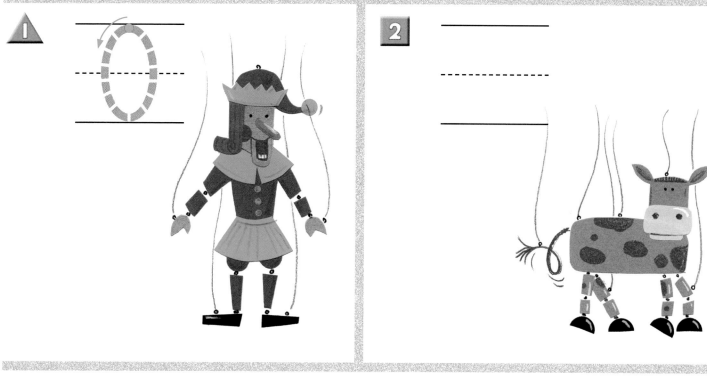

▲ 1 _____

2 _____

3

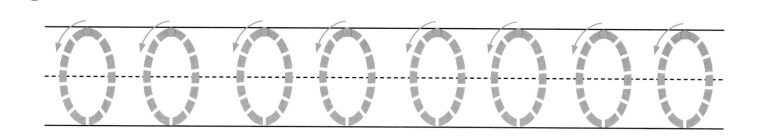

Directions 1—2 Look for the same puppet in the picture. Write the number to show how many you find. 3 Write the number.

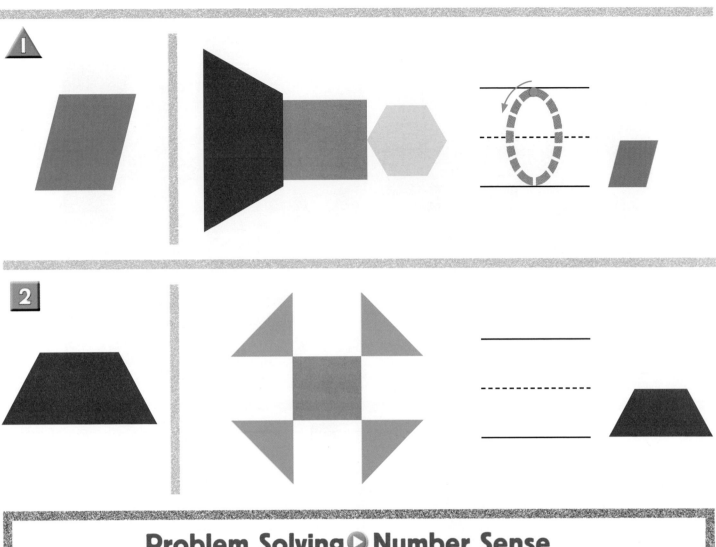

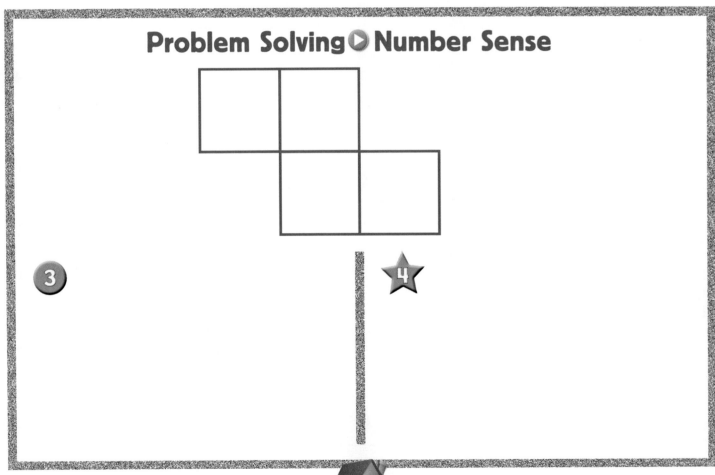

Problem Solving ▶ Number Sense

Directions 1–2 Look for the same block in the picture. Write the number to show how many you find. 3–4 Draw the same number of squares in a different way.

At Home Have your child tell you what zero means and what items you have zero of in your home. Have your child practice writing 0.

68

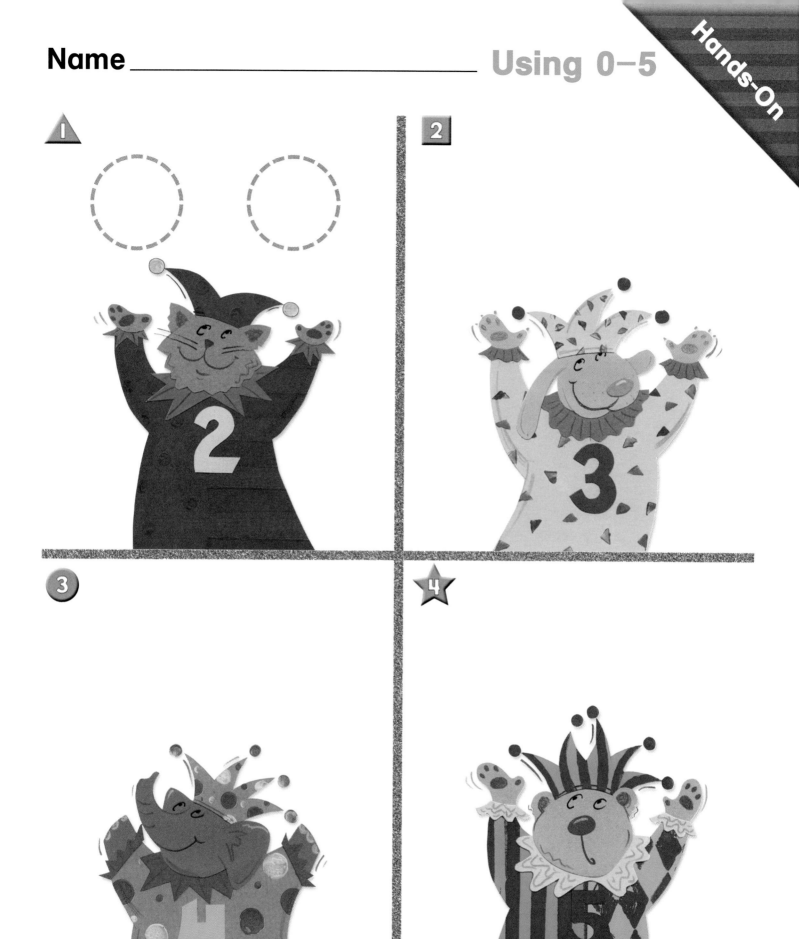

Directions 1–4 Use counters to show the number. Draw.

1

3

2

_____

_____

3

_____

_____

4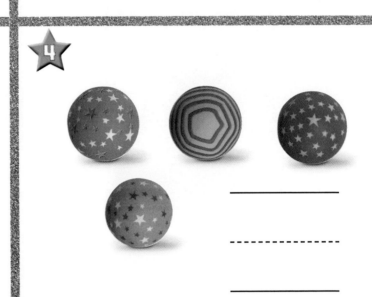

_____

_____

5

_____

_____

6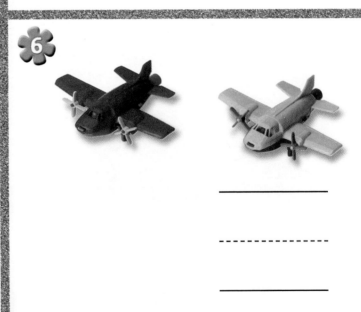

_____

_____

Directions 1–6 Count. Write the number of items in the set.

At Home Write a number from 0 to 5 and have your child show that number, using small items such as pennies or buttons.

Name _____

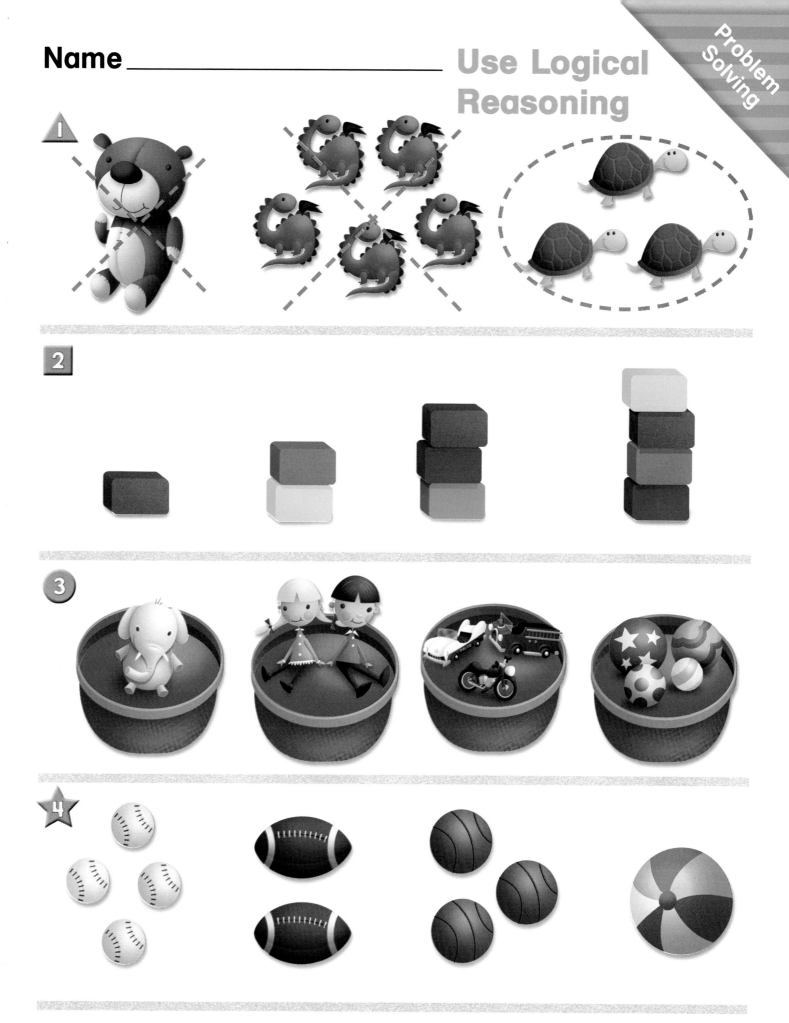

Directions 1–4 Listen to each clue. Cross out what does not match each clue. Circle
what matches all the clues.

Chapter 4

71

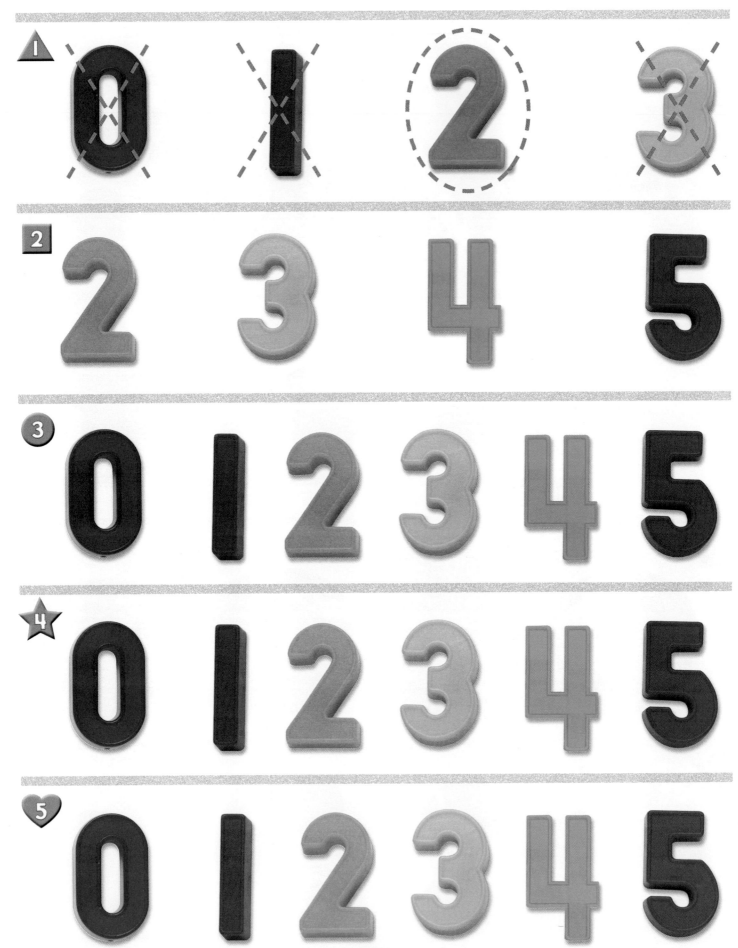

Directions 1–5 Listen to each clue. Cross out what does not match each clue. Circle what matches all the clues.

At Home Give your child two clues to guess a number from 0 to 5. For example: It is more than 3. It is fewer than 5. What is it?

72

Name _____

1

2

3

4

Directions 1 Circle the fourth bear. 2 Circle the third person. 3 Circle the fifth bug.
4 Circle the first person.

Directions 1 Circle the fifth person. 2 Circle the second bee. 3 Circle the first turtle. 4 Circle the fourth ant.

At Home Have your child line up five toys. Ask which is first? third? fifth? fourth? second?

74

All Dressed Up

This take-home book will help you review concepts you learned in Chapter 4.

1

How many hats does Tim have? _____

3

Let's see what Rosa and Tim find in this trunk.

2

How many gloves is Rosa wearing?

4

How many hats does Tim have now?

How many buttons does Rosa have?

Count the shoes you see.

6

How many clothes are inside the trunk?

8

Name_____

 **Chapter Review/Test**

 1

_____
- - - - - - - -
_____

 **2**

_____
- - - - - - - -
_____

3

4 5

5

6 0 1 2 3 4 5

Directions 1 Circle the group that shows 4. Write the number. 2 Circle the group that shows 2. Write the number. 3–4 Draw dots to show the number. 5 Circle the second turtle. 6 Circle the number that matches both clues. It is more than 3. It is not 5.

Chapter 4

75

MATCH-UP

What You Need

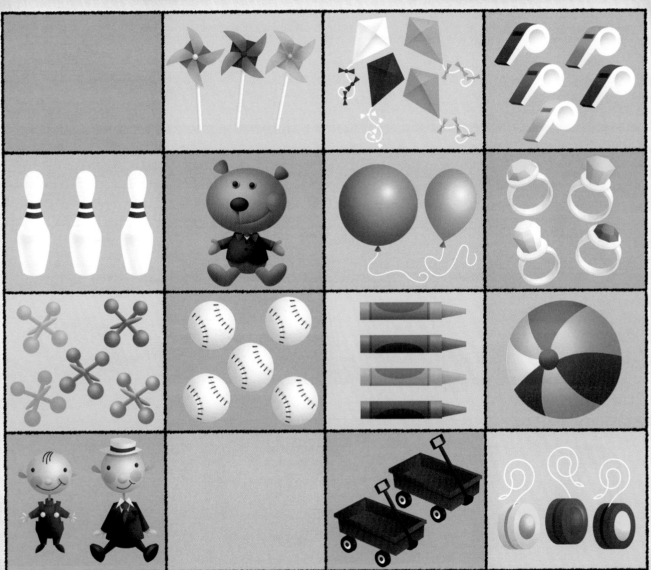

How to Play | Take turns with a partner. 2 Spin the spinner. Place a counter on a space that has that number of objects. 3 Play until all the spaces are covered.

Name _____

Directions 1 Draw the same number of counters. 2 Circle the set with more. 3 Circle the set with fewer. 4 Circle the third carriage. Draw a line under the fifth carriage.

5

Which Has More?

6

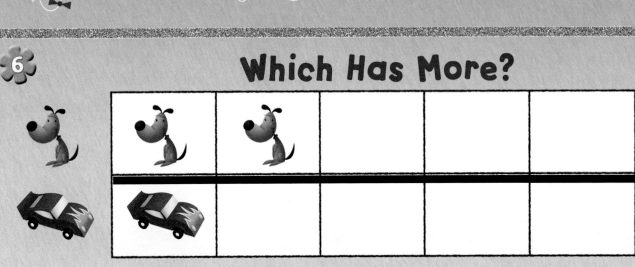

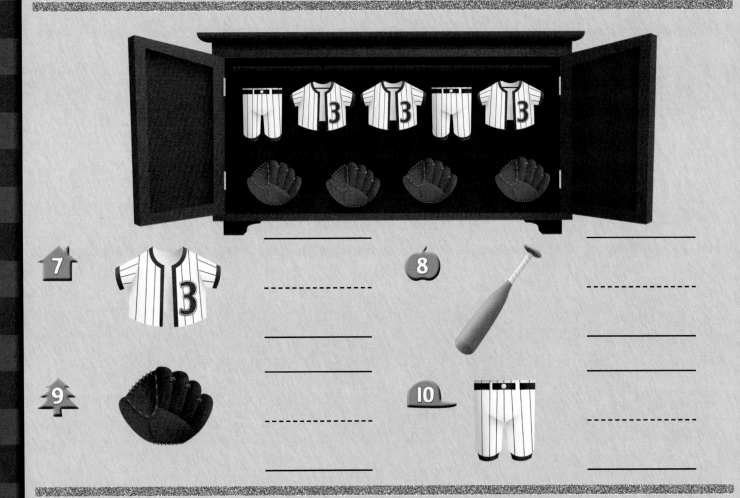

7

8

9

10

Directions 5 Circle the set that shows 5. 6 Circle the row with more. 7–10 Look for each item in the picture. Write the number to show how many you find.

Name _____

Make a Table and Graph

Number of Toys

Toy	Number
(car)	_____
(airplane)	_____
(car)	_____

Number of Toys

(car)			
(airplane)			
(car)			

Directions Count the number of each kind of toy. Write the numbers in the table.
Use the table to complete the graph. Tell about the graph.

Favorite Toy

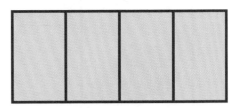

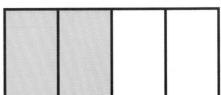

Directions 1 Circle the animal that is the same as the first one. Cross out the one that is different.
2 Circle the boat that is between the others. 3 Color to continue the pattern. 4 Match the items one to one.
Circle the set that has fewer. 5 Circle the favorite toy.

Photography Credits: 46(bm) © Ken Karp. 47 © Ken Karp. 48(t) © Ken Karp. 48(bl) © Radlund & Associates/Brand X Pictures/PictureQuest. 48(bmr) Corbis Images. 48(bml) © www.comstock.com. 48(br) © Corbis Images. 53(t) © Tony Freeman/PhotoEdit. 53(b) © Susan Van Etten/PhotoEdit. 54(t) © Mary Kate Denny/PhotoEdit. 54(m) © David Harrison/Index Stock Imagery. 54(b) © Jack Hollingsworth/Corbis. 55(t) © www.comstock.com. 55(mtr) © Ken Karp. 55(mbr) © Ken Karp. 62 © Ken Karp. 70(tl) © Radlund & Associates/Brand X Pictures/PictureQuest. 70(tr) © www.comstock.com. 70(b) © Ken Karp. 72 © Ken Karp. 75 © Ken Karp. 77(tm) © Ken Karp. 80(t) © Ken Karp. **Illustration Credits:** 42 © Chris Lensch. 43-44 © Dorothy Donohue. 47-48 © Dorothy Donohue. 49-50 © Ethan Long. 52-54 © Dorothy Donohue. 55 © Ethan Long. 56 © Bari Weissman. Chapter 3 Story © Dorothy Donohue. 57-58 © Chris Lensch. 59 © Liz Conrad. 60 © Ethan Long. 63-66 © Chris Lensch. 67 © Liz Conrad. 69 © Liz Conrad. 71 © Chris Lensch. 73-74 © Liz Conrad. 75(t) © Chris Lensch. 75(b) © Liz Conrad. 76 © Chris Lensch. 77 © Ethan Long. 78 © Chris Lensch. 79 © Liz Conrad. 80(t) © Richard Garland. 80(bl) © Chris Lensch. Chapter 4 Story © Liz Conrad.

Geometry, Fractions, and Probability

From the Read-Aloud Anthology

THE SHAPE OF THINGS

by Dayle Ann Dodds
illustrated by Julie Lacome

Access Prior Knowledge
This story will help you review
- Shapes

The Shape of Things, by Dayle Ann Dodds, illustrated by Julie Lacome. Text copyright © 1994 by Dayle Ann Dodds. Illustrations copyright © 1994 by Julie Lacome. Reproduced by permission of Candlewick Press Inc., Cambridge, MA.
ISBN: 0-618-33873-X   Printed in the U.S.A.

MATH at Home

Dear Family,

We are starting a new unit called Geometry, Fractions, and Probability. In Chapter 5, we will identify plane shapes, equal parts, and symmetry. We will explore probability. In Chapter 6, we will learn about solid shapes.

Love, _____

Vocabulary

plane shape
A two-dimensional figure.

circle   **square**   **triangle**   **rectangle**

solid shape
A three-dimensional figure.

sphere   **cone**   **cube**   **rectangular prism**   **cylinder**

symmetry
When a figure can be divided in half so that it has two mirrored parts.

equal parts
When a whole object is divided into two or more parts that are the same size and shape.

Vocabulary Activities

- Help your child find, describe, and identify plane and solid shapes in your home or neighborhood.

- Give your child a mirror to hold at the middle of a picture to explore mirror images and symmetry.

- Let your child help cut foods into equal parts such as halves.

Visit *Education Place* **at eduplace.com/parents/mw/ for** *e • WordGame*, *e • Glossary* **and more.**

Literature to Read Together

- **Bear in a Square**
by Stella Blackstone
(Barefoot Books, 1998)

- **Shapes**
by Dr. Alvin Granowsky
(Copper Beech, 2001)

- **Eating Fractions**
by Bruce McMillan
(Scholastic, 1991)

82

Plane Shapes and Fractions

CHAPTER 5

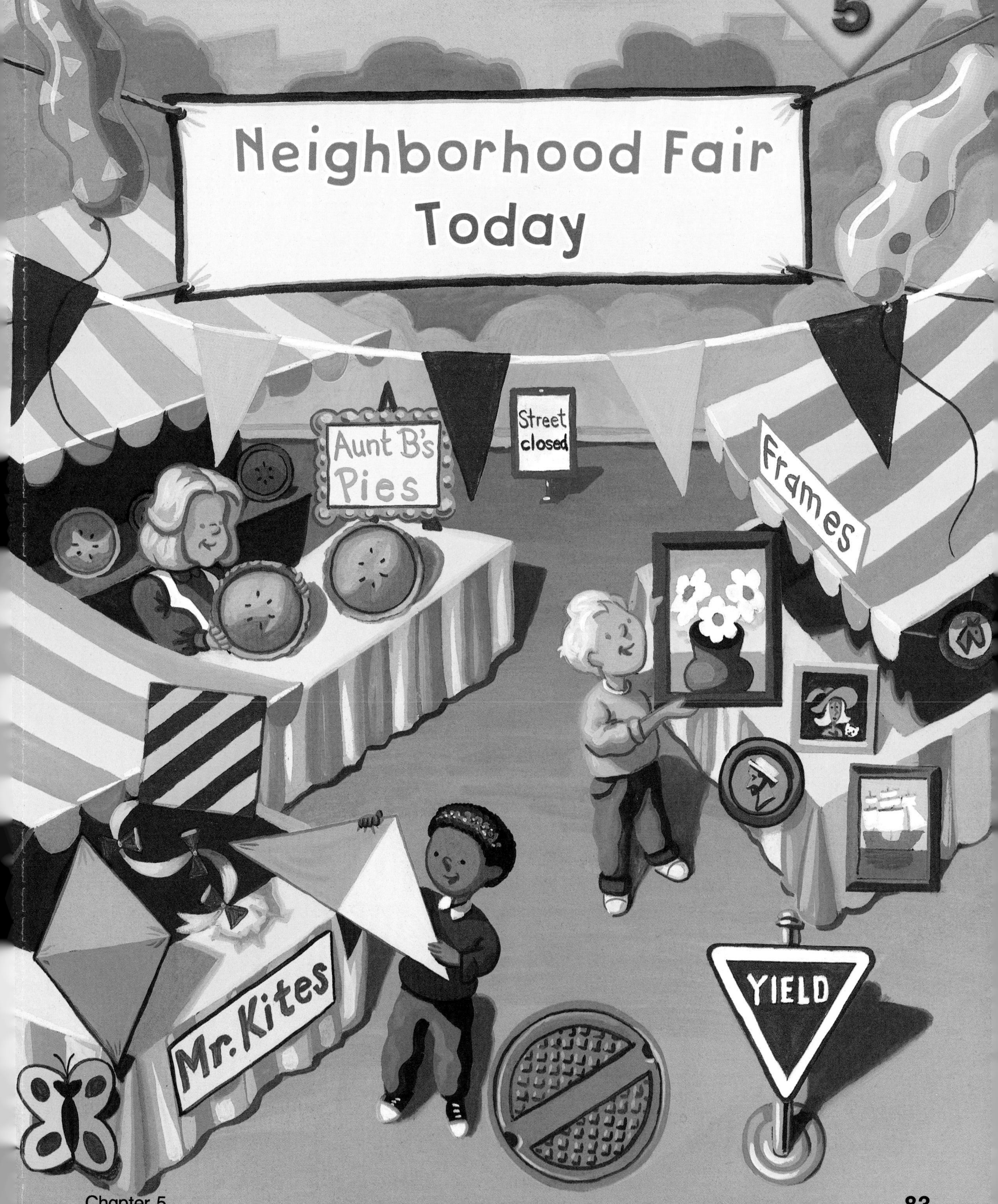

Neighborhood Fair Today
Street closed
Aunt B's Pies
Frames
Mr. Kites
YIELD

Directions Place an attribute block of the same shape in each section. Draw the block.
Tell how the shapes are alike.

84

Name _____

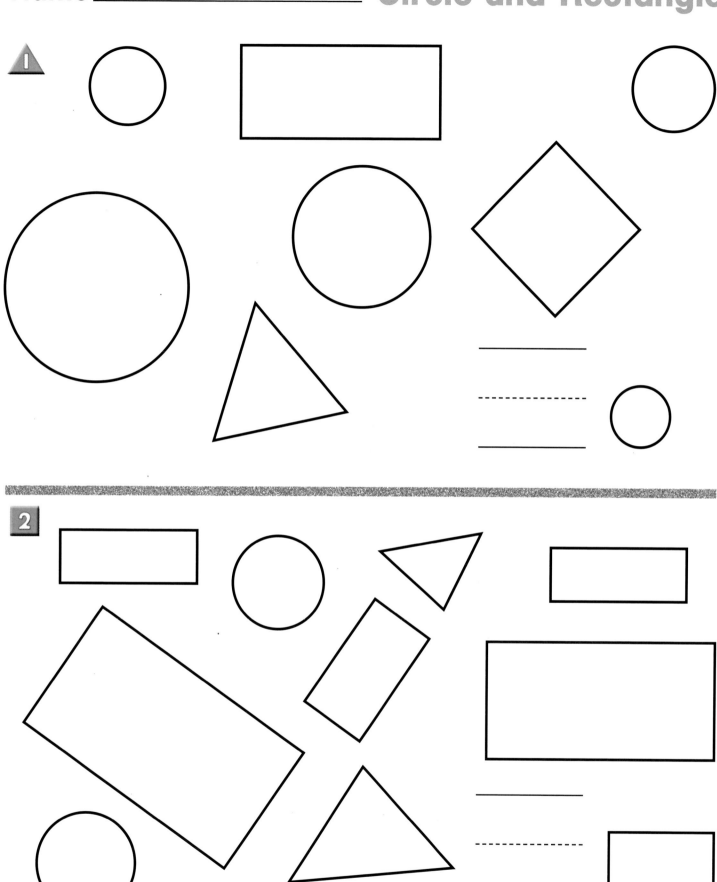

Directions 1 Color the circles red. Count. Write the number. 2 Color the rectangles blue.
Count. Write the number.

Directions Color the circles red. Color the rectangles blue. Count. Write the number of each shape.

At Home Have your child find examples of circles and rectangles around your home, and then explain how he or she knew what each shape was.

Name _____ **Square and Triangle**

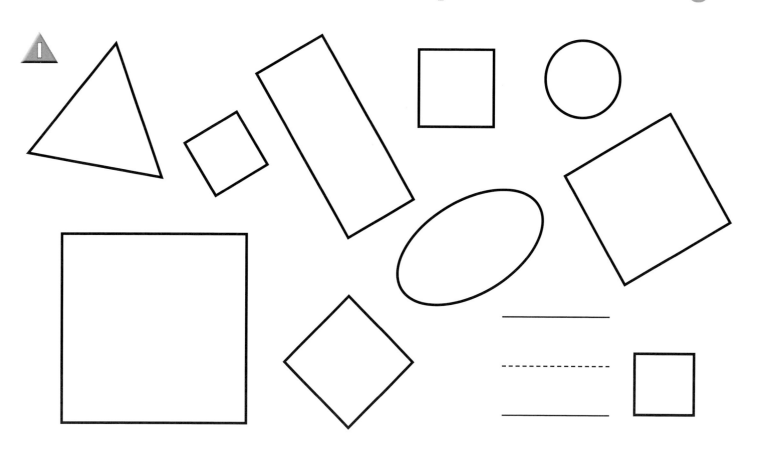

Directions I Color the squares green. Count. Write the number. 2 Color the triangles orange.
Count. Write the number.

_____   _____

- - - - - - - - - - ☐   - - - - - - - - - - △

_____   _____

Directions Color the squares green. Color the triangles orange. Count. Write the number of each shape.

At Home Have your child find examples of squares and triangles around your home. Have him or her tell you how a square and a triangle are different.

Name _____

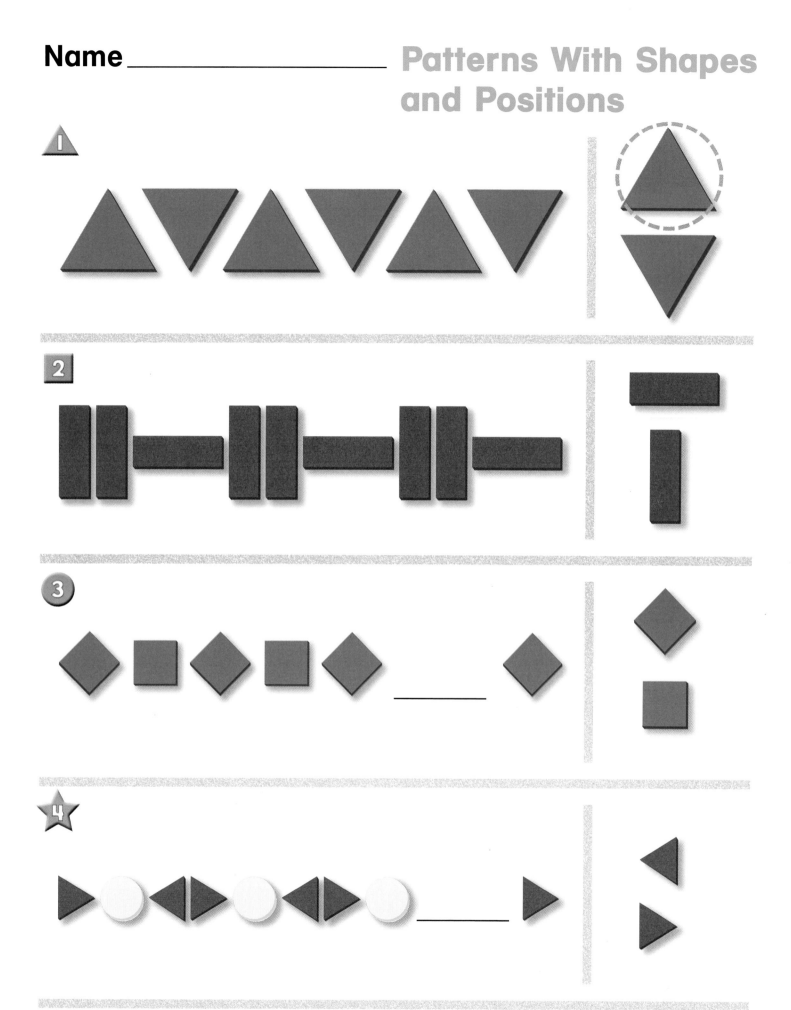

Directions Describe the positions of the shapes. 1–2 Circle the shape that is likely to come next.
3–4 Circle the missing shape.

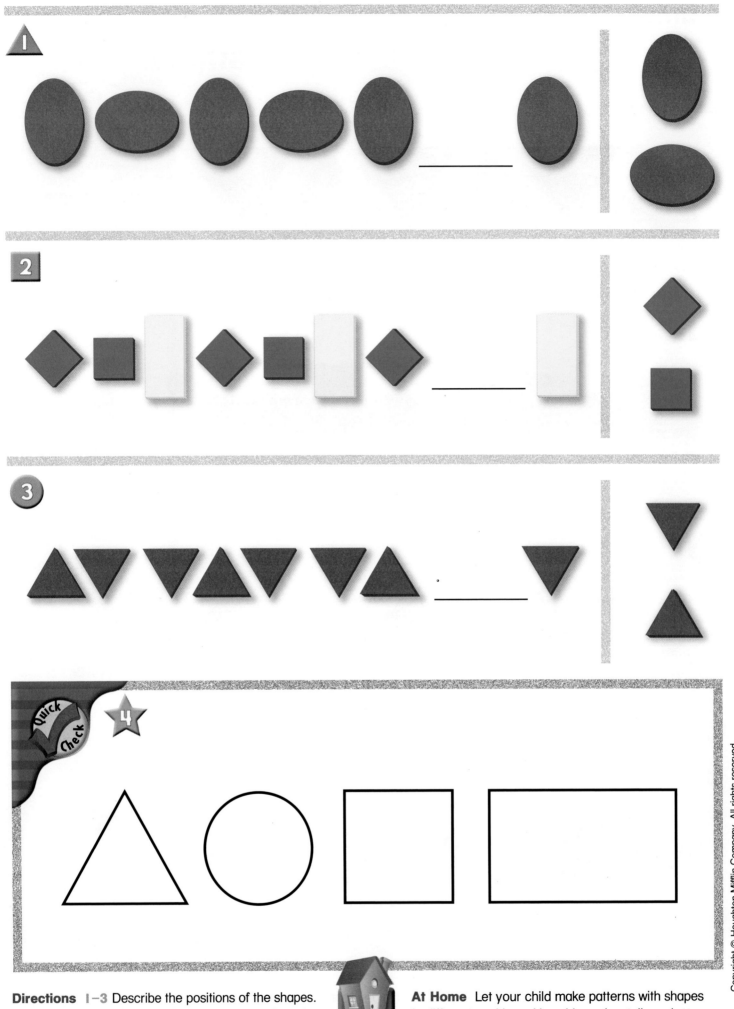

Directions 1–3 Describe the positions of the shapes. Circle the missing shape. 4 Color the circle yellow, the square red, the triangle blue, and the rectangle green.

At Home Let your child make patterns with shapes in different positions. Have him or her tell you how the patterns repeat.

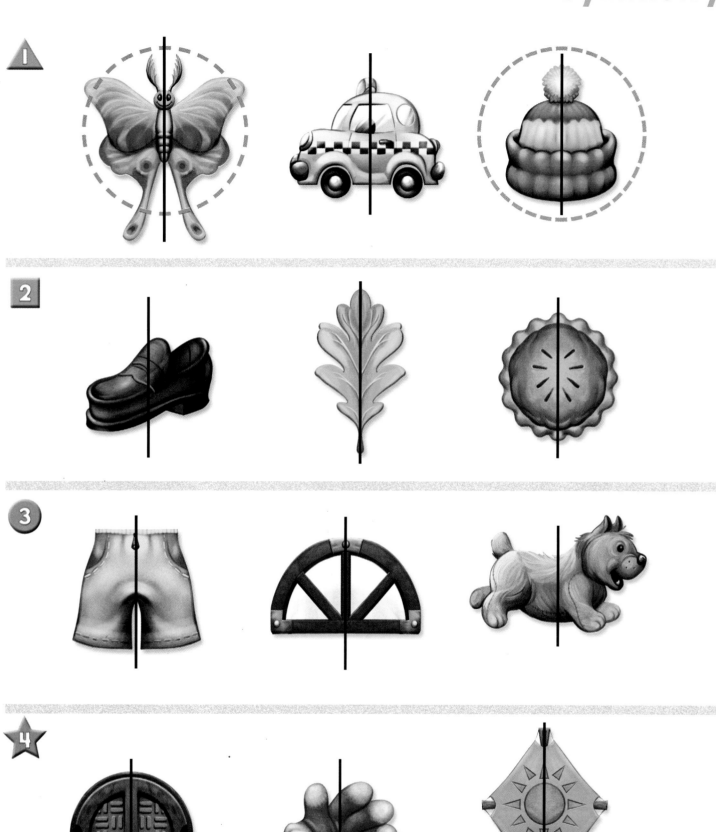

Directions 1–4 Circle the ones with symmetry.

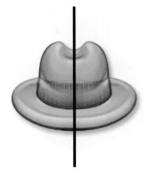  

2

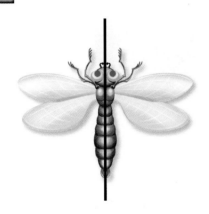  

Problem Solving ▶ Visual Thinking

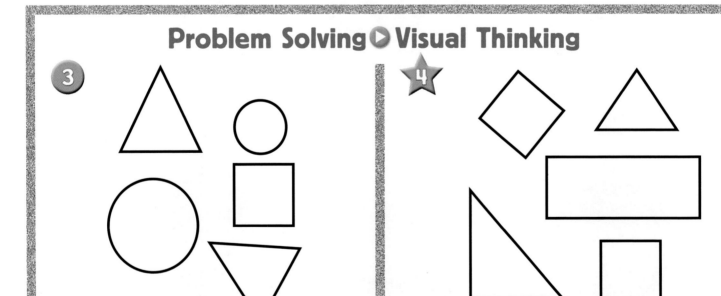

Directions 1–2 Circle the ones with symmetry.
3–4 Color the ones that are the same size and
same shape.

At Home Help your child fold a paper in half and cut
out a shape on the fold. Open the paper and have
your child show you the mirrored parts.

Name _____ Equal Parts

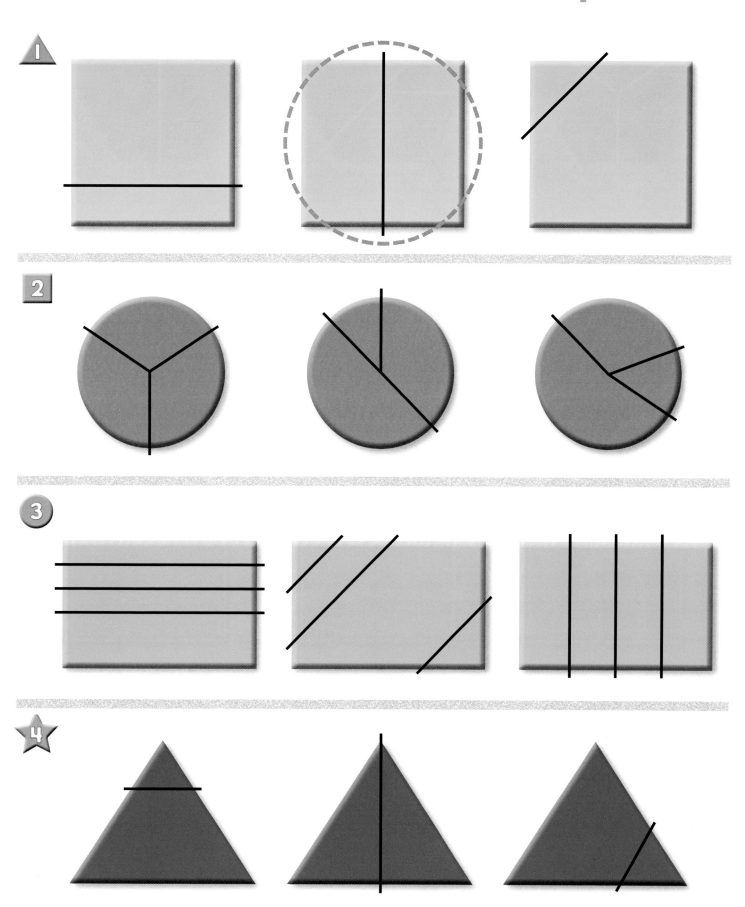

1

2

3

4

Directions 1–4 Circle the one that shows equal parts.

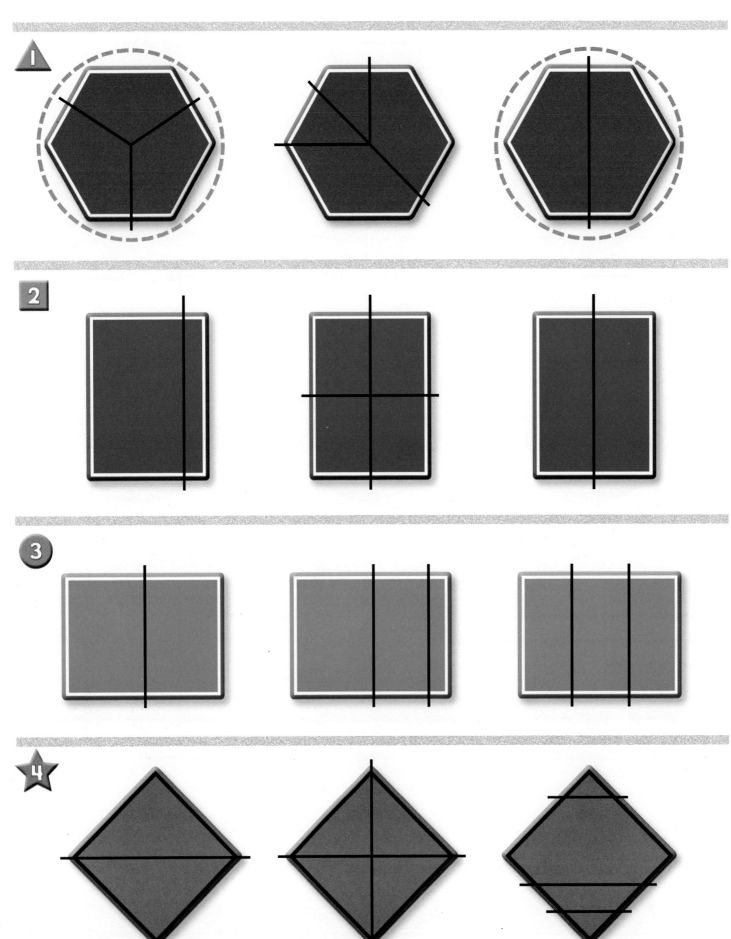

Directions 1–4 Circle the ones that show equal parts.

At Home Have your child find examples of items that are divided into parts, such as windows and sofa cushions. Have him or her tell whether or not the items show equal parts.

Directions Circle the foods that show halves.

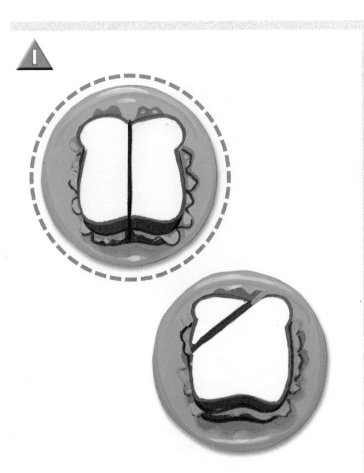

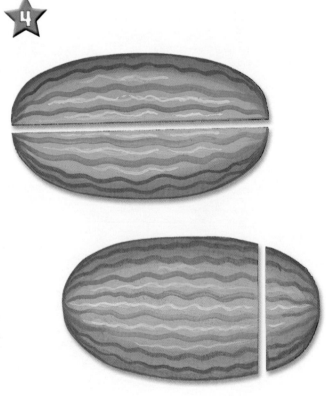

Directions 1–4 Circle the item that shows halves. Tell why the two parts are halves.

At Home Have your child explain which items in this lesson show halves and which don't. Discuss with your child foods that you might separate into halves.

Name _____ **Use a Picture**

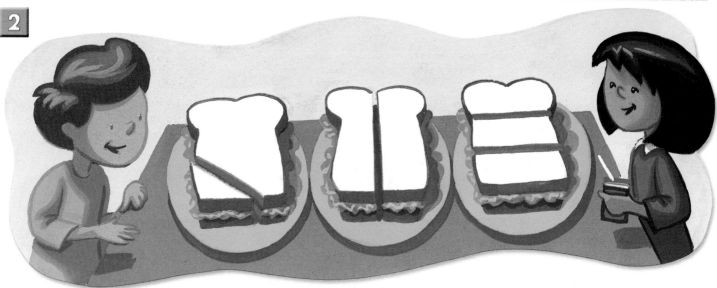

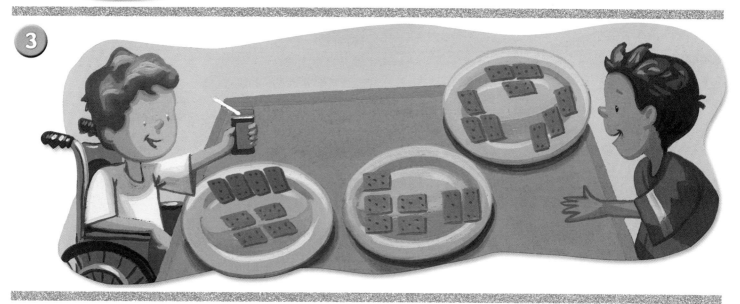

Directions 1–3 Count the number of children shown. Circle the plate of food that would give each child an equal part.

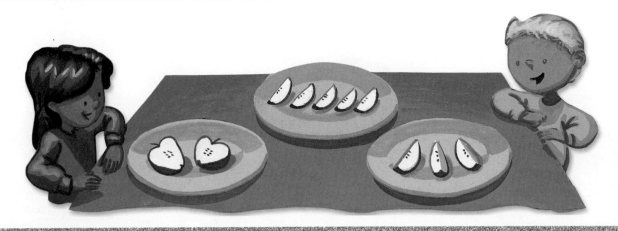

Directions 1–4 Count the number of children shown. Circle the plate of food that would give each child an equal part.

At Home Have your child help you cut and serve foods in equal parts for your family members.

98

Name _____

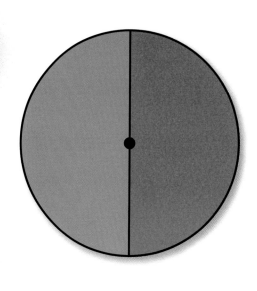

Spin and Tally

Color	Predict	Record

Directions Predict how many times the spinner will land on each color if you spin five times. Make a tally mark after each spin. Record the number of tally marks. Compare your predictions to the outcomes.

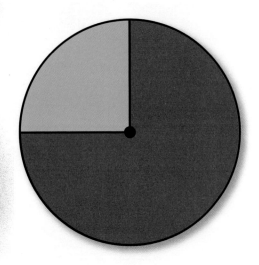

Spin and Tally

Color	Predict	Record
	_____ ------------ _____	_____ ------------ _____
	_____ ------------ _____	_____ ------------ _____
	_____ ------------ _____	_____ ------------ _____

Directions Predict how many times the spinner will land on each color if you spin five times. Spin and tally. Write the number of tallies. Compare to your predictions.

At Home Draw spinners like the ones in this lesson. Use a paper clip held by a pencil to spin. Have your child predict and record the outcomes.

I See Shapes!

This take-home book will help you review concepts you learned in Chapter 5.

1

I see rectangles.
How many do you see?

3

I see circles.
How many do you see?

2

I see squares.
How many do you see?

4

I see triangles.
How many do you see?

5

I see shapes with symmetry.
Which are the shapes with symmetry?

7

I see a shape pattern.
Draw the shapes that will likely come next.

6

I see shapes with equal parts.
Which shapes have equal parts?

8

Name _____

Chapter Review / Test

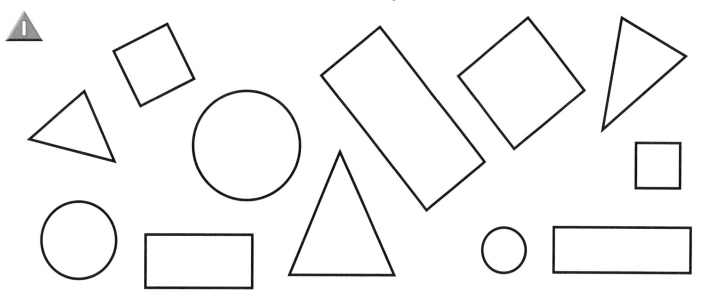

2

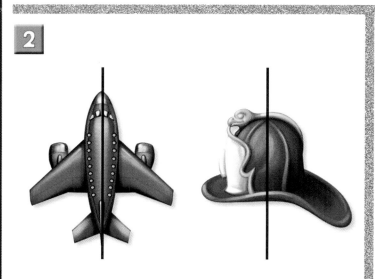

3

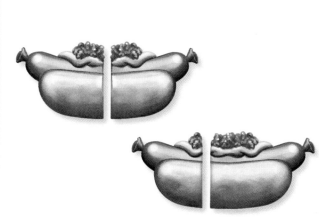

4

5

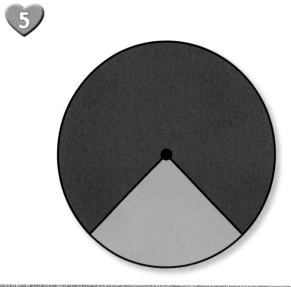

Directions 1 Color the rectangles blue, the triangles yellow, the circles green, and the squares red. 2 Circle the one with symmetry. 3 Circle the one that shows equal parts. 4 Circle the food that would give each child an equal part. 5 Put an X on the color you are more likely to spin.

Art
Connection

eduplace.com/kids/mw/

Directions Tell about the plane shapes you see in the paintings. Draw your own picture
using at least two different shapes.

102

Solid Shapes

CHAPTER 6

Directions Find your way through the maze. Follow the path of cubes. Color the path. What is at the end?

104

Name _____

Roll

Slide

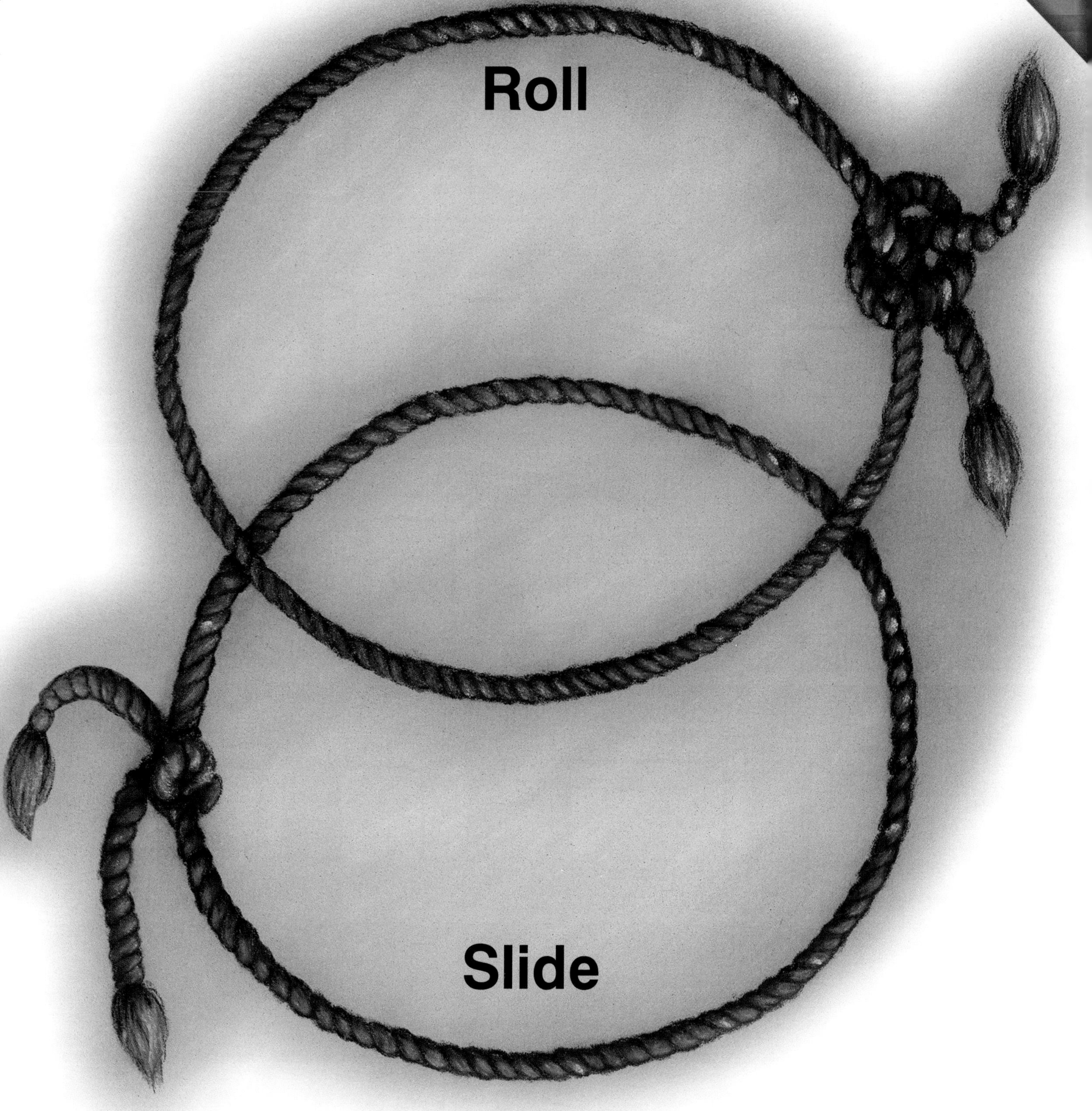

Directions Cut out the shapes. In the top section, put the shapes that roll. In the bottom section, put the shapes that slide. In the middle, put the shapes that both roll and slide. Glue the shapes in place.

105

Directions Color the shapes that have corners red. Color the shapes that have curves blue.

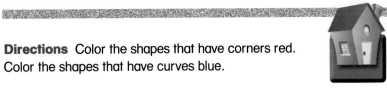

At Home Give your child a variety of boxes and cans to sort into two groups.

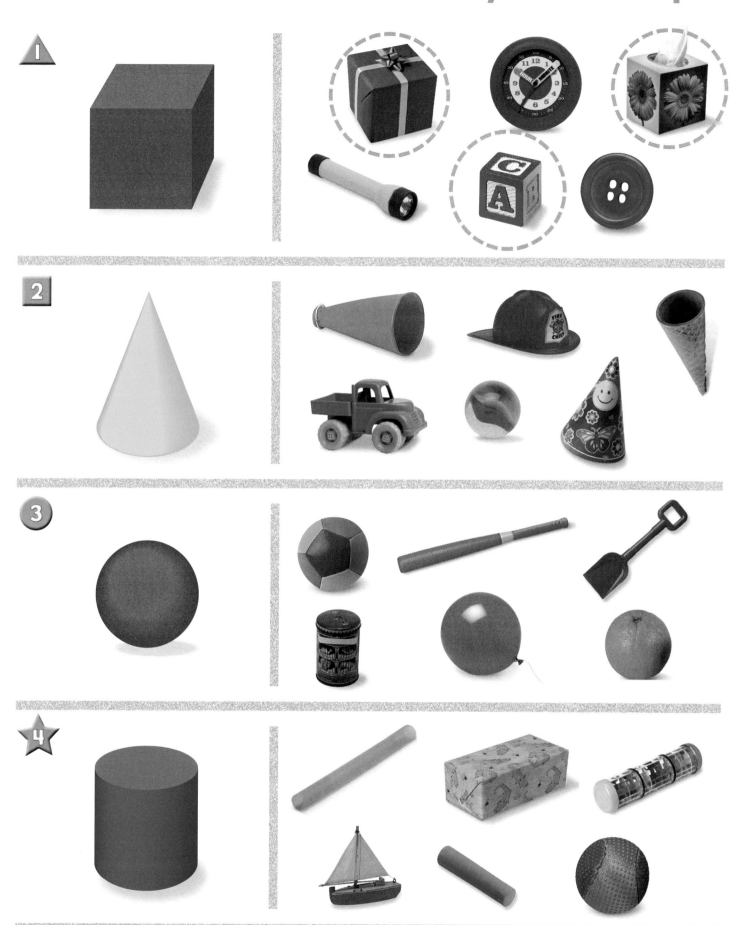

1

2

3

4

Directions 1–4 Name and describe the solid shape. Circle the objects that are like the solid shape.

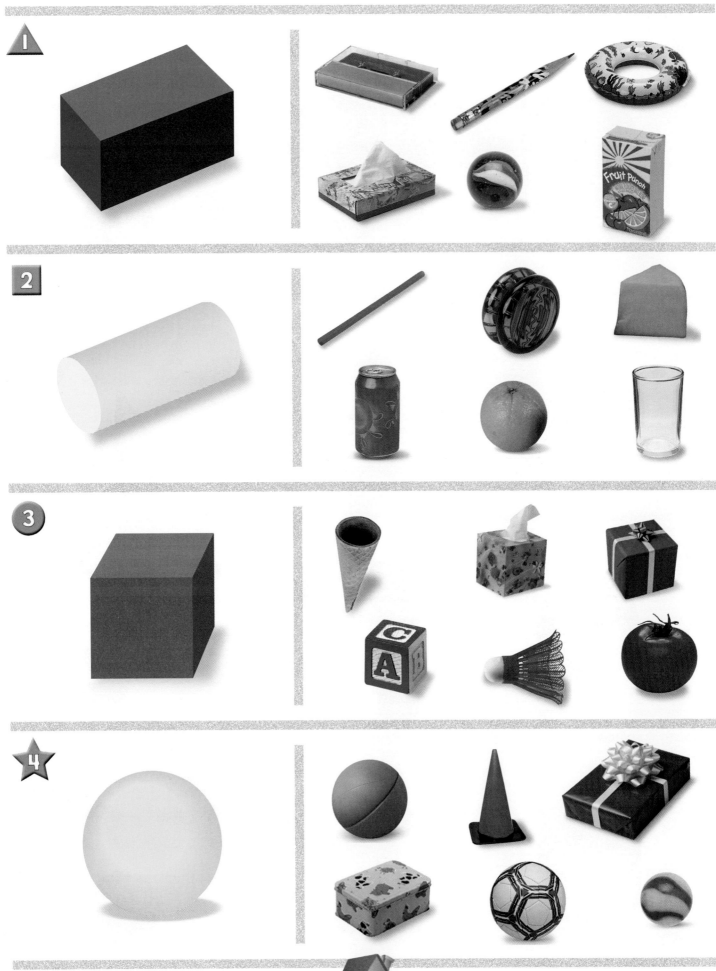

1

2

3

4

Directions 1-4 Name and describe the solid shape. Circle the objects that are like the solid shape.

At Home Help your child gather objects such as balls, boxes, and cans; sort them by shape and identify their mathematical names—spheres, rectangular prisms, cubes, and cylinders.

Name_____

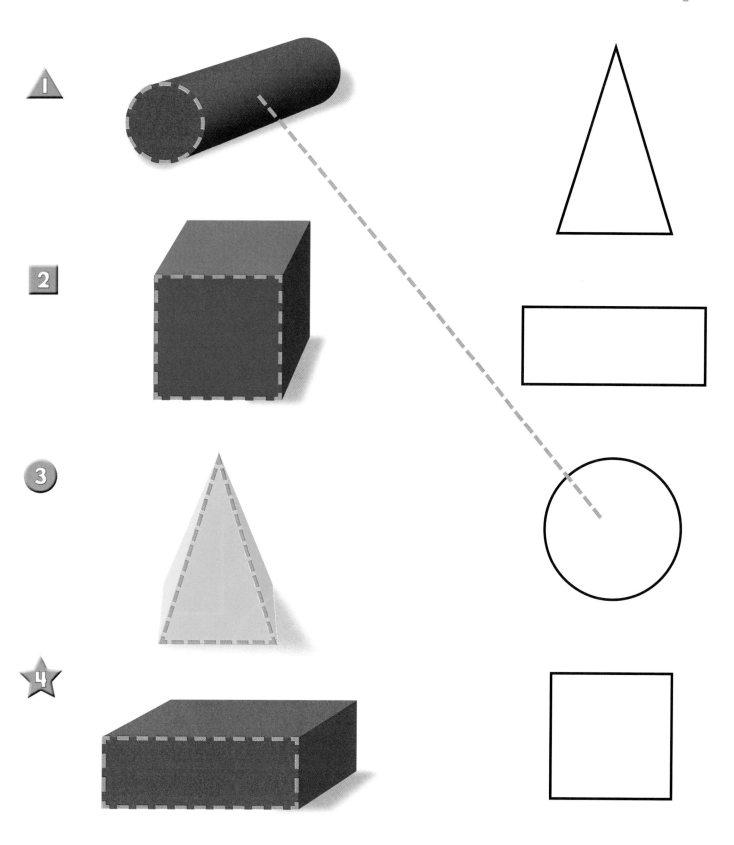

1

2

3

4

Directions 1–4 Trace the dotted line on the surface of the solid shape.
Draw a line to the matching plane shape.

Chapter 6

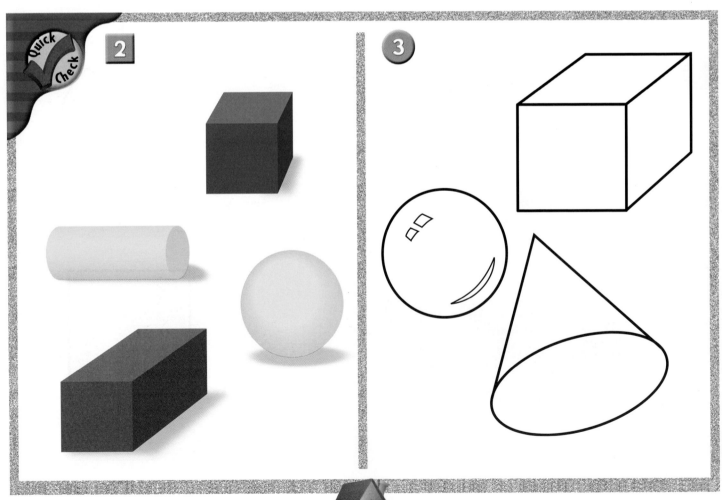

Directions 1 Circle the shapes that have a square surface. 2 Circle the shapes that have corners. 3 Color the sphere blue, the cube red, and the cone yellow.

At Home Examine a can and a box with your child. Have your child identify the surfaces that are circles, rectangles, and squares.

110

Name _____

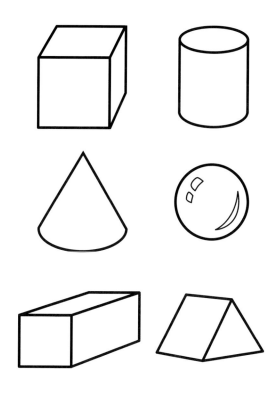

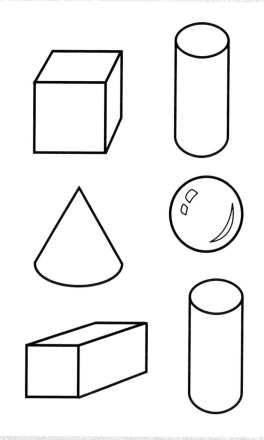

Directions 1 Color the shapes to match the ones that were used to make the barn and silo.
2 Color the shapes to match the ones that were used to make the wagon.

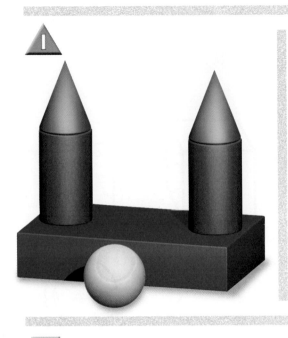

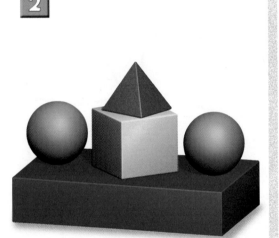

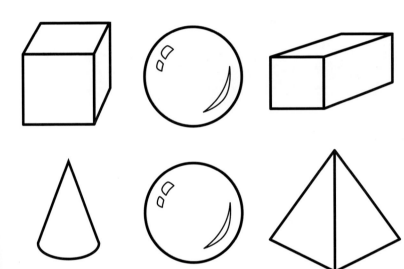

Problem Solving ▶ Visual Thinking

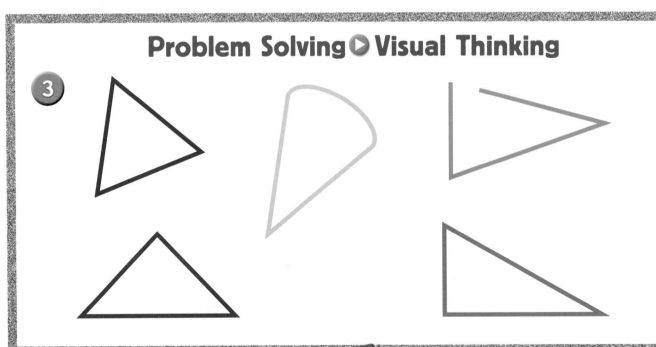

Directions 1–2 Color the shapes to match the ones that were used to make the building. 3 Circle the triangles.

At Home Have your child combine solid shapes to make a single object. Then have your child identify the different shapes that were used.

112

Make a Graph

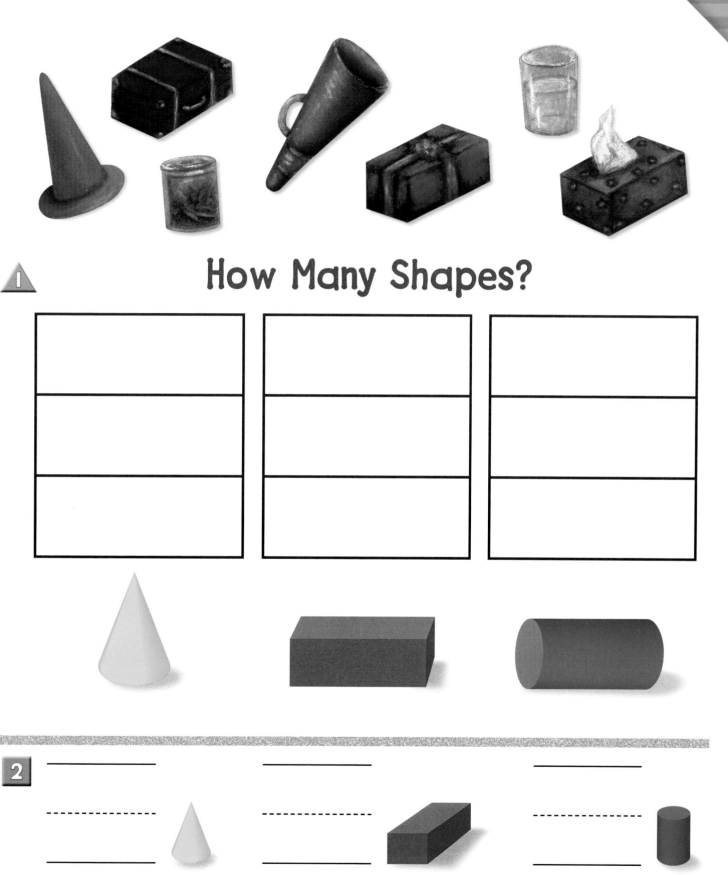

How Many Shapes?

1

2 _____   _____   _____

- - - - - - -   - - - - - - -   - - - - - - -

_____   _____   _____

Directions 1 Color one box in the graph for each item that is like the solid shape. 2 Count the colored boxes and write the numbers. Compare the numbers of shapes.

How Many of Each Shape?

△ 1

2

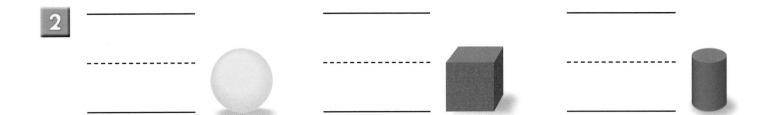

3

⭐ 4

Directions 1 Color one box for each item like the solid shape. 2 Count the colored boxes. Write the numbers. 3 Circle the shape that has more. 4 Circle the shape that has fewer.

At Home Ask your child to tell you about the graphs and what they show.

A Shape Hunt With Patches

This take-home book will help you review concepts you learned in Chapter 6.

1

Snow Cones
1.00

Find the ⬤ spheres.

3

Patches is on a shape hunt.
Help Patches find each shape.

2

Find the cubes.

4

Find the  rectangular prisms.

Which shapes can slide?
Which shapes can roll?

Find the  cones and the cylinders.

6

Which solid shape made each shape print?

8

Name _____

1

2

3

⭐4

How many 🔲 and ⚪ ?

_____

- - - - - - - - - - - - - - - -

_____

- - - - - - - - - - - - - - - -

_____

Directions 1 Circle the shapes that roll. 2 Color the sphere red, the cylinder yellow, and the rectangular prism blue. 3 Draw a line from the surface of the solid to the matching plane shape.
4 Color a box for each shape. Write how many.

What You Need

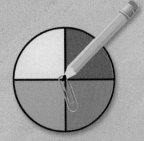

SHAPE-O!

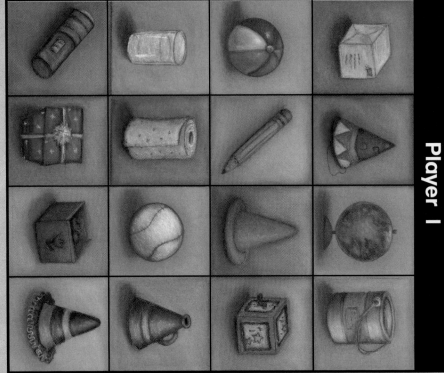

Player 1

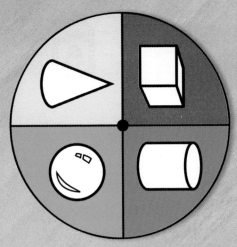

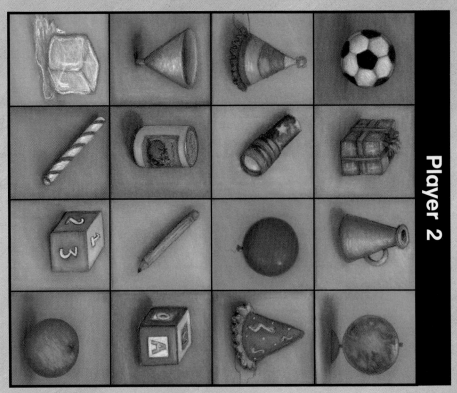

Player 2

How to Play **1** Take turns with a partner. **2** Spin the spinner and name the shape. Both players place a counter on a space that has that shape. **3** The first player to get 4 in a row calls out "Shape-O" and wins.

116

Name _____

1

2

3

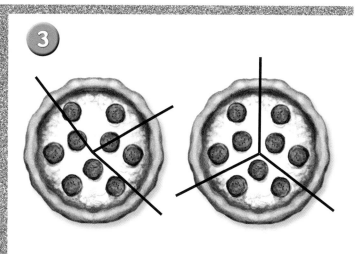

4

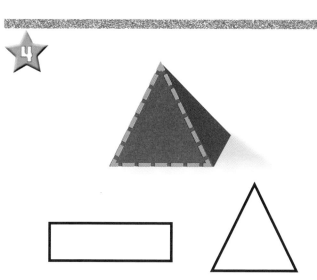

5

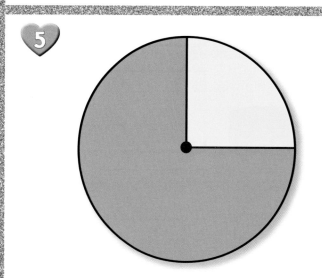

Directions 1 Color the circles red, the squares blue, the triangles green, and the rectangles yellow.
2 Circle the one with symmetry. 3 Circle the one that shows equal parts. 4 Draw a line from the
surface of the solid to the matching plane shape. 5 Put an X on the color you are more likely to spin.

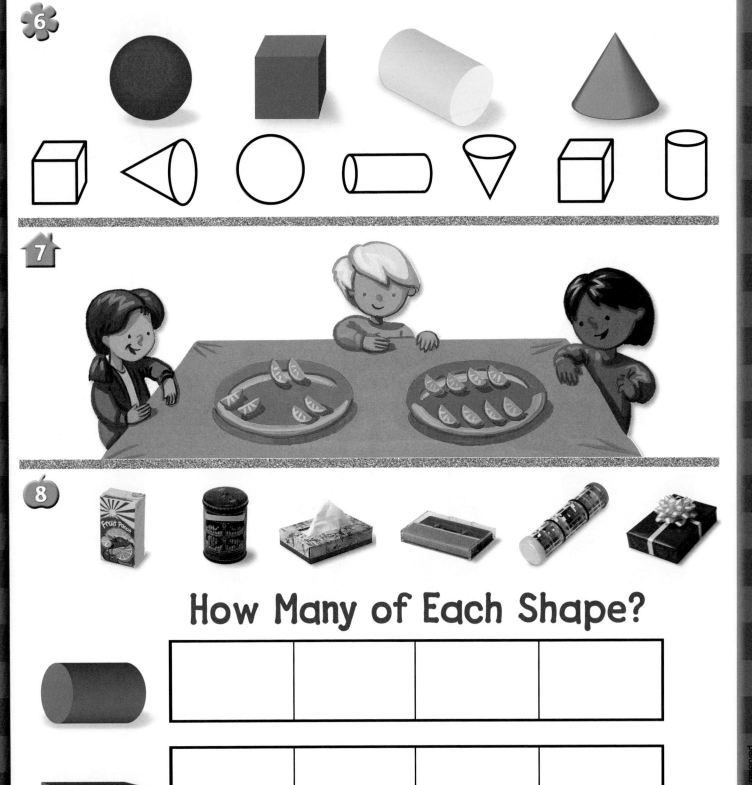

How Many of Each Shape?

Directions 6 Color the shapes to match the shapes at the top. 7 Circle the plate of food that would give each child an equal part. 8 Color a box for each shape. Write how many.

118

Name _____

Paths and Mazes

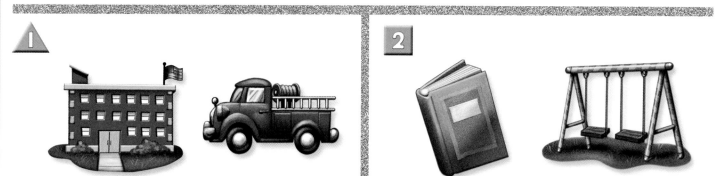

1

2

3

4 ★
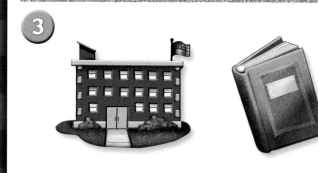

Directions Start at the house each time. Follow the directions. Circle where you stop.
1 Go left 2 and up 1. 2 Go right 2 and down 1. 3 Go down 1 and left 3. 4 Go up 2 and right 3.

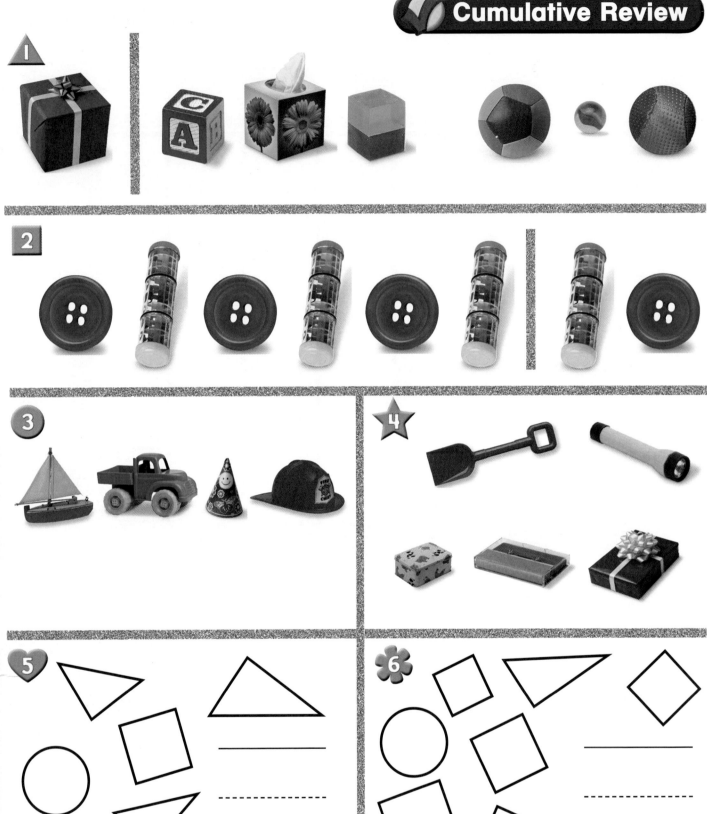

Directions 1 Circle the group where the shape belongs. 2 Circle the item that is likely to come next in the pattern. 3 Draw balls to show the same number. 4 Circle the set with more. 5 Color the triangles. Write the number. 6 Color the squares. Write the number.

Photography Credits: 102(bl) © 2005 Artists Rights Society (ARS), New York/ADAGP, Paris/Superstock. 102(tl) © 2005 Mondrian/Holtzman Trust/Artists Rights Society (ARS), New York/Giraudon/Art Resource, NY. 102(tr) © 2005 Artists Rights Society (ARS), New York/VG Bild-Kunst, Bonn/Giraudon/Art Resource. 107(1tl); 107(2tm); 107(2bl); 107(4bl); 108(3tr); 108(4tr); 110(br); 115(rm); 118(r); 120(1l); 120(3l); 120(3ml); 120(3r); 120(4br) © C Squared Studios/PhotoDisc/Getty Images. 107(3tr) © Stockbyte/ PictureQuest. 107(3br); 108(2bm); 108(3br) © www.comstock.com. 108(2tr) © Burke/Triolo/Brand X Pictures/PictureQuest. 108(3bm); 108(4tl); 110(bl) © Corbis Images. 108(4tm) © Siede Preis/PhotoDisc/Getty Images. 108(4bm) © Radlund & Associates/Brand X Pictures/PictureQuest. 120(4tl) © Stockbyte/ Picturequest. All remaining photographs © Ken Karp.
Illustration Credits: 82-84; 95-98; 101(bl); 102; 118 © Kenneth Spengler. 91-92; 101(ml); 101(mr); 117; 119; Mark and Rosemary Jarman. 99-100; Chapter 5 Story © Benrei Haung. 103-106; 113-114; 116 © Marisol Sarrazin. 111-112 © Patrick Gnan. Chapter 6 Story © Wayne Parmenter.

120

Numbers Through 12

From the Read-Aloud Anthology

James AND THE Rain

by Karla Kuskin

illustrated by Reg Cartwright

Access Prior Knowledge
This story will help you review
- Counting to 5
- Comparing Groups

James and the Rain, by Karla Kuskin, illustrated by Reg Cartwright. Text copyright © 1957, 1995 by Karla Kuskin. Illustrations copyright © 1995 by Reg Cartwright. Originally published in 1957 by Harper and Brothers Publishers with illustrations by Karla Kuskin. Reprinted by permission of Simon & Schuster Books for Young Readers, an imprint of Simon & Schuster Children's Publishing Division.
ISBN: 0-618-33874-8   Printed in the U.S.A.

MATH at Home

Dear Family,

We are starting a new unit called Numbers Through 12. In Chapter 7, we will count, read, and write numbers 6 through 12. In Chapter 8, we will name, order, and compare numbers through 12. We will also estimate numbers of objects in a group.

Love, _____

Vocabulary

number pattern
A sequence of numbers arranged according to some rule.

12, 11, 10, 9, 8, 7, 6
backward by ones

2, 4, 6, 8, 10, 12
forward by twos

more, fewer
Words used to compare numbers of objects.

There are more frogs than ducks.
There are fewer ducks than frogs.

greater than, less than
Words used to compare numbers.

7 is greater than 5.
5 is less than 7.

Vocabulary Activities

• Help your child look for numbers on grocery items and buildings.

• Write a sequence of numbers leaving out one number. Have your child find the missing number.

• Give your child two groups of items. Have your child tell which group has more and which has fewer.

Visit *Education Place* at
eduplace.com/parents/mw/
for *e* • WordGame,
e • Glossary **and more.**

Literature to Read Together

● **Feast for 10**
by Cathryn Falwell
(Clarion Books, 1993)

● **Anno's Counting Book**
by Mitsumasa Anno
(HarperCollins, 1977)

● **Little Rabbits' First Number Book**
by Alan Baker
(Kingfisher, 1998)

Represent and Read Numbers 6–12

Directions Count and compare the numbers of animals in each group. Circle the group that has five. Use counters to show a group with one more. Draw the group.

124

Name _____

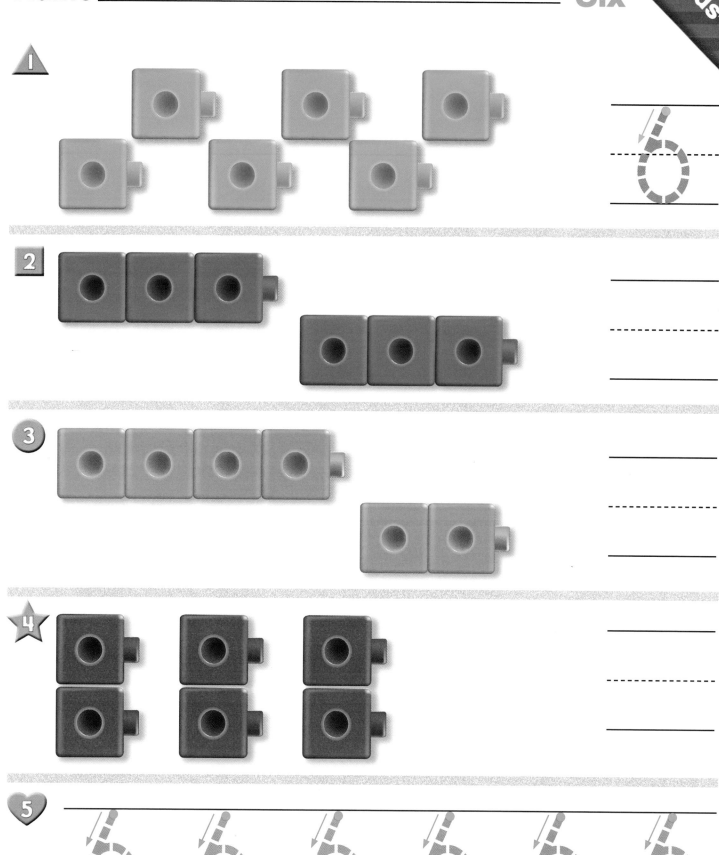

Six

Directions 1–4 Place cubes on the pictured cubes. Count and write the number.
5 Write the number.

125

1

_____

- - - - - - - - - - -

_____

2

_____

- - - - - - - - - - -

_____

3

_____

- - - - - - - - - - -

_____

4

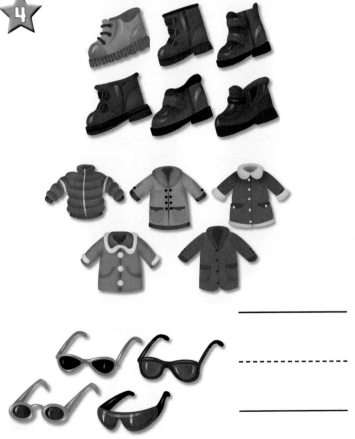

_____

- - - - - - - - - - -

_____

Directions 1–4 Circle the sets of 6. Write the number.

At Home Display different arrangements of 6 items and have your child count them each time. Have your child practice writing the number 6.

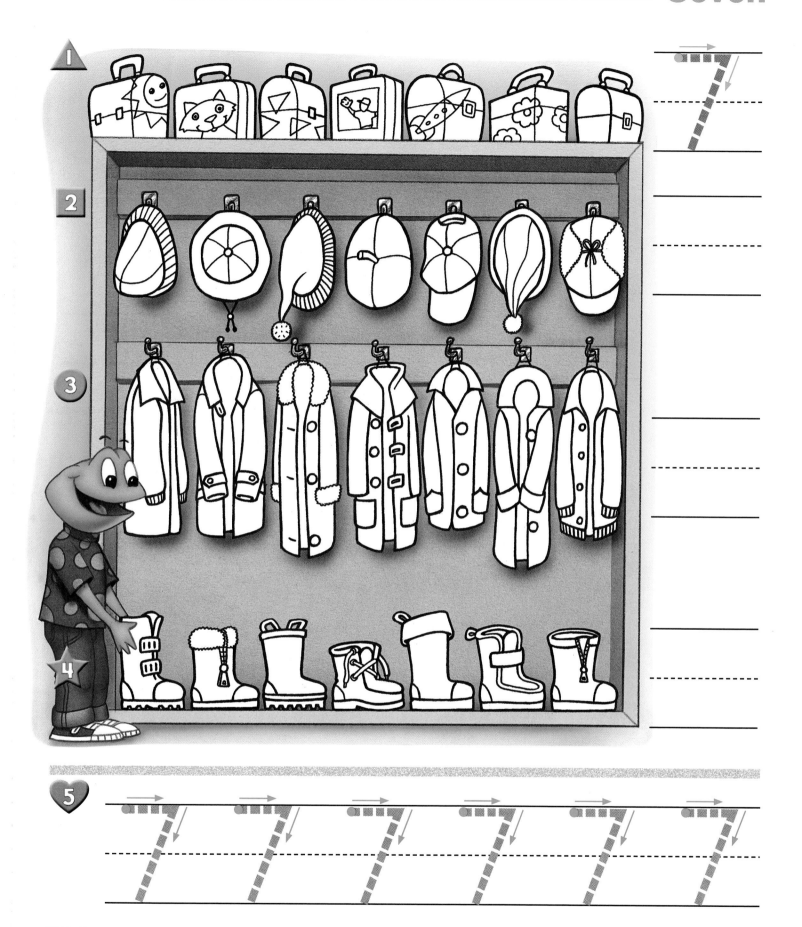

Directions 1–4 Color the items. Count. Write the number. 5 Write the number.

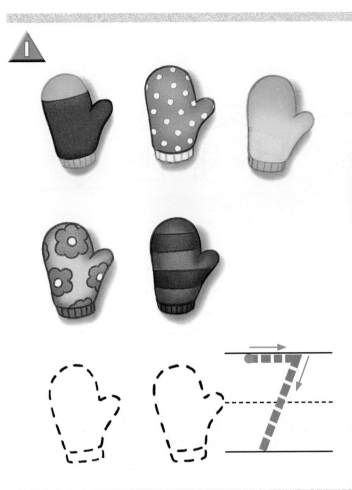

Directions 1–4 Count the items. Draw more to make a set of 7. Write the number.

At Home Help your child use a calendar to count the number of days in a week. Have your child practice writing the number 7.

128

Eight

Directions 1 Circle the groups of 8. 2 Write the number.

1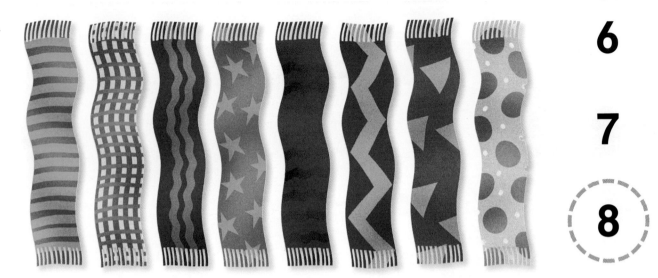

6

7

8

2

6

7

8

3

6

7

8

4

6

7

8

Directions 1–4 Count the items. Circle the number.

At Home Give your child a handful of pennies and have your child count out 8. Then ask your child to arrange the pennies in different groups—7 and 1, 4 and 4, 5 and 3, and so on.

Name _____

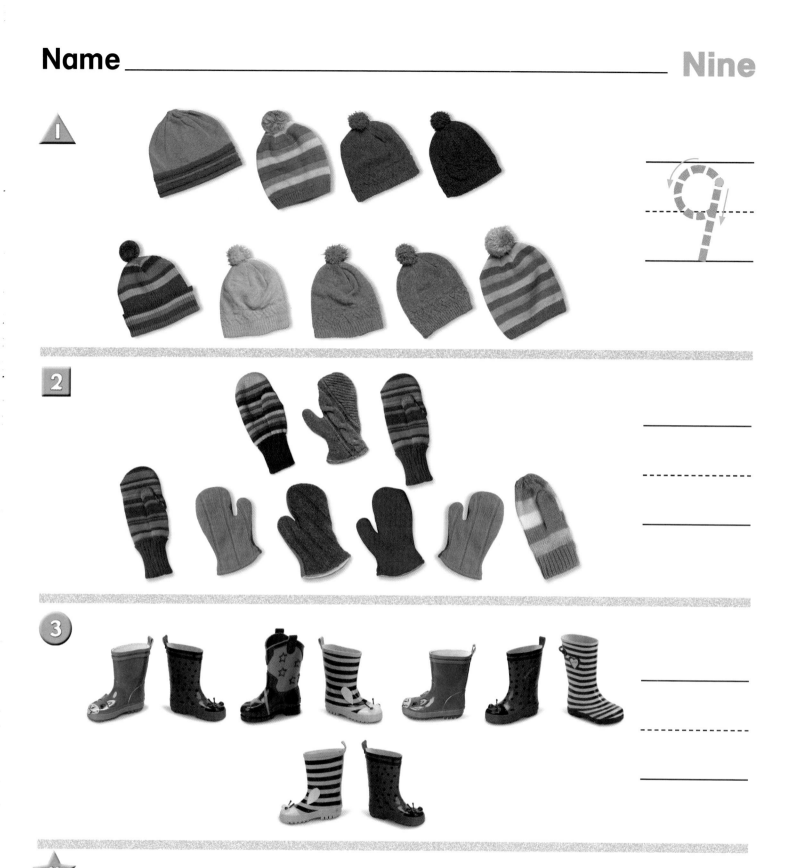

Nine

Directions 1–3 Count the items. Write the number. 4 Write the number.

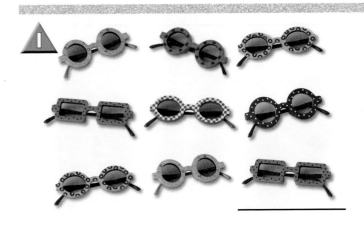

1

_____

_____

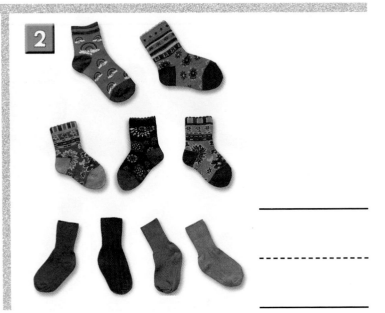

2

_____

_____

Quick Check

3

_____

_____

4

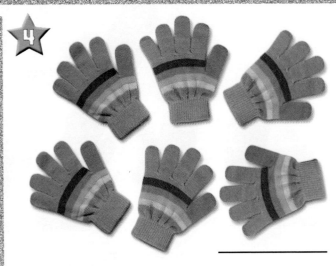

_____

_____

5

_____

_____

Directions 1–5 Count the items. Write the number.

At Home Have your child separate 9 crayons into 2 groups and join them to see that there are still 9. Have your child practice writing numbers.

Name _____

 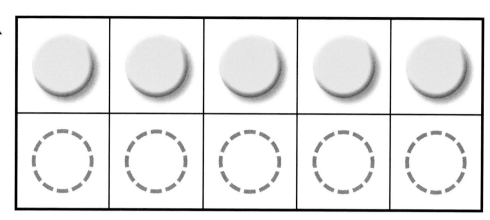 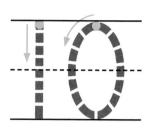

2

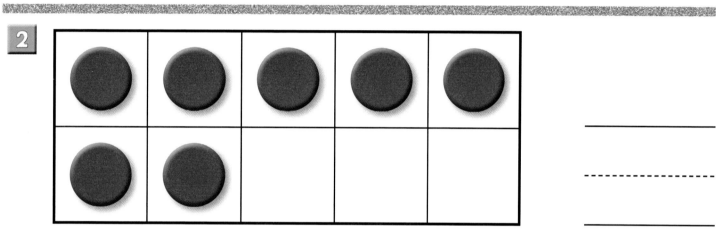

3

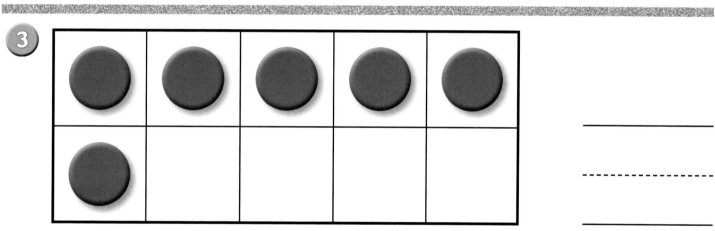

4

Directions 1–3 Place counters in the ten-frame to make 10. Draw. Write the number.
4 Write the number.

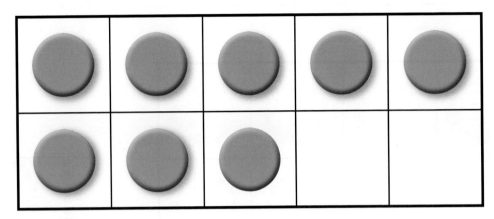

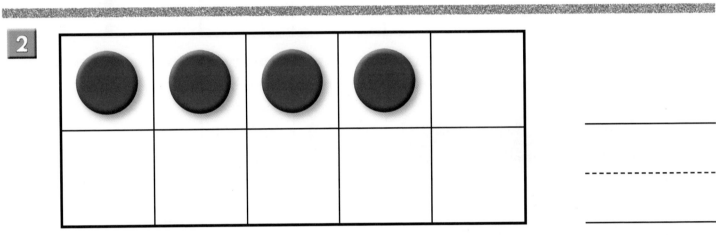

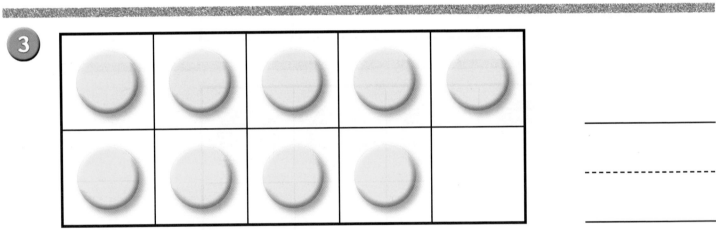

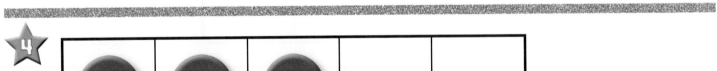

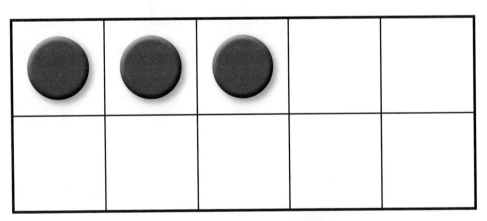

Directions 1–4 Place counters in the ten-frame to make 10. Draw. Write the number.

At Home Have your child point to and count the circles in each ten-frame. Have your child draw 10 objects and practice writing the number 10.

Name _____

Problem Solving

1 2 3 4 5 6

2

7 6 5 4 3 ___

3

1 3 5 ___ 9

Directions 1–3 Count the items. Look for a pattern. Write the missing number.

5   6   7   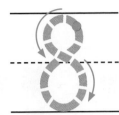   9   10

2

3   4   5   6   _____   _____

3

10   9   8   7   _____   _____

4

9   8   _____   6   5   _____

5

2   4   _____   8   _____   12

Directions 1–5 Look for a pattern in the numbers. Write the missing numbers.

At Home Have your child read the numbers and explain the patterns in each exercise. Start a number pattern and have your child tell you the number that comes next.

Name _____

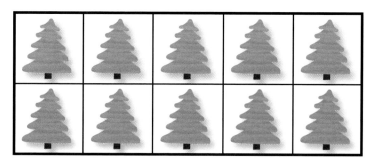

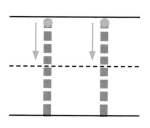

Eleven

2

_____

- - - - - - - - - - - -

_____

3

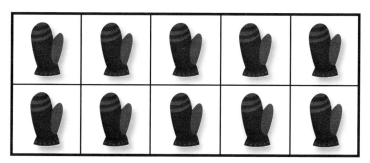

_____

- - - - - - - - - - - -

_____

4

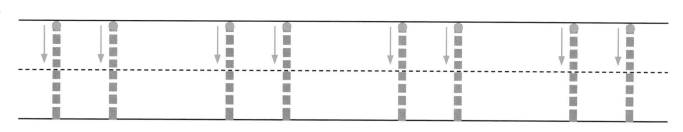

Directions 1–3 Count the items. Write the number. 4 Write the number.

1

9

10

(11)

2

9

10

11

3

9 10 11

4

9 10 11

Directions 1–4 Count the items. Circle the number.

At Home Have your child point out the groups of 11 on this page. Listen as your child points to and counts the items one by one.

138

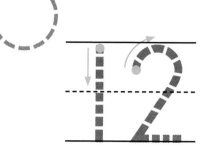

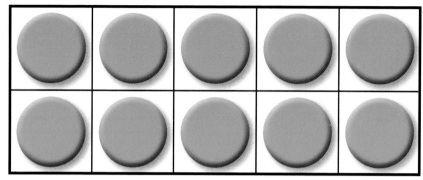

2

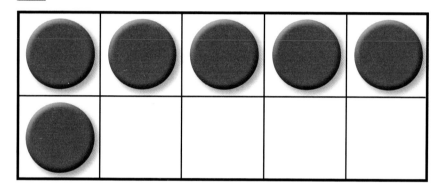

3

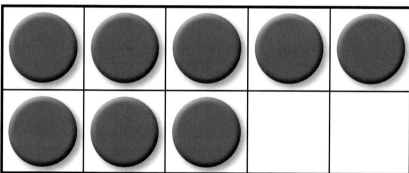

Directions 1–3 Use counters to make 12. Draw the counters. Write the number.
4 Write the number.

1 _____

- - - - - - - - - - - -

_____

2 _____

- - - - - - - - - - - -

_____

Problem Solving ▶ Reasoning

3

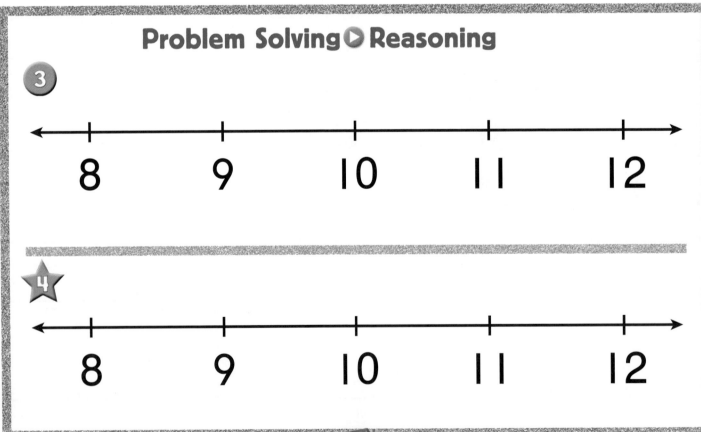

8   9   10   11   12

4

8   9   10   11   12

Directions 1–2 Count the items. Draw more to make 12. Write the number. 3–4 Listen to each clue. Cross out what does not match each clue. Circle what matches all the clues.

At Home Let your child count a dozen eggs, 12 pieces of silverware, and 12 pennies. Have your child show you how to write 12.

FOLLOW THE TRACKS

This take-home book will help you review concepts you learned in Chapter 7.

Follow the tracks to the grass.
How many tracks do you see?

Follow the tracks to the tree.
How many tracks do you see?

2

Follow the tracks to the berries.
How many tracks do you see?

4

Follow the tracks to the carrot.
How many tracks do you see?

Follow the tracks to the corn.
How many tracks do you see?

Follow the tracks to the acorns.
How many tracks do you see?

6

Follow the tracks to the seeds.
Draw more tracks to make 12.

8

Name _____

1

_____

- - - - - - - - - -

_____

2

_____

- - - - - - - - - -

_____

3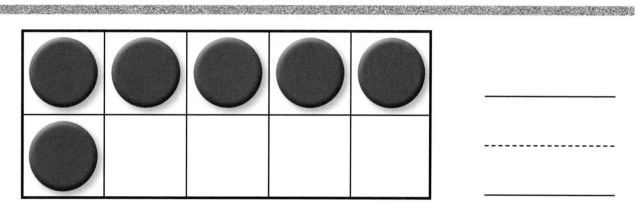

_____

- - - - - - - - - -

_____

4

10

11

12

5

_____ _____

- - - - - - - - - - - -

12 11 10 _____ _____ **7**

Directions 1 Circle the group that shows 7. Write the number. 2 Circle the group that shows 9. Write the number. 3 Place counters in the ten-frame to make 10. Draw. Write the number. 4 Count the trees. Circle the number. 5 Look for a pattern. Write the missing numbers.

November

Sunday	Monday	Tuesday	Wednesday	Thursday	Friday	Saturday
	1	2	3	4	5	6
7	8	9	10	11	12	13
14	15	16	17	18	19	20
21	22	23	24	25	26	27
28	29	30				

1

_____

- - - - - - - - - - - - -

_____

2

_____

- - - - - - - - - - - - -

_____

3

_____

- - - - - - - - - - - - -

_____

4

_____

- - - - - - - - - - - - -

_____

Directions 1–4 Look for the weather symbol on the calendar. Count. Write the number you find.

142

Using Numbers 0-12

CHAPTER 8

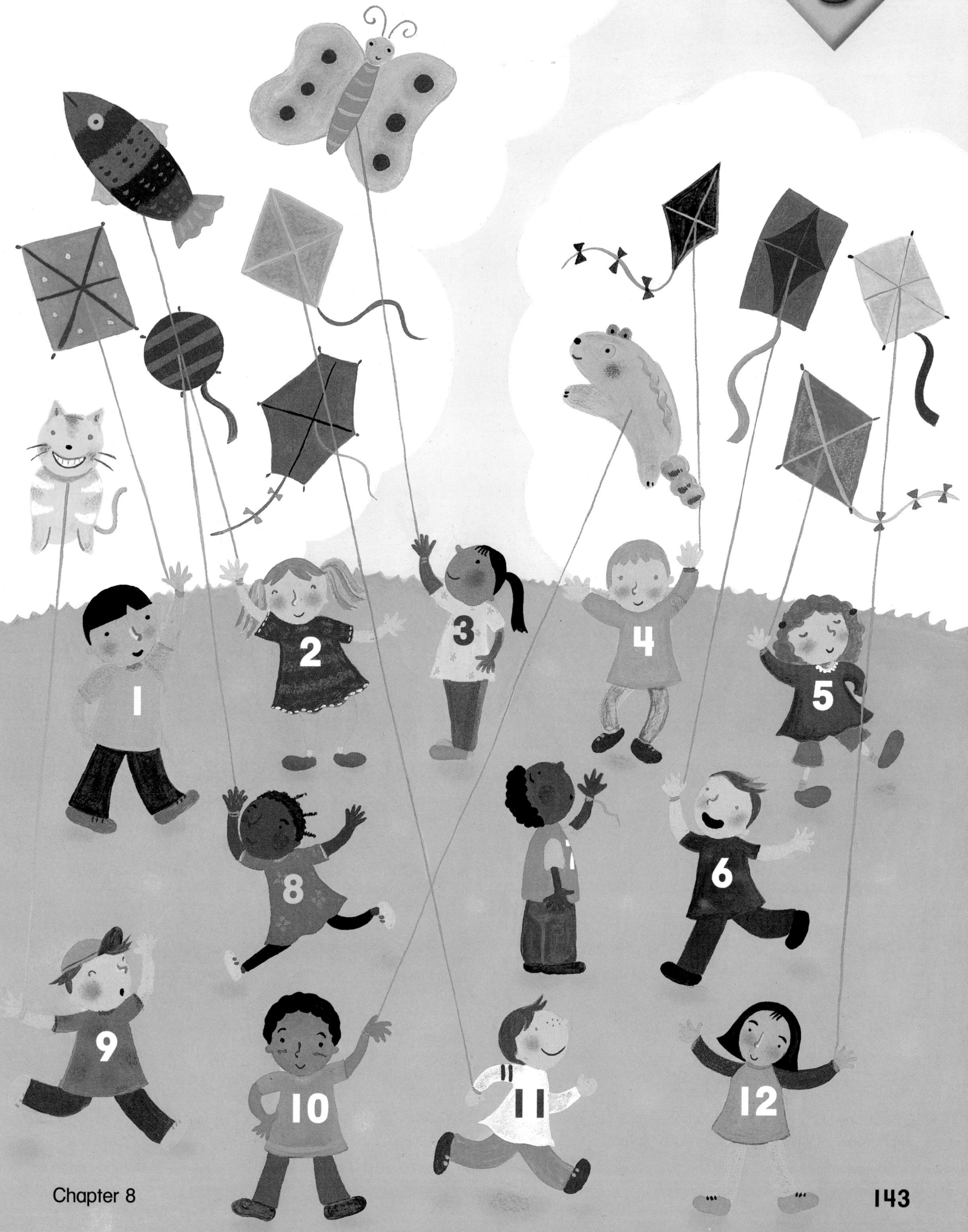
1
2
3
4
5
6
8
9
10
11
12

8

7

6

9

Directions Draw more kites to show each number. Talk about the number of kites shown and the number of kites you drew in each picture.

144

Name _____

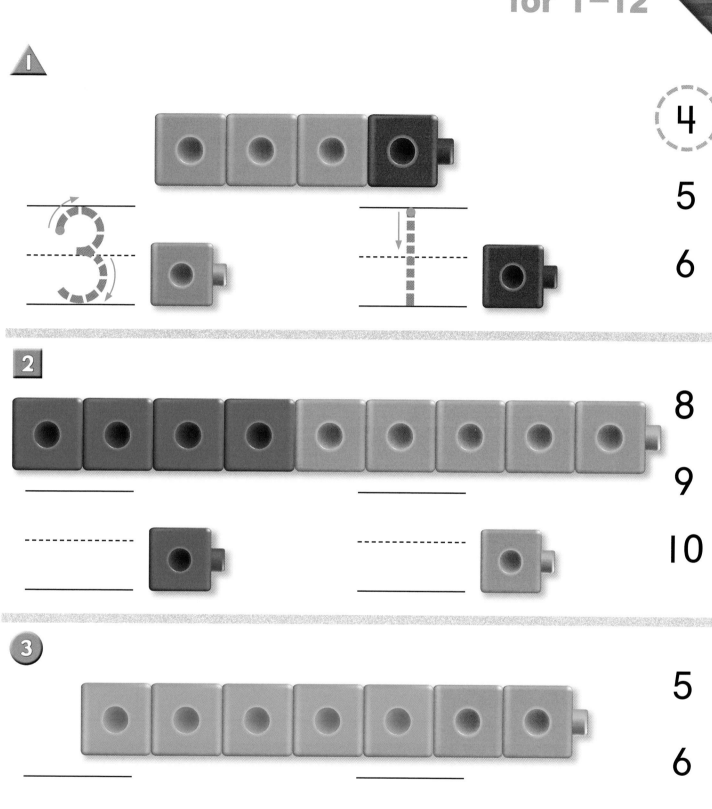

⚠ ①

4

5

6

②

8

9

10

③

5

6

7

Directions 1–3 Build the cube train. Count the cubes. Circle the number.
Count the cubes of each color. Write the numbers.

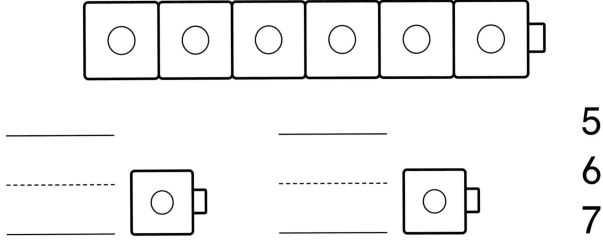

1

2   8   10
          11
          12

2

5
6
7

3

7
8
9

Directions 1–3 Count the cubes. Circle the number.
Color some cubes one color and the rest another color.
Write the number of each color.

At Home Have your child divide 12 pennies into
2 groups and tell how many are in each group. For
example, 11 and 1, 10 and 2, 9 and 3, 8 and 4, 7
and 5, 6 and 6.

Name _____

Order Numbers to 12

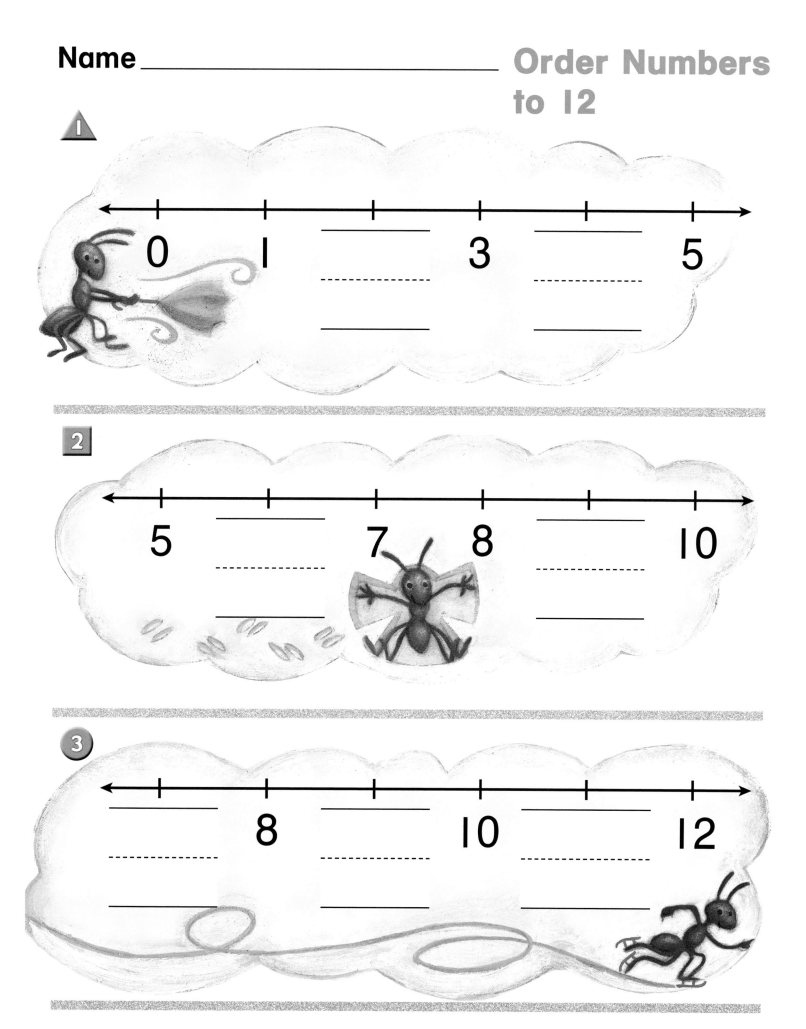

1

0   1   ___   3   ___   5

2

5   ___   7   8   ___   10

3

___   8   ___   10   ___   12

Directions 1–3 Write the missing numbers.

Chapter 8   147

Directions Connect the dots. Color the picture.

At Home Help your child write the numbers 1 through 12 on small pieces of paper, mix them up, and put them in order.

Directions Circle sets of 7 with red. Circle sets of 10 with blue.

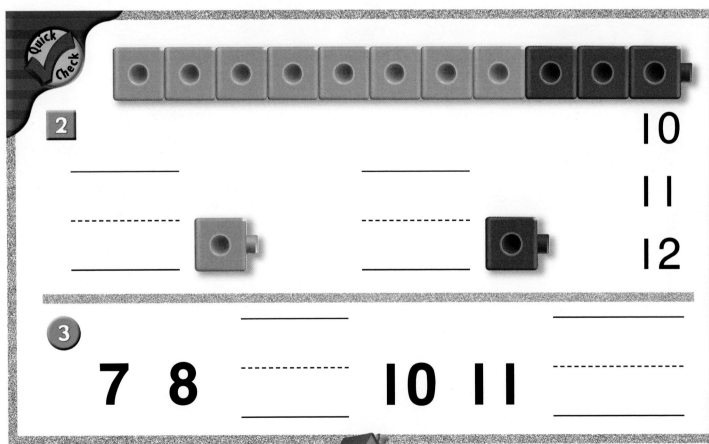

| 10 |
| 11 |
| 12 |

7 8 _____ 10 11 _____

Directions 1 Circle sets of 4 with red. Circle sets of 6 with blue. 2 Build the cube train. Circle the number. Count the cubes of each color. Write the numbers. 3 Write the missing numbers.

At Home Using small items such as buttons, make two sets of 5 and two sets of 7. Have your child count each set and tell which sets have the same number.

150

Name _____ More and Fewer

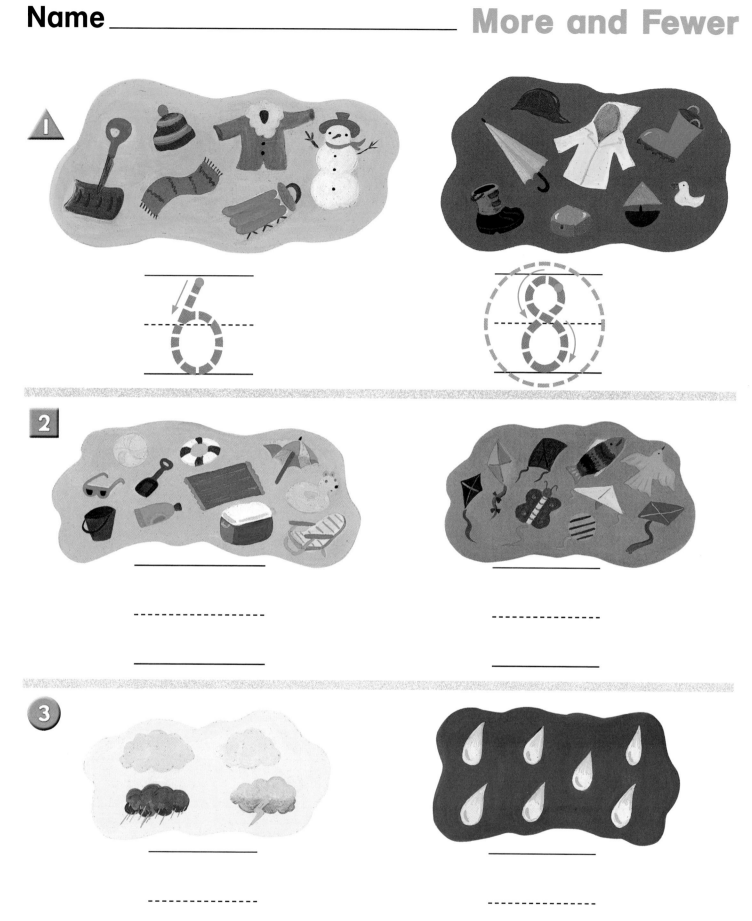

Directions 1–3 Count. Tell which set has more and which has fewer. Write each number.
Circle the greater number.

1

_____

- - - - - - - - - - - - - - -

_____

                                     _____

                                     - - - - - - - - - - - - - - -

                                     _____

2

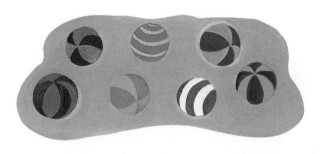

_____

- - - - - - - - - - - - - - -

_____

                                     _____

                                     - - - - - - - - - - - - - - -

                                     _____

Algebra Readiness ▶ Functions

3

1 More

10	6	9	11

Directions 1–2 Count. Tell which set has more and which has fewer. Write each number. Circle the greater number. 3 Follow the rule to fill in the missing numbers.

At Home Have your child count 10 pieces of pasta and 8 dry beans. Have your child tell which set has more and which has fewer. Have your child tell which number is greater.

152

Name _____

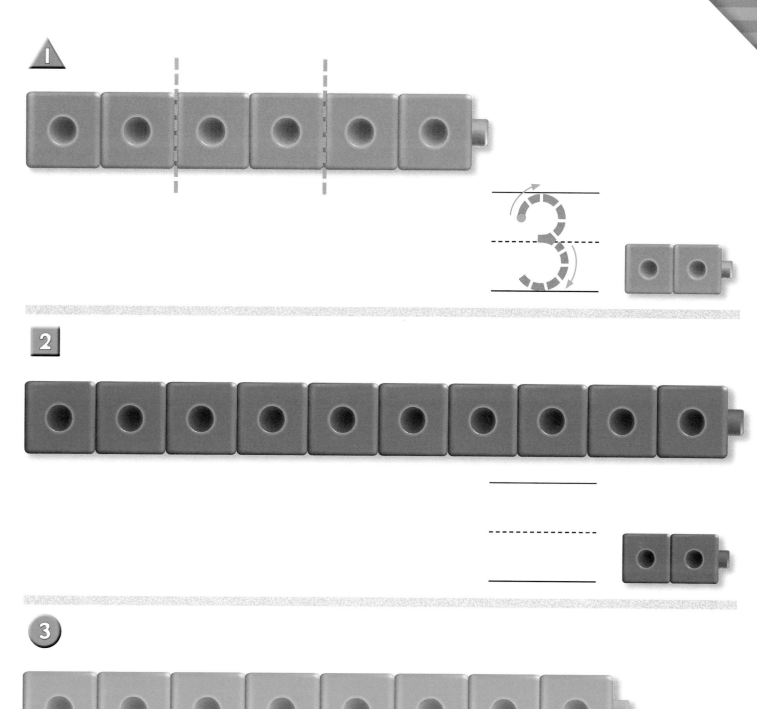

1

2

3

Directions 1–3 Build the cube train. Break it into groups of 2 cubes. Draw lines to show where you broke the train. Write the number of equal groups you made.

▲1

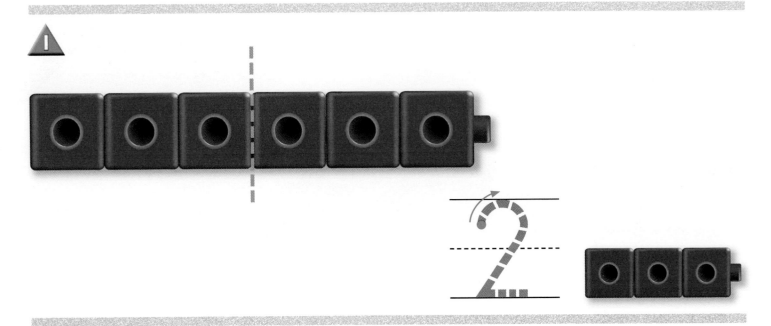

2

2

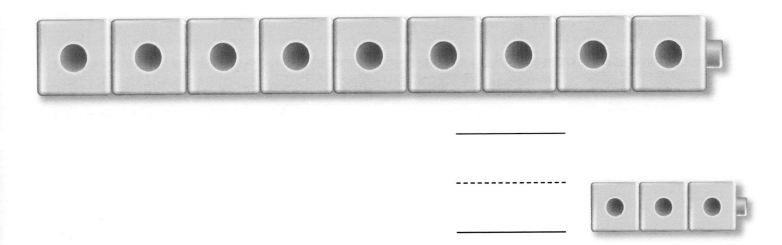

_____

- - - - - - - - - - -

3

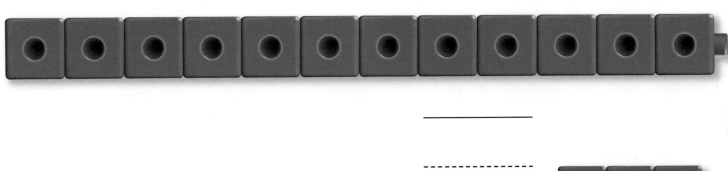

_____

- - - - - - - - -

Directions 1–3 Build the cube train. Break it into groups of 3 cubes. Draw lines to show where you broke the train. Write the number of equal groups you made.

At Home Have your child divide 12 paper clips into groups of 2, 3, and 4. Have your child tell how many groups there are.

154

Pitter, Patter Raindrops

This take-home book will help you review concepts you learned in Chapter 8.

1

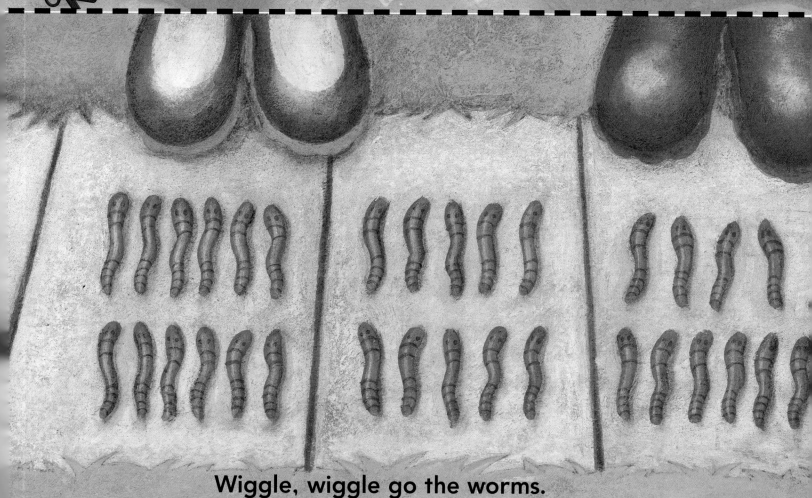

Wiggle, wiggle go the worms.
Which sets of worms show twelve?

Pitter, patter goes the rain.
Which sets of raindrops show seven?

2

1 ___ 3 4 ___ 6

7 8 ___ 10 ___ 12

Splash, splash in the puddles.
Write the missing numbers.

4

_____ 5 6 _____ 8

6 7 _____ 9 _____

Snap, snap go the turtles.
Write the missing numbers.

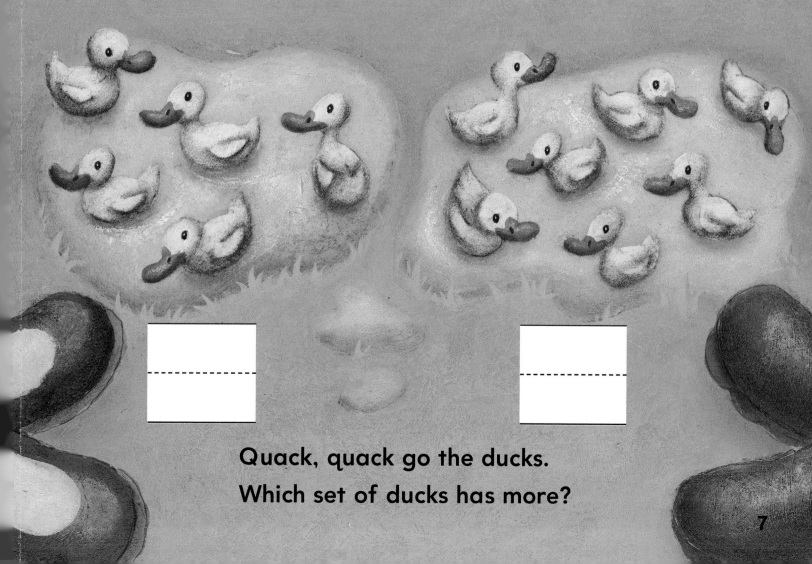

Quack, quack go the ducks.
Which set of ducks has more?

Croak, croak go the frogs.
Which sets have 8 frogs?

6

Pitter, patter goes the rain.
Which umbrella has fewer raindrops?

8

Name _____

7   **8**   _____   **10**   _____

_____   _____

_____   _____

_____

_____

Directions 1 Write the missing numbers. 2 Circle sets of 6 in red. Circle sets of 7 in blue. 3 Count.
Write the numbers. Circle the greater number. 4 Build the cube train. Break it into groups of 2 cubes.
Draw lines to show where you broke the train. Write the number of equal groups you made.

SPIN AND COUNT!

Start

What You Need

Finish

How to Play 1 Take turns with a partner. 2 Spin the spinner. Move your marker to the first space that has the same number of objects as the number on the spinner. 3 The first player to reach Finish wins.

1

_____

- - - - - - - - - - - - - - -

_____

2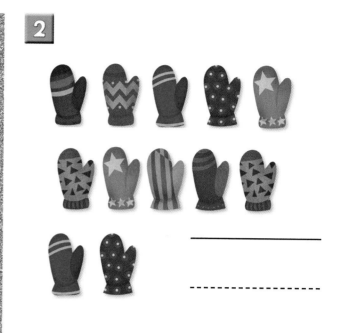

_____

- - - - - - - - - - - - - - -

_____

3

7   **8**   **9**

4

10   **11**   **12**

5

_____   _____

- - - - - - - - -   - - - - - - - - -

2   4 _____ **8** _____ **12**

Directions 1–2 Count the items. Write the number. 3–4 Count the items. Circle the number.
5 Look for a pattern. Write the missing numbers.

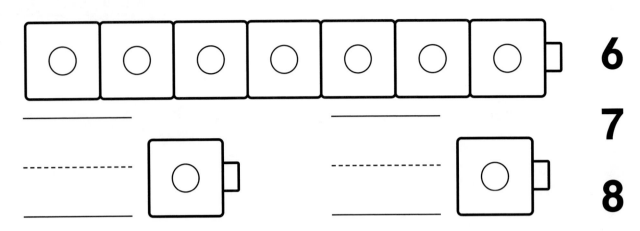

6
7
8

4 _____ 6 7 8 _____

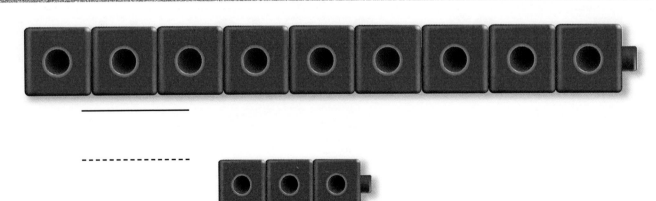

Directions 6 Count the cubes. Circle the number. Color some cubes one color and the rest another color. Write the numbers. 7 Write the missing numbers. 8 Count and write the numbers. Circle the greater number. 9 Build the cube train. Break it into groups of 3 cubes. Draw lines to show where you broke the train. Write the number of equal groups.

Name _____

Odd and Even Numbers

 1

5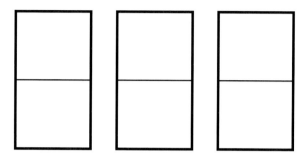

Odd

Even

2

6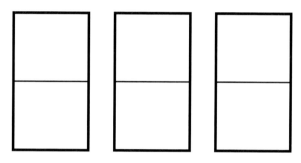

Odd

Even

3

7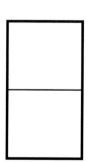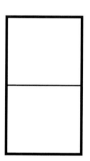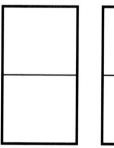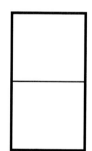

Odd

Even

4

8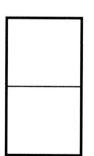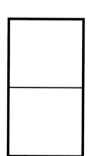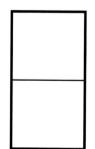

Odd

Even

Directions 1–4 Count out cubes to match the number. Place pairs of two cubes in each frame. If each frame has a pair of cubes, circle Even. If not, circle Odd.

Name _____

_____   _____

- - - - - - - - - - -   - - - - - - - - - - -

_____   _____

4

8

Directions 1 Count and write the number in each set. Circle the set that has fewer. 2 Cross out the item that does not belong in a set of cylinders. 3 Circle the third mouse. 4 Circle the shape that is likely to come next. 5–6 Draw raindrops to show each number.

Photography Credits: 131-132 © Ken Karp. 140(t) © Ken Karp. 140(b) © Siede Preis/PhotoDisc/Getty Images. **Illustration Credits:** 122 © Mircea Catusanu. 123-124 © Promotion Studios. 126 © Mircea Catusanu. 127-128 © John Berg. 129-130 © Mircea Catusanu. 135 © Mircea Catusanu. 137-138 © Mircea Catusanu. Chapter 7 Story © Promotion Studios. 141(t) © Mircea Catusanu. 141(m) © John Berg. 141(b) © Mircea Catusanu. 142(t) © John Berg. 143-144 © Sachiko Yoshikawa. 147-148 © Wallace Keller. 149-152 © Sachiko Yoshikawa. Chapter 8 Story © Wallace Keller. 155(t) © John Berg. 155(m) © Mircea Catusanu. 156 © Sachiko Yoshikawa. 157-158(tl) © Mircea Catusanu. 160(t) © Mircea Catusanu. 60(m) © Wallace Keller.

HOUGHTON MIFFLIN MATH

UNIT 5

Time and Money

From the Read-Aloud Anthology

Bunny Day

by Rick Walton
illustrated by
Paige Miglio

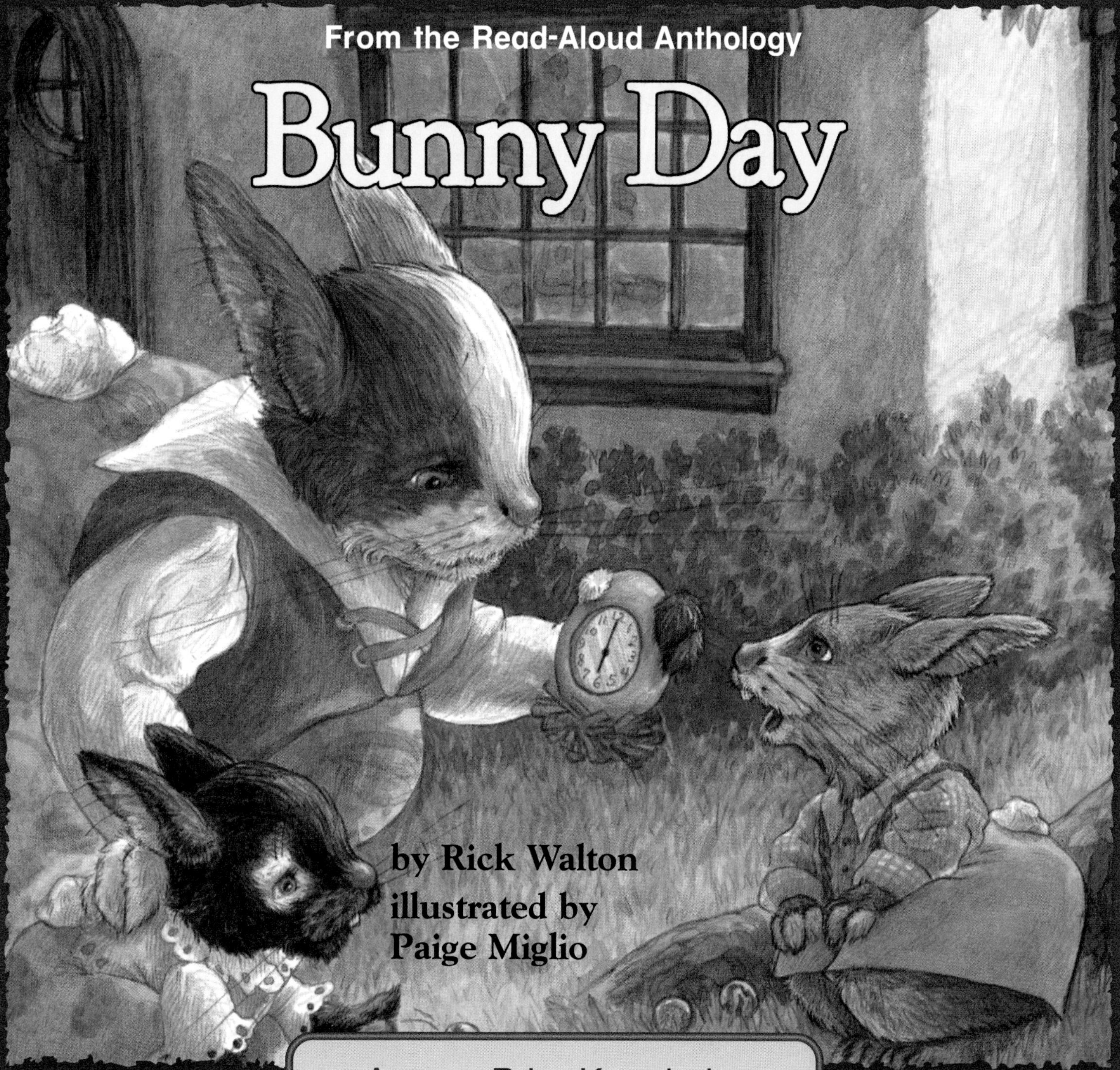

Access Prior Knowledge

This story will help you review

- Times of day

ISBN: 0-618-33875-6 Printed in the U.S.A.

MATH at Home

Dear Family,

We are starting a new unit called Time and Money. In Chapter 9, we will work with calendars and learn how to tell time to the nearest hour on a clock. In Chapter 10, we will identify coins and learn about the value of different coins.

Love, _____

Vocabulary

calendar
A chart showing the days of the week and the months of the year.

clock
A tool to measure and record time.

minute hand

hour hand

3 o'clock

3 o'clock

penny, nickel, dime, quarter
Coins with the value of one cent, five cents, ten cents, and twenty-five cents, respectively.

1¢

5¢

10¢

25¢

Vocabulary Activities

- Have your child use a calendar to name the days of the week and the months of the year.

- Help your child read times to the hour on clocks around your home.

- Let your child sort, identify, and compare different coins. Help your child trade 5 pennies for 1 nickel.

Visit *Education Place* at **eduplace.com/parents/mw/** for *e* • WordGame, *e* • Glossary **and more**.

Literature to Read Together

- **A Chair for My Mother** by Vera B. Williams (*Greenwillow Books, 1982*)

- **Just a Minute!** by Anita Harper (*Putnam, 1987*)

- **The Pig Is in the Pantry, The Cat Is on the Shelf** by Shirley Mozelle (*Clarion Books, 2000*)

Time

CHAPTER 9

Which Does Your Family Use More?

Directions Think about the things that help us tell time. Ask 5 classmates whether their families use clocks or calendars more. Color a box for each response. Tell about your graph.

164

3

Directions Circle the picture that shows: **1** the morning; **2** the afternoon; **3** the evening.

1

morning

2

afternoon

evening

Directions 1–3 Draw something you do at the time of day pictured.

At Home Name some daily events such as going to school or having dinner. Have your child use the words *day, night, morning, afternoon,* and *evening* to identify the time of day each event happens.

166

Comparing Temperature

1

2

3

Directions 1-3 Color a red frame around the picture that shows a hotter day. Color a blue frame around the picture that shows a colder day.

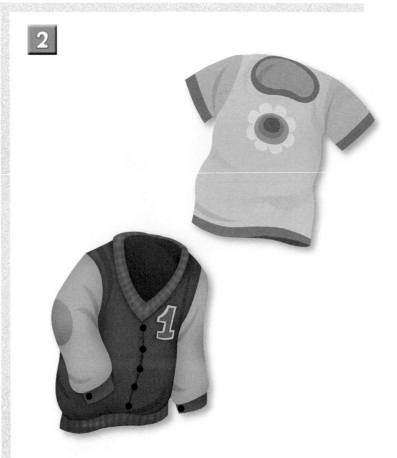

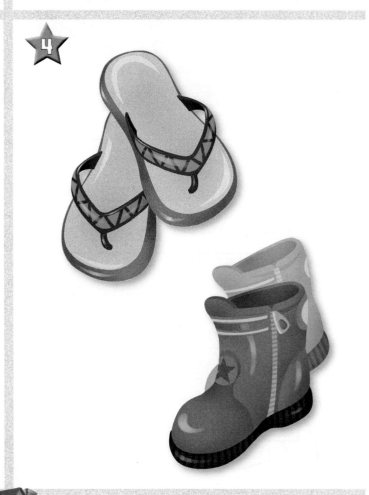

Directions 1–4 Circle in red the clothing worn on a warmer day. Circle in blue the clothing worn on a cooler day.

At Home Help your child use the words *warmer* and *cooler* to compare the temperature during the four seasons. For example, it is cooler in spring than in summer.

Name _____

JANUARY

Sunday	Monday	Tuesday	Wednesday	Thursday	Friday	Saturday
	1	2	3	4	5	6
7	8	9	10	11	12	13
14	15	16	17	18	19	20
21	22	23	24	25	26	27
28	29	30	31			

1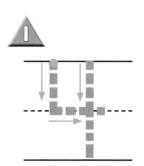

_____ Sundays

2

_____ Tuesdays

3

_____ Fridays

4

_____ days in a week

Directions Count and write the number of: 1 Sundays; 2 Tuesdays; 3 Fridays; 4 days in a week. Circle the first Sunday in red, all the Tuesdays in blue, and the last Friday in green.

APRIL

Sunday	Monday	Tuesday	Wednesday	Thursday	Friday	Saturday
				1	2	3
4	5	6	7	8	9	10
11	12	13	14	15	16	17
18	19	20	21	22	23	24
25	26	27	28	29	30	

⚠ 1

_____

_____ Mondays

2

_____

_____ Thursdays

③ 3

_____

_____ Wednesdays

★ 4

_____

_____ Saturdays

Directions Write the number of: 1 Mondays;
2 Thursdays; 3 Wednesdays; 4 Saturdays. Circle the
second Monday in red, all the Thursdays in blue, the third
Wednesday in green, and the last Saturday in yellow.

At Home Help your child point to and read the
numbers on this month's calendar. Have your child
find different days such as the first Tuesday.

More Time, Less Time

Hands-On

1 △

2

3

Directions 1–3 Underline the activity you predict will take more time. Do the activities. Circle in red the activity that took more time. Circle in blue the activity that took less time.

Directions 1–2 Circle in red the activity that takes more time. Circle in blue the activity that takes less time. 3 Circle the picture that shows the afternoon. 4 Circle the clothing worn on a warmer day.

At Home Let your child compare two home activities. Talk about which takes more time and which takes less time.

172

Name _____

 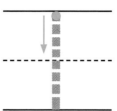 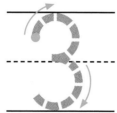

2

Directions 1–2 Write the numbers *1*, *2*, and *3* to show the order of events from first to last.

_____   _____   _____

- - - - - - - -   - - - - - - - -   - - - - - - - -

_____   _____   _____

_____   _____   _____

- - - - - - - -   - - - - - - - -   - - - - - - - -

_____   _____   _____

Problem Solving ▶ Visual Thinking

Directions 1–2 Write the numbers *1*, *2*, and *3* to show the order of events from first to last. **3** Circle the one that is likely to come next.

At Home Have your child tell you some events of his or her day in order. Encourage your child to use the words *first*, *next*, and *last*.

174

_____

_____ o'clock

Directions Write the missing numbers on the clock. Write the time shown on the clock.

1  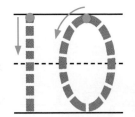 o'clock

2  _____ o'clock

3  _____ o'clock

4  _____ o'clock

5  _____ o'clock

Directions 1–5 Write the time shown on the clock.

At Home Fold this page lengthwise so only the clocks are showing. Point to each clock and have your child tell you the time that is shown.

176

Name_____

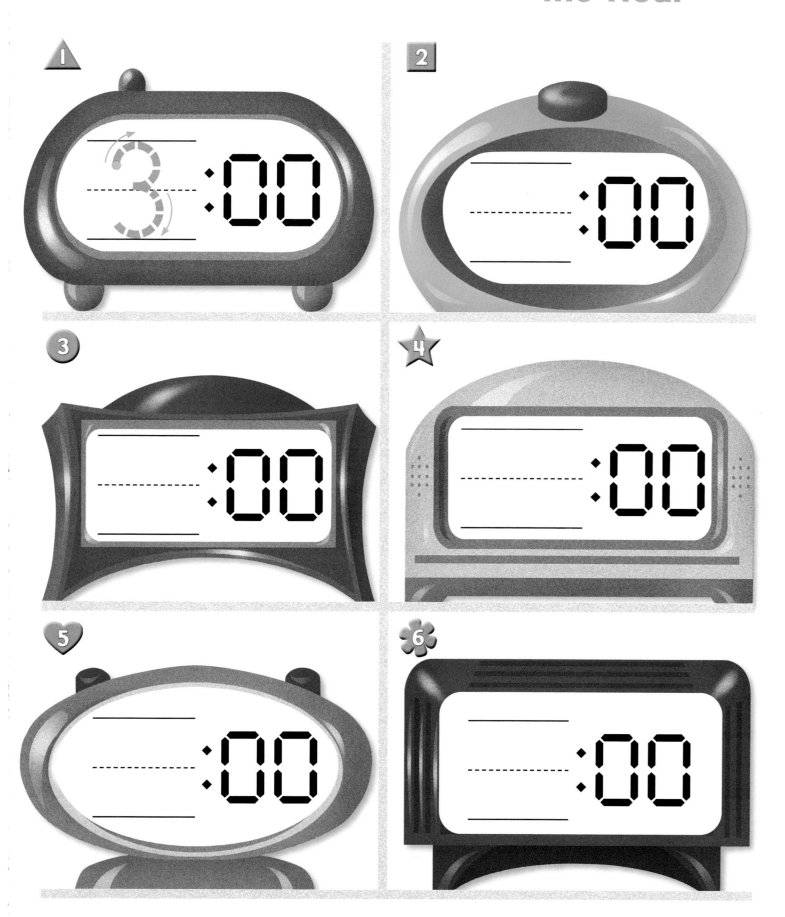

Directions Show the following times on the clocks: 1 3 o'clock, 2 7 o'clock, 3 4 o'clock,
4 11 o'clock, 5 2 o'clock, and 6 9 o'clock.

1  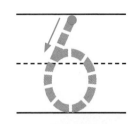 _____ o'clock

2  _____ o'clock

3  _____ o'clock

4  _____ o'clock

5  _____ o'clock

Directions 1–5 Write the time shown on the clock.

At Home Have your child point to each clock and tell you the time. Talk about things that he or she might do at each time shown.

178

Name _____

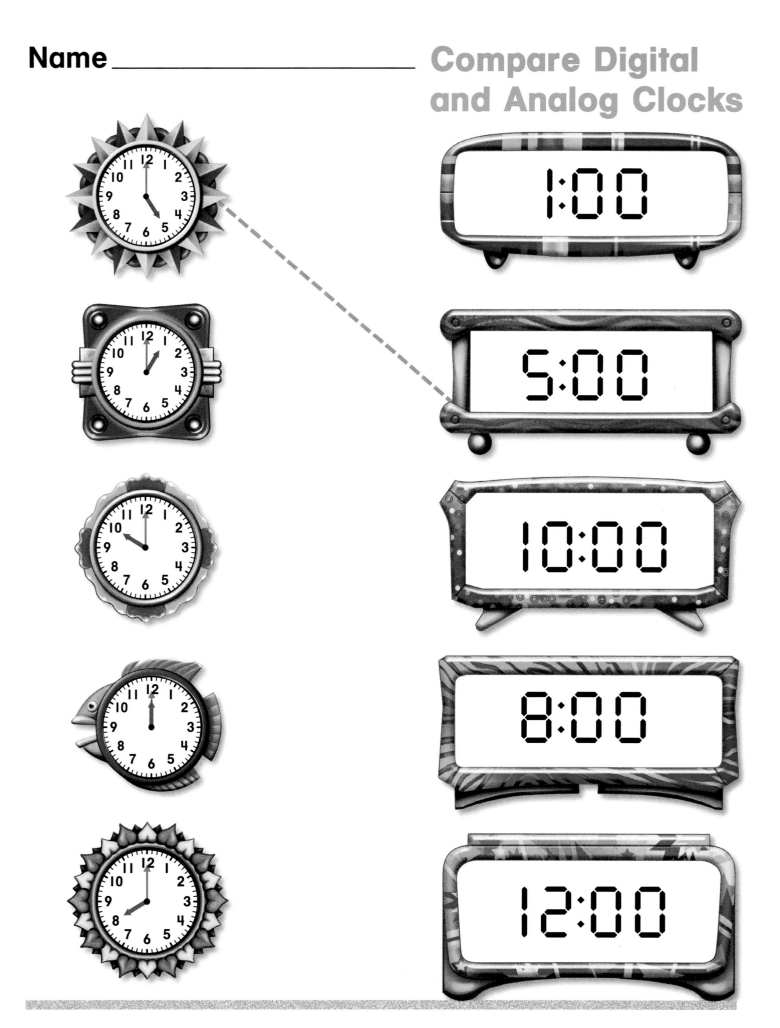

Directions Draw lines to match the clocks that show the same time.

Directions 1–5 Write the time on the digital clock to match the time shown.

At Home Draw attention to clocks in your home and neighborhood. Help your child read times on the hour.

Polly Piglet's Day

This take-home book will help you review concepts you learned in Chapter 9.

MARCH

day	Thursday	Friday	Saturday
	1	2	3 CARLOS
	8		10
	16	17	
	22		24
28	29		

MILK

cereal

Yesterday was Friday.
What day is it today?

3

It is time for Polly Piglet to get up.
Is it morning, afternoon, or evening?

2

Carlos Cow has come to play.
Is it cooler inside or outside?

4

Polly and Carlos play with blocks.
Which tower took more time to make?

Polly says goodbye to Carlos.
What time is it?

_____ :00

It is lunchtime.

What happens first, next, and last?

6

Polly loves bedtime stories.

What time is it?

8

o'clock

Name _____

1

2

3

_____ _____ _____

- - - - - - - - - - - - - - - - - - - - - - - - - - - - - - - - -

4

5

March

Sunday	Monday	Tuesday	Wednesday	Thursday	Friday	Saturday
			1	2	3	4
5	6	7	8	9	10	11
12	13	14	15	16	17	18
19	20	21	22	23	24	25
26	27	28	29	30	31	

Directions 1 Circle the picture that shows the afternoon. 2 Circle the activity that takes more time.
3 Write *1*, *2*, and *3* to show the order of events from first to last. 4 Write the time. 5 Circle the last
Tuesday in red. Circle the first Thursday in blue.

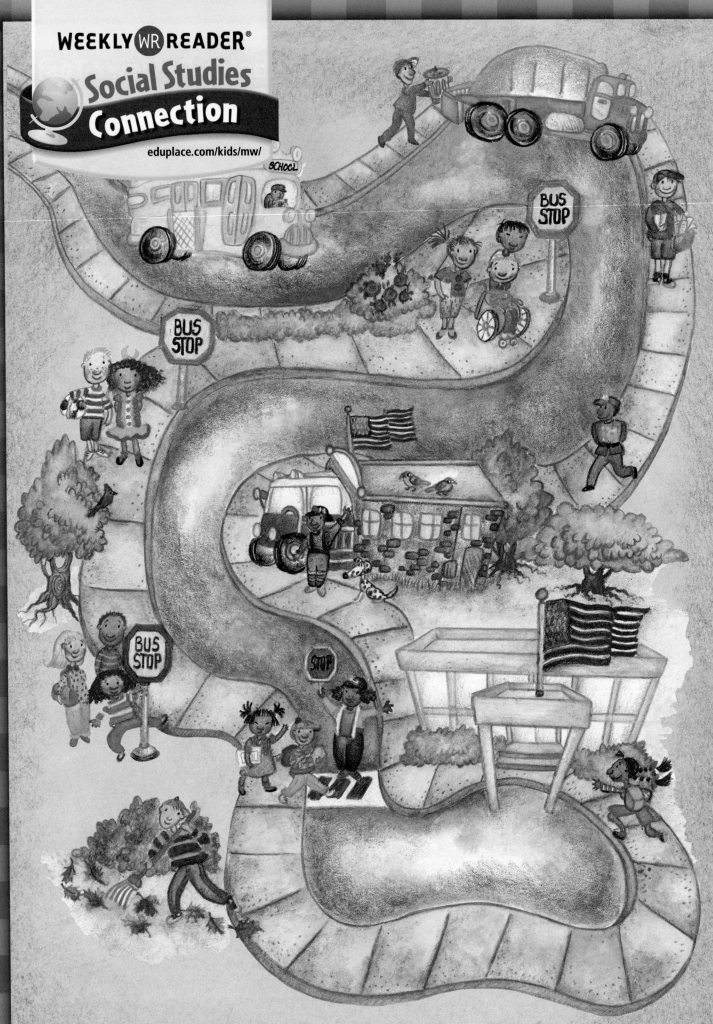

Directions Follow the bus route to school. Circle in red the group that will get on first. Circle in blue the group that will get on next. Circle in green the group that will get on last. Talk about the community helpers along the way.

182

Money

LEMONADE

2¢
5¢
10¢

Coin tally

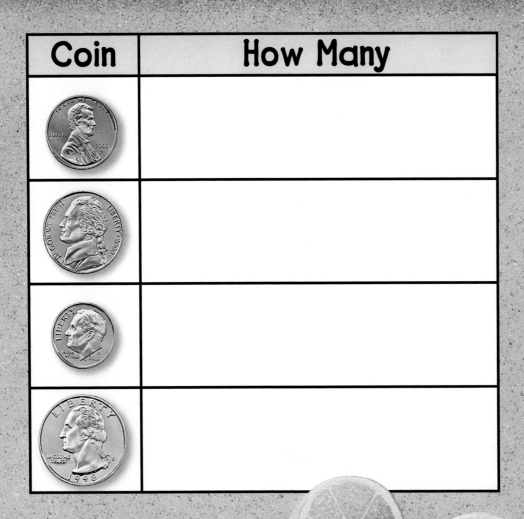

Coin	How Many

Directions Make a tally chart of the coins. Cross out each coin as you make a tally mark in the chart. Tell what you know about the different coins.

Name ______________________ **Penny**

1

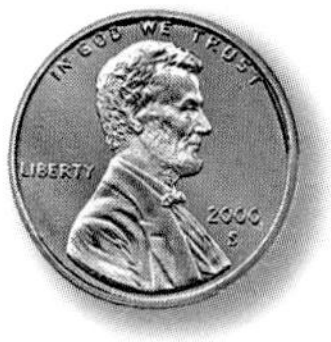

___ ¢

2

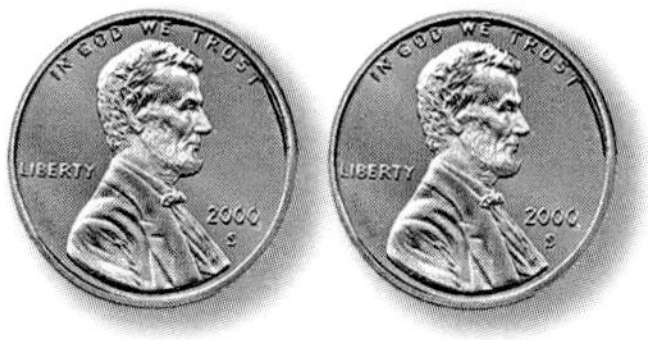

___ ¢

3

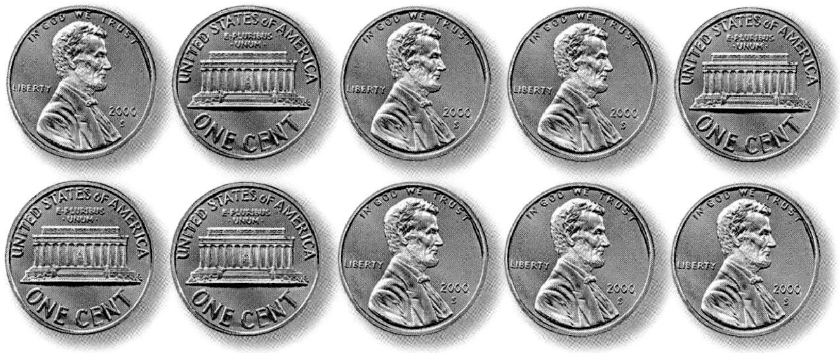

___ ¢

4

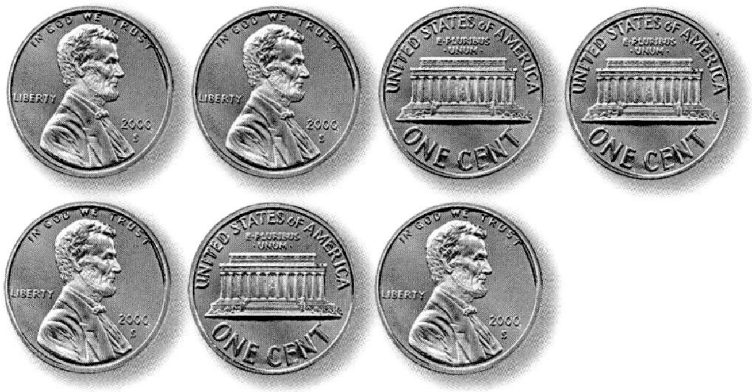

___ ¢

5

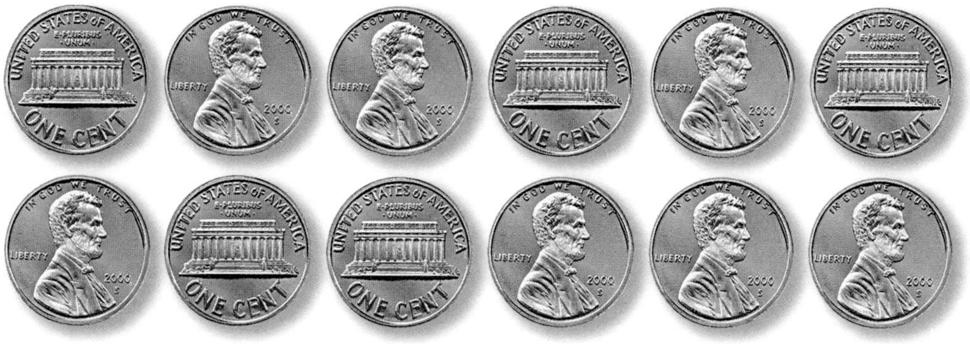

___ ¢

Directions 1–5 Write the number of cents.

1

3¢

2

2¢

3

5¢

4

8¢

5

6¢

Directions: 1–5 Use pennies to show each price. Draw the pennies.

At Home Have your child separate the pennies from a handful of coins. Let your child use pennies to count out groups of 5¢, 8¢, 10¢, and 12¢.

186

Name ______________________ **Nickel**

1

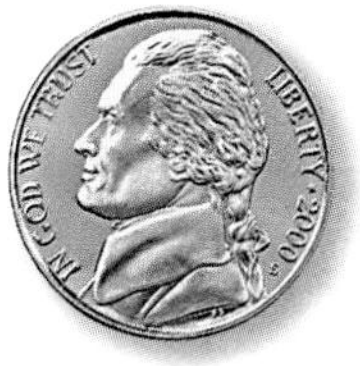

5 ¢

2

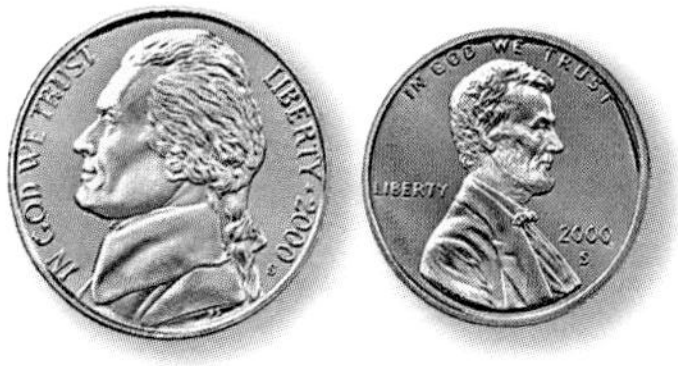

______ ¢

3

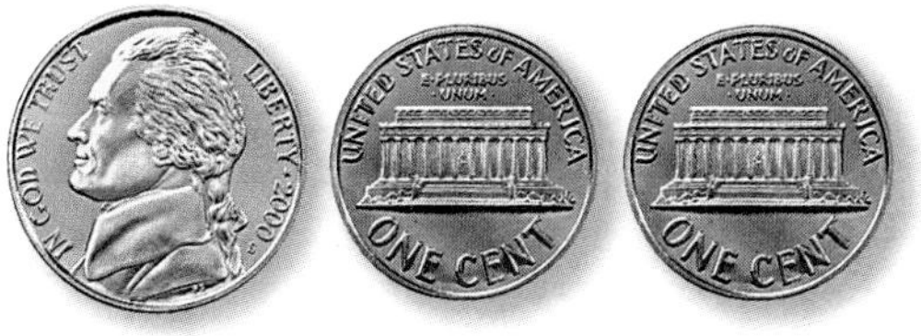

______ ¢

4

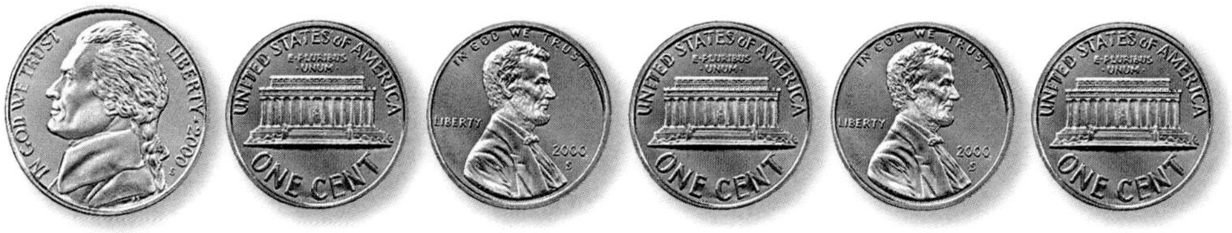

______ ¢

5

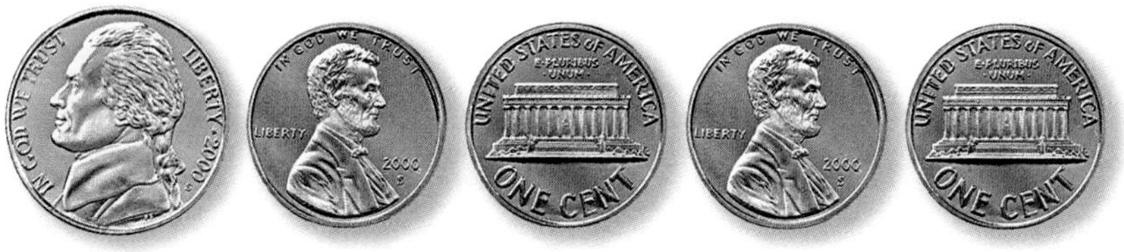

______ ¢

Directions 1–5 Write the number of cents.

1

6¢ (**7¢**) **8¢**

2

1¢ **5¢** **10¢**

3

4¢ **5¢** **9¢**

4

8¢ **7¢** **4¢**

Directions 1–4 Circle the price tag that matches the number of cents.

At Home Have your child identify all the nickels in a handful of coins. Then have your child make and count groups of coins that include 1 nickel and up to 5 pennies.

188

Dime

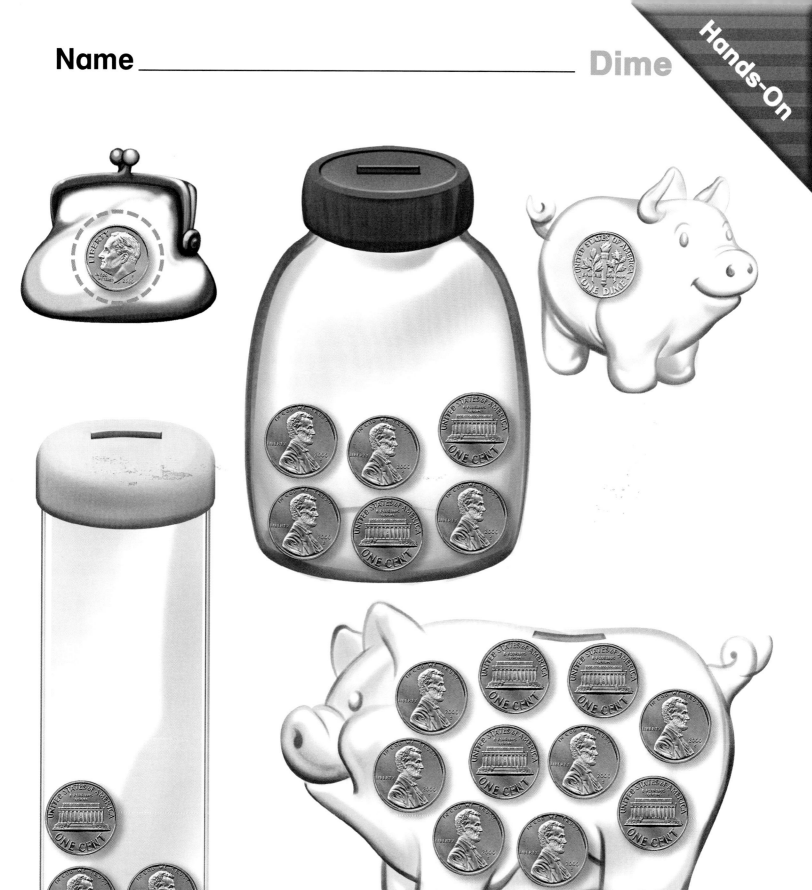

Directions Circle the groups that show 10¢. Use pennies to make all groups show 10¢.
Draw the pennies you used.

1

1¢   5¢   (10¢)

2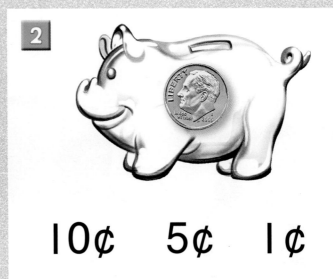

10¢   5¢   1¢

3

6¢   10¢   5¢

4

8¢   9¢   10¢

5

_____
- - - - - - -
_____ ¢

6

_____
- - - - - - -
_____ ¢

Directions 1–4 Circle the number of cents. 5–6 Write the number of cents.

At Home Have your child separate the dimes from a handful of coins. Then have your child make groups of pennies that equal 10 cents.

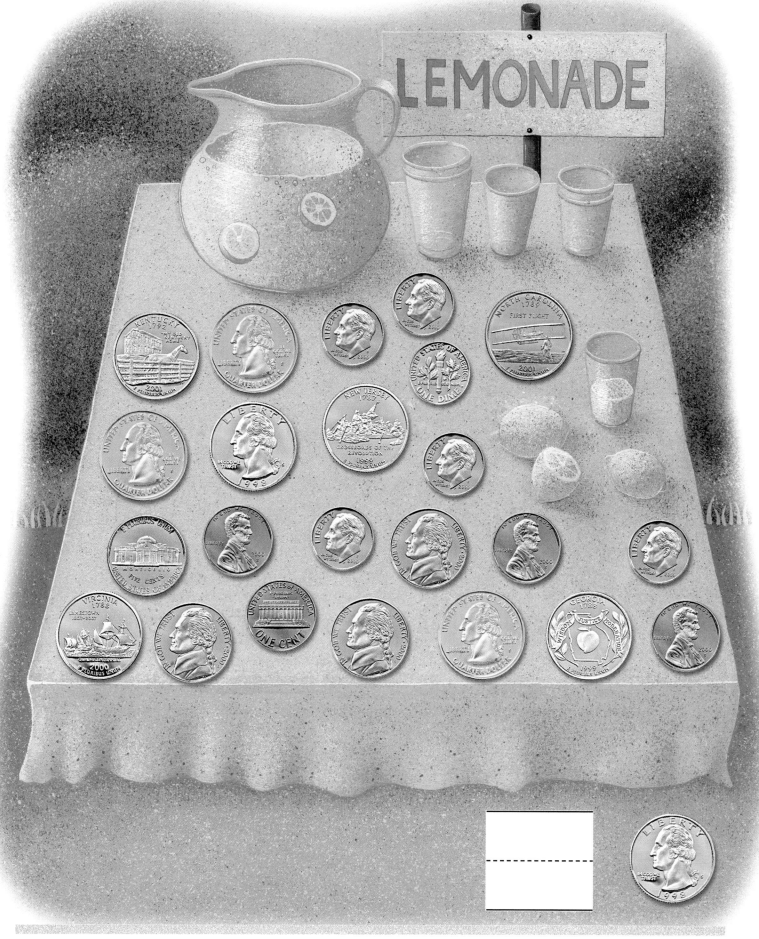

Directions Circle all the quarters. Count and write the number of quarters.

Problem Solving ▷ Number Sense

2

3

Directions | Circle the quarters in red, the dimes in blue, and the nickels in yellow. 2–3 Circle the group that will buy more.

At Home Have your child separate the quarters from a handful of coins. Talk about how a quarter differs from both a dime and a nickel.

192

_____
- - - - - - - - - -
_____ ¢

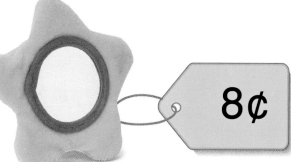 8¢

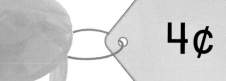 4¢

 3¢

_____
- - - - - - - - - -
_____ ¢

Directions Place 10 pennies on the purse. Circle an item you want to buy. Move that many cents to the cash register. Write how much you spent. Write what you have left in the purse.

_____
- - - - - - - - - - -
_____ ¢

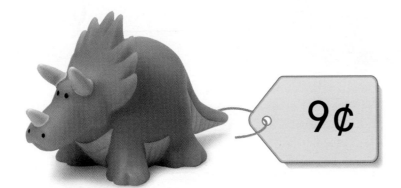

9¢

5¢

6¢

_____
- - - - - - - - - - -
_____ ¢

Directions Place 10 pennies on the coin purse. Circle an item you want to buy. Move that many cents to the cash register. Write how much you spent. Write what you have left in the coin purse.

At Home Have your child use 10 pennies to act out purchasing different items. Have your child tell how much he or she spent and how much is left.

194

Sam's Coins

This take-home book will help you review concepts you learned in Chapter 10.

1

Sam finds more coins.
Name the coins.

3

Grandpa hides coins for Sam to find.
Name the coins.

2

Sam counts his pennies.
Write the number of cents.

_____ ¢

4

Grandpa holds a coin.
Write the number of cents.

_____ ¢

5

Sam buys a pencil.
Which coins show 8¢?

7

Grandpa holds more coins.
Write the number of cents.

_____ ¢

6

Grandpa gives Sam a bank.
Which coin does Sam save?

8

Name _____

1

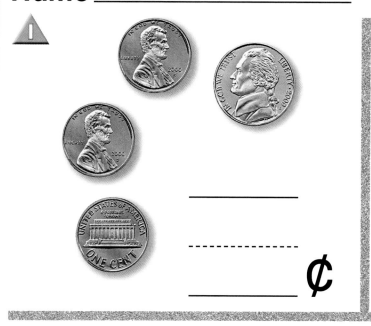

_____

- - - - - - - - - - - - - -

_____ ¢

2

_____

- - - - - - - - - - - - - -

_____ ¢

3

4

5¢

_____

- - - - - - - - - - - - - -

_____ ¢

Directions 1–2 Write the number of cents. 3 Circle the pennies in red, the nickels in blue, the dimes in yellow, and the quarters in green. 4 Circle the pennies used to buy the item. Write the cents left.

Chapter 10

195

MONEY MATCH

What You Need

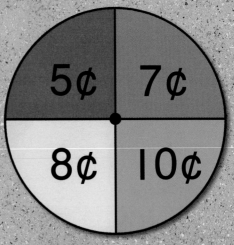

5¢	7¢	
8¢	10¢	

How to Play 1 Take turns with a partner. 2 Spin the spinner. Place a counter on a space that shows that number of cents. 3 Play until all the spaces are covered.

196

Name _____

_____

- - - - - - - - - -

_____ o'clock

⭐

APRIL

Sunday	Monday	Tuesday	Wednesday	Thursday	Friday	Saturday
					1	2
3	4	5	6	7	8	9
10	11	12	13	14	15	16
17	18	19	20	21	22	23
24	25	26	27	28	29	30

_____

- - - - - - - - - -

_____

Directions 1 Circle the picture that shows morning. 2 Circle the activity that takes less time.
3 Write the time. 4 Circle the first Monday in red. Circle the first day of the month in blue.
Write the number of days in a week.

5

6

7

_____

- - - - - - - - - - - - - - -

_____ ¢

8

_____

- - - - - - - - - - - - - - -

_____ ¢

9

7¢

_____

- - - - - - - - - - - - - - -

_____ ¢

Directions 5 Circle the dime. 6 Circle the quarter. 7–8 Write the number of cents.
9 Circle the pennies used to buy the item. Write the cents left.

198

1

Dollar

2

Directions 1 Discuss the dollar coins and bills. 2 Circle the dollars. Cross out the ones that are not dollars.

Cumulative Review

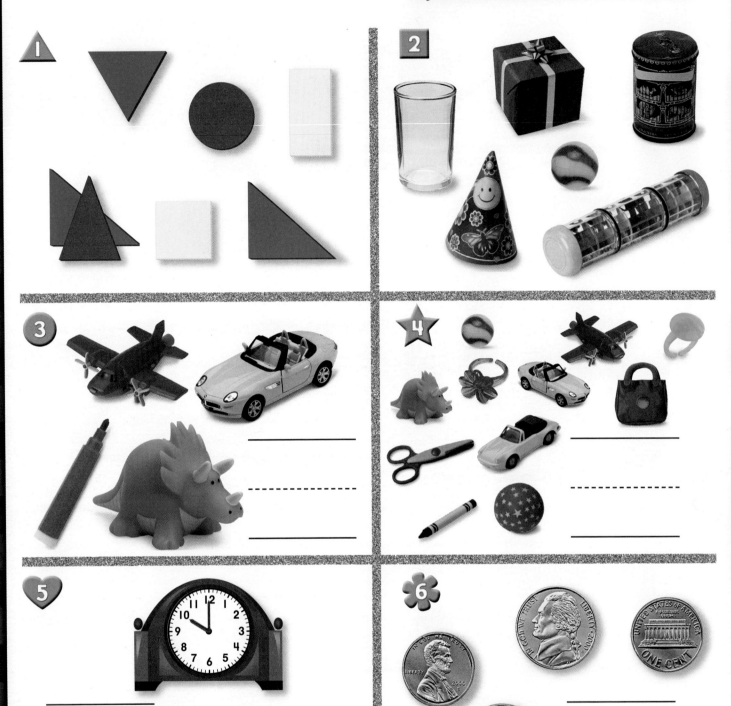

o'clock

¢

Directions 1 Circle the triangles. 2 Circle the cylinders. 3–4 Count. Write the number.
5 Write the time. 6 Write the number of cents.

Measurement

From the Read-Aloud Anthology

Flower Garden

by Eve Bunting
illustrated by Kathryn Hewitt

Access Prior Knowledge
This story will help you review
• Comparing objects

MATH at Home

Dear Family,

We are starting a new unit called Measurement. In Chapter 11, we will compare, order, and measure the length and height of objects. In Chapter 12, we will compare, order, and measure the weight and capacity of objects. In both chapters, we will estimate before we measure.

Love, _____

Vocabulary

longer, shorter, taller
Words used to compare length and height.

shorter

longer

shorter

taller

heavier, lighter
Words used to compare weight.

heavier

lighter

holds more, holds less
Words used to compare capacity.

holds less

holds more

Vocabulary Activities

- Help your child compare lengths of household objects, using the words *longer, shorter, longest,* and *shortest.*

- Let your child lift two objects to find which is heavier and which is lighter.

- Show your child different-sized containers. Let your child tell which holds more and which holds less.

Visit *Education Place* at
eduplace.com/parents/mw/
for *e •* WordGame,
e • Glossary **and more.**

Literature to Read Together

- **The Best Bug Parade**
by Stuart J. Murphy
(HarperCollins, 1996)

- **A Pig Is Big**
by Douglas Florian
(Greenwillow, 2000)

- **If the Shoe Fits**
by Gary Soto
(Putnam, 2002)

Length

Directions Place a cube on each square. Compare the cube trains.

Compare Length

Directions 1–4 Circle the taller one. Underline the shorter one. 5 Circle the longer one.
Underline the shorter one.

1

2

3

4

Directions 1–4 Circle the longer one. Underline the shorter one.

At Home Help your child find items both taller and shorter than he or she is. Then help your child find items that are longer or shorter than his or her arm.

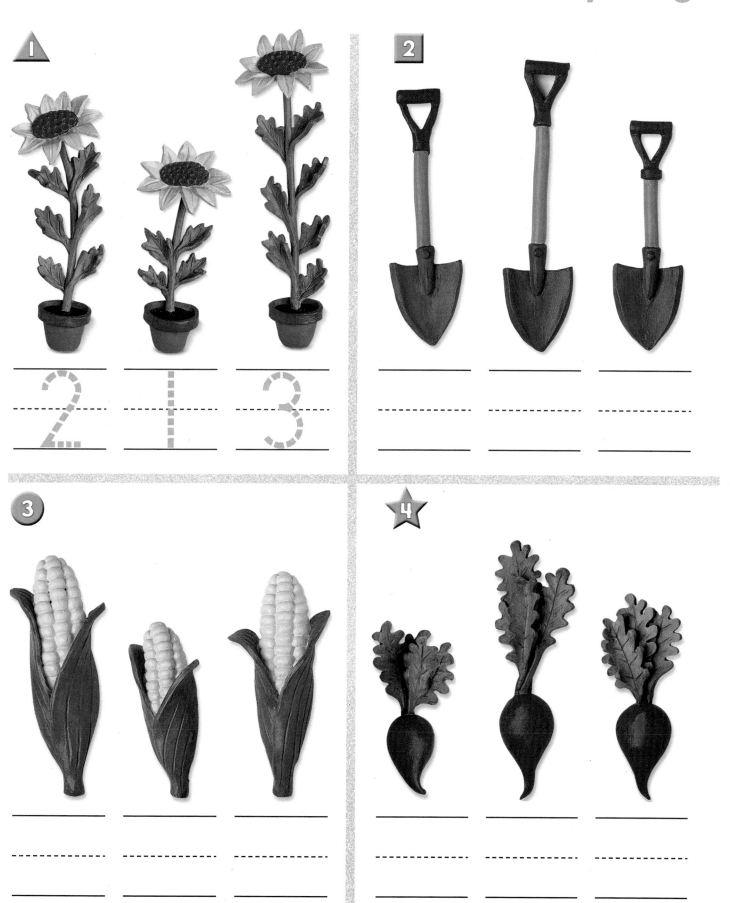

▲ 1

2

3

★ 4

Directions 1–4 Write the numbers *1*, *2*, and *3* to order the items from shortest to tallest.

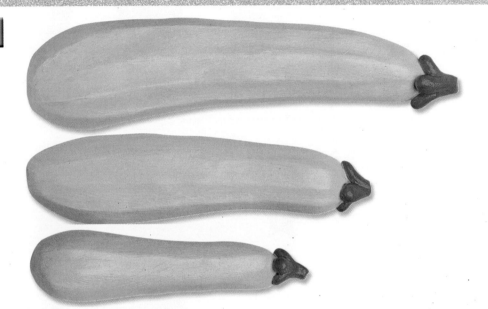

Directions 1–3 Write the numbers *1*, *2*, and *3* to order the items from shortest to longest.

At Home Help your child find 3 objects of different lengths and put them in order from shortest to longest.

Name _____

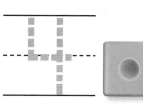
Hands-On

about _____

 2

about _____

3

about _____

4

about _____

Directions 1–4 Use cubes to measure the length. Record the length.

about _____

2

about _____

3

4

Directions 1–2 Use cubes to measure the length. Record the length. 3 Circle the taller one. Underline the shorter one. 4 Write the numbers 1, 2, and 3 to order the items from shortest to longest.

At Home Draw lines of different lengths on paper. Have your child use paper clips or pennies to measure each length and tell which is longer or shorter.

210

Name ____________________

Estimate and Measure Length

Hands-On

1

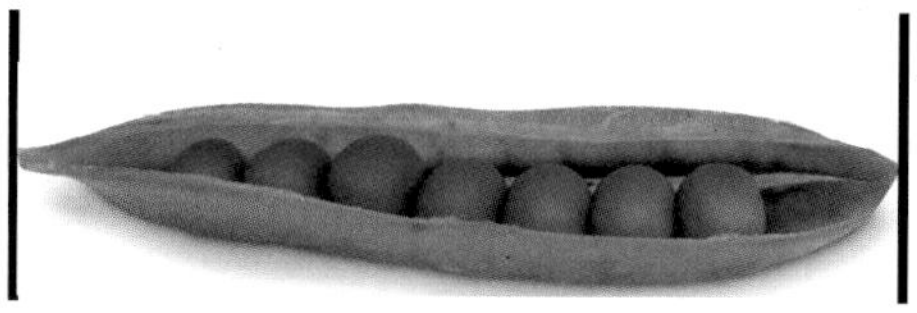

Estimate

about ______ 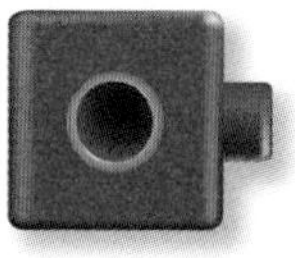

Measure

about ______ 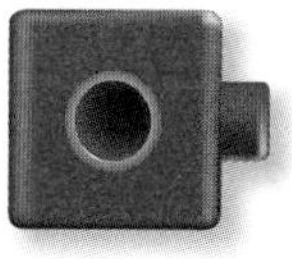

2

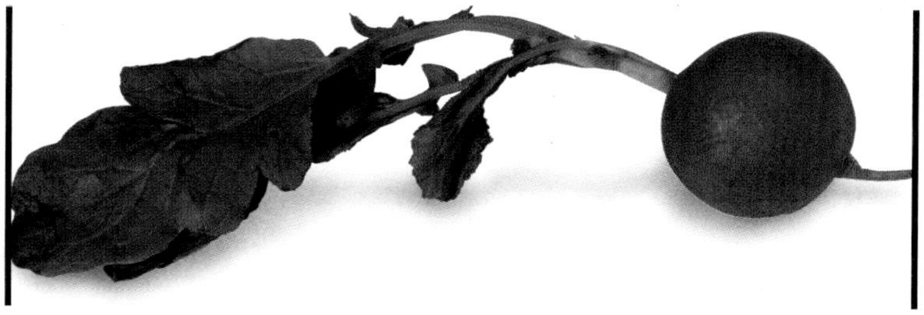

Estimate

about ______ 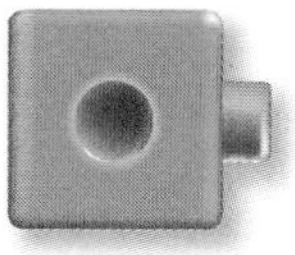

Measure

about ______ 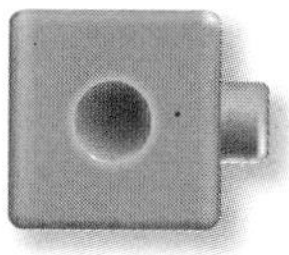

3

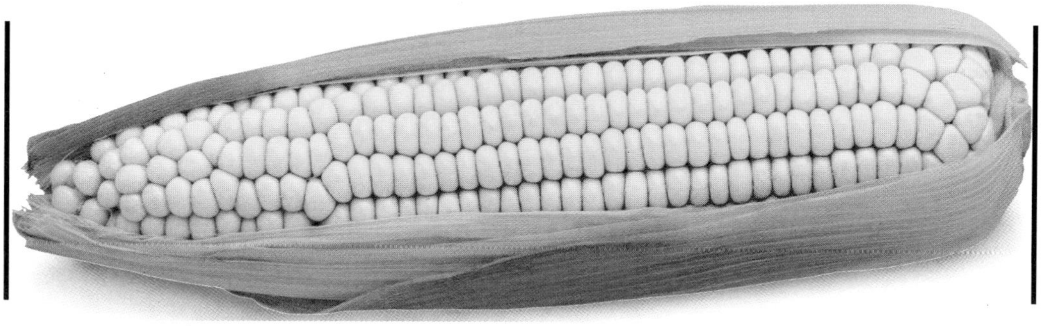

Estimate

about ______ 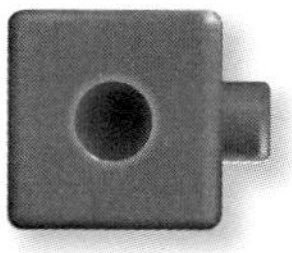

Measure

about ______ 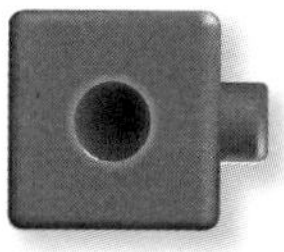

Directions 1–3 Estimate how many cubes long. Measure. Record the length. Compare the measurement to the estimate.

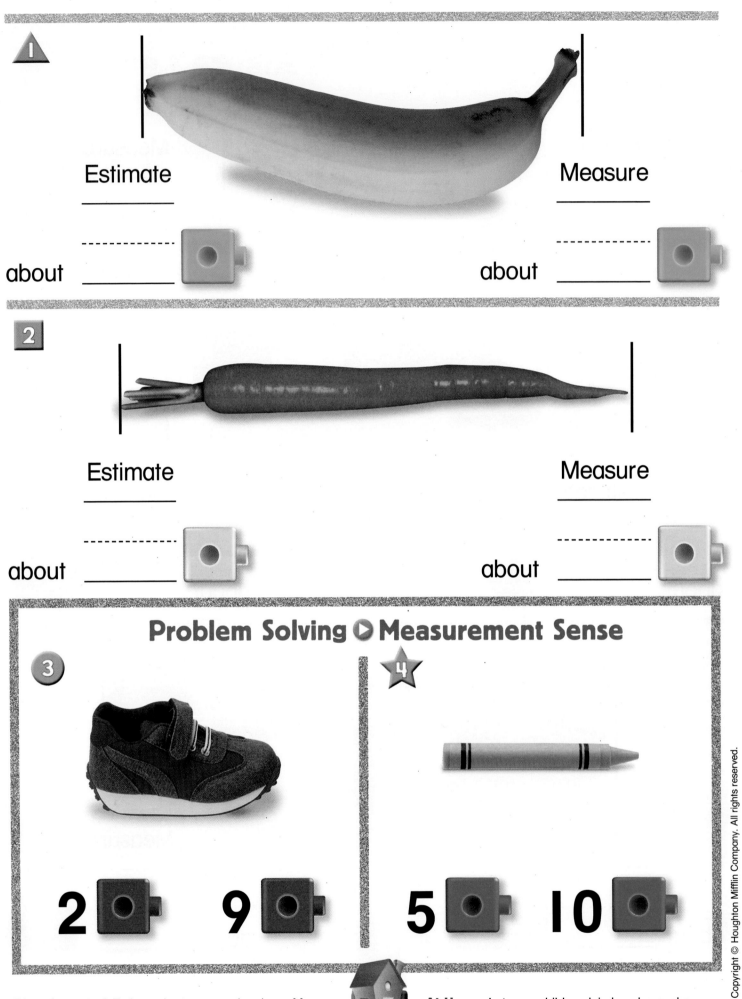

1

Estimate   Measure

about _____   about _____

2

Estimate   Measure

about _____   about _____

Problem Solving ▷ Measurement Sense

3

2   **9**

4

5   **10**

Directions 1–2 Estimate how many cubes long. Measure. Record the length. Compare the measurement to the estimate. **3–4** Circle the most likely length of the real item.

At Home Let your child explain how he or she estimated and measured the lengths above.

1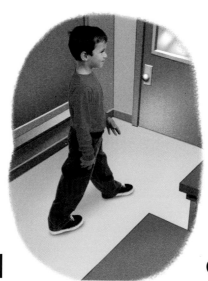

Estimate

_____

- - - - - - - - - - -

about _____

Measure

_____

- - - - - - - - - - -

about _____

2

Estimate

_____

- - - - - - - - - - -

about _____

Measure

_____

- - - - - - - - - - -

about _____

3

Estimate

_____

- - - - - - - - - - -

about _____

Measure

_____

- - - - - - - - - - -

about _____

Directions Estimate the number of: 1 giant steps to cross the classroom; 2 forearms long the board is;
3 hand spans long the table is. Measure and record. Compare measurements to estimates.

1

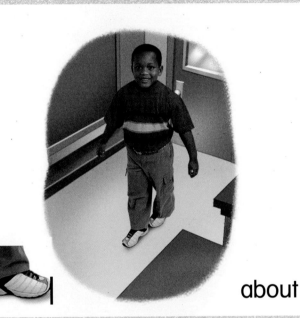

Estimate

_____

about .... _____

Measure

_____

about .... _____

2

Estimate

_____

about .... _____

Measure

_____

about .... _____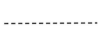

3

Estimate

_____

about .... _____

Measure

_____

about .... _____

Directions Estimate the number of: **1** hand spans wide the door is; **2** foot lengths long the board is; **3** hand spans high the bookcase is. Measure and record. Compare measurements to estimates.

At Home Let your child explain how he or she estimated and measured in this lesson. Estimate and measure some similar lengths at home.

Cali meets Sal Snake.
Who is longer?

2

Up the vines they race.
Which vine is taller?

4

The cornstalks are tall.
Which is the tallest?

The beans taste good.
Which bean is the longest?

Picking flowers is fun.

Which flower is the shortest?

6

It's time to take a rest.

Whose bed is the shortest?

8

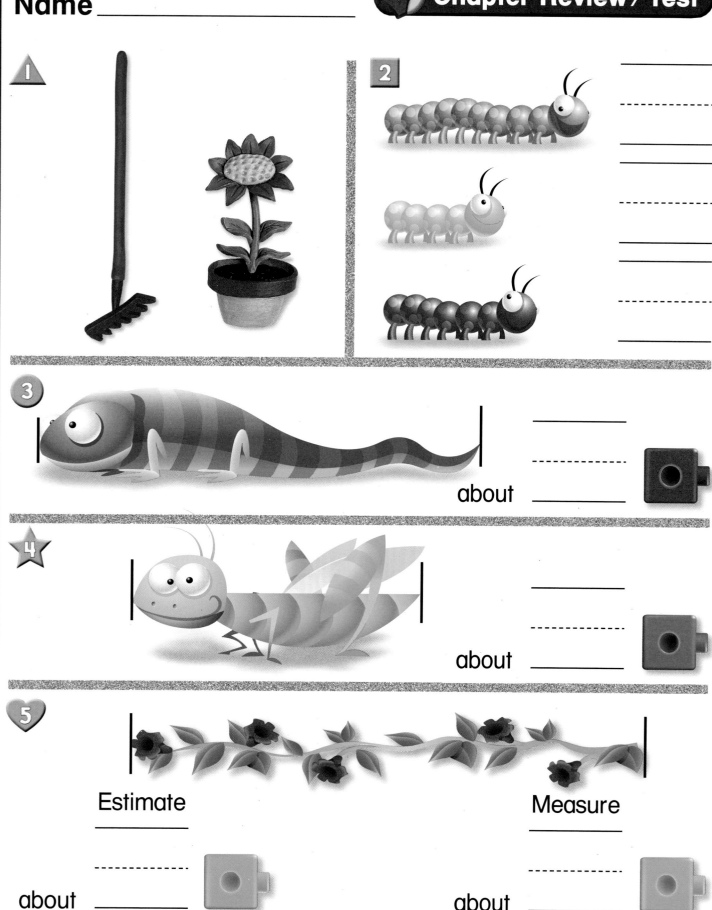

Directions 1 Circle the taller one. Underline the shorter one. 2 Write the numbers *1*, *2*, and *3* to order the items from shortest to longest. 3–4 Use cubes to measure the length. Record the length. 5 Estimate how many cubes long. Measure. Record the length.

Directions Compare the plants in the picture. Tell how they are alike and different. 1 Circle in red the plant that is the tallest. 2 Circle in blue the plant with the thickest stem. 3 Circle in yellow the plant with the smallest leaves.

216

Weight and Capacity

Big or Small?

big						

small						

Directions Circle in red all the big items. Circle in blue all the small items. Color one box to match each item you circled. Tell about your graph.

Name_____ Compare Weight

Directions 1–4 Circle the heavier one. Underline the lighter one. 5 Circle the two that are about the same weight.

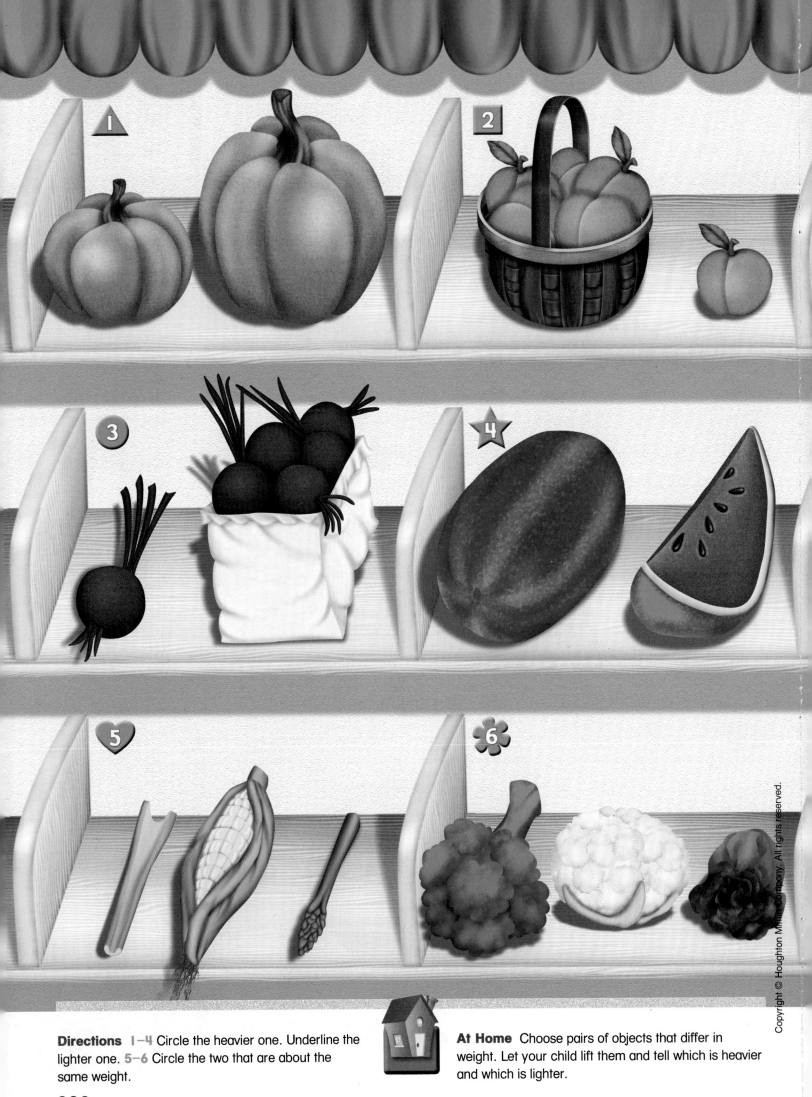

Directions 1—4 Circle the heavier one. Underline the lighter one. 5—6 Circle the two that are about the same weight.

At Home Choose pairs of objects that differ in weight. Let your child lift them and tell which is heavier and which is lighter.

220

Name_____

3   2   1

2

3

Directions 1–3 Write the numbers 1, 2, and 3 to order the items from lightest to heaviest.

——————— ——————— ———————

- - - - - - - - - - - - - - - - - - - - - - - - - - -

——————— ——————— ———————

2

——————— ——————— ———————

- - - - - - - - - - - - - - - - - - - - - - - - - - -

——————— ——————— ———————

Algebra Readiness ▶ Relationships

3

Directions 1–2 Write the numbers *1*, *2*, and *3* to order the items from lightest to heaviest. 3 Circle the heavier one.

At Home Have your child find and lift 3 objects of different weights and put them in order from lightest to heaviest.

222

Name _____

Hands-On

Estimate

_____

- - - - - - - - - - - -

about _____

Measure

_____

- - - - - - - - - -

about _____

2

Estimate

_____

- - - - - - - - - - - -

about _____

Measure

_____

- - - - - - - - - -

about _____

3

Estimate

_____

- - - - - - - - - - - -

about _____

Measure

_____

- - - - - - - - - -

about _____

4

Estimate

_____

- - - - - - - - - - - -

about _____

Measure

_____

- - - - - - - - - -

about _____

Directions 1–4 Use objects like the ones shown. Estimate how many cubes are needed to balance the buckets. Measure. Record the number of cubes. Compare the measurement to the estimate.

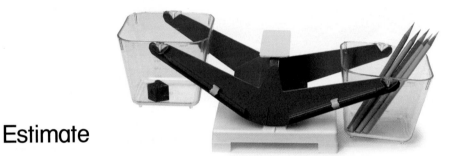

1

Estimate

about _____

Measure

about _____

2

Estimate

about _____

Measure

about _____

Directions 1–2 Use objects like the ones shown. Estimate and measure how many cubes are needed to balance the buckets. **3** Circle the heavier one. **4** Write 1, 2, and 3 to order the items from lightest to heaviest.

At Home Have your child explain how he or she estimated and measured the weight of each object using cubes.

Name _____ **Compare Capacity**

Directions 1–4 Compare the sizes of the two containers. Circle the one that holds more. Underline the one that holds less.

Chapter 12 **225**

Directions 1–2 Draw something that holds more.
3–4 Draw something that holds less.

At Home Let your child examine two containers of different sizes, such as a bowl and a cup, and tell which holds more and which holds less.

226

Name _____

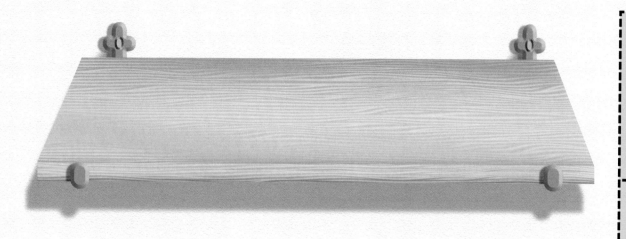

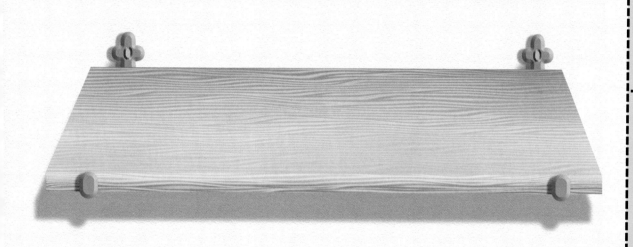

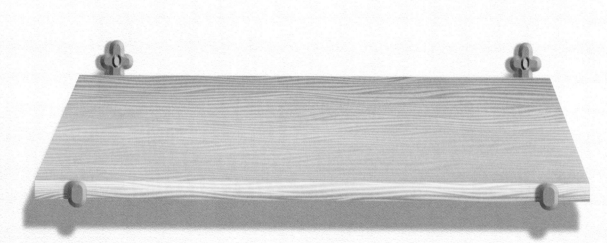

Directions Cut out the pictures. Sort them by kind. Glue them on the shelves in order from the one that holds the least to the one that holds the most.

 Directions Circle the shelves that have the items in order from the one that holds the least to the one that holds the most.

At Home Help your child find three containers of different sizes, and order them from the one that holds the least to the one that holds the most.

228

Estimate and Measure Capacity

Hands-On

1

Estimate

_____

- - - - - - - - - - - -

about _____

Measure

_____

- - - - - - - - - - - -

about _____

2

Estimate

_____

- - - - - - - - - - - -

about _____

Measure

_____

- - - - - - - - - - - -

about _____

3

Estimate

_____

- - - - - - - - - - - -

about _____

Measure

_____

- - - - - - - - - - - -

about _____

Chicken Noodle SOUP
Free Range Chicken
NET WT 15 OZ

4

Estimate

_____

- - - - - - - - - - - -

about _____

Measure

_____

- - - - - - - - - - - -

about _____

Directions 1–4 Use a container like the one shown. Estimate how many cups of beans are needed to fill the container. Measure. Record the number of cups. Compare the measurement to the estimate.

1 ▲

Estimate

about _____

Measure

about _____

2

Estimate

about _____

Measure

about _____

VITAMIN D **MILK**
GRADE A
PASTEURIZED HOMOGENIZED
HALF PINT (236 mL)

3

Estimate

about _____

Measure

about _____

Coffee

4 ★

Estimate

about _____

Measure

about _____

Directions 1–4 Use a container like the one shown. Estimate and measure how many cups of beans are needed to fill it. Compare the measurement to the estimate.

At Home Have your child estimate how many cups of rice, beans, or pasta are needed to fill a large container. Let your child show you how to use the cup to measure how much the container holds.

Name

1

2

3

4

Directions Circle the tool used to: 1 find the date of the second Saturday; 2 find out if a rock is heavier than a shoe; 3 find how long a rake is; 4 tell what time it is.

1

2

JANUARY

SUN.	MON.	TUES.	WED.	THURS.	FRI.	SAT.
		1	2	3	4	5	6
7	8	9	10	11	12	13
14	15	16	17	18	19	20
21	22	23	24	25	26	27
28	29	30	31			

3

4

Directions Circle the tool used to: 1 tell if it is hot or cold outside; 2 measure the length of a pencil; 3 measure flour and sugar for a recipe; 4 find out if a pencil is heavier than a marker.

At Home Ask your child to tell you about the different measuring tools shown above. Help your child find examples of measuring tools in your home.

232

1

2

Directions Listen carefully for what to draw.   Draw Flower A taller than Flower B and B taller than Flower C. Circle the shortest one.   On the cloth, draw a blue basket that holds more than a red basket. Draw a green basket that holds less than the red basket. Circle the basket that holds the most.

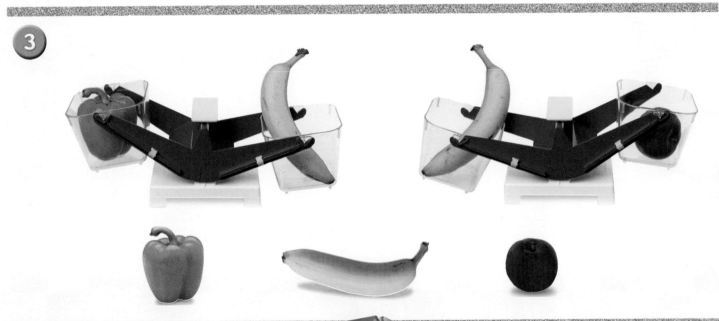

Directions Circle the item that is: 1 heavier; 2 lighter;
3 heaviest.

At Home Have your child explain how he or she
solved one of the problems on the front of this page
and one of the problems on the back.

234

Gardening Pals

This take-home book will help you review concepts you learned in Chapter 12.

They pick fruit.
Draw a fruit that is heavier.

3

Tracy and Beth plant seeds.
Which is lighter, the seeds or the pot?

2

They pick vegetables.
Which one is the lightest?

4

They water the plants.
Which watering can holds more?

They pick bunches of grapes.
Which basket holds the least?

They fill many bowls.
Which bowl holds the most?

6

Tracy and Beth work together.
Draw a pail that holds less.

8

Name _____

1

2

3

_____   _____   _____

- - - - - -   - - - - - -   - - - - - -

_____   _____   _____

4

about **2**

about **12**

5

Directions 1 Circle the heavier one. Underline the lighter one. 2 Circle the one that holds more.
Underline the one that holds less. 3 Write *1*, *2*, and *3* to order the items from lightest to heaviest.
4 Circle the number of cups needed to fill the can. 5 Circle the lighter one.

LONGER, SHORTER, SAME?

What You Need

How to Play | Take turns with a partner. 2 Roll the number cube and move your cube train that number of spaces. 3 Use your cube train to measure. If the animal is longer, move ahead 1 space. If the animal is shorter, go back 1 space. If it is the same length, stay.

236

Name _____

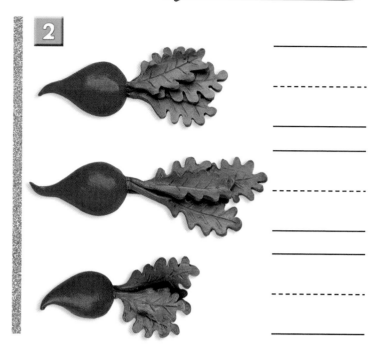

_____
- - - - - - - - - -
_____
_____
- - - - - - - - - -
_____
_____
- - - - - - - - - -
_____

_____

- - - - - - - - - -
about _____

Estimate   Measure

_____   _____

- - - - - - - - - -   - - - - - - - - - -
about _____   about _____

Directions: 1 Circle the longer one. Underline the shorter one. 2 Write the numbers *1*, *2*, and *3* to order the items from shortest to longest. 3 Use cubes to measure the length. Record the length. 4 Estimate how many cubes long. Measure. Record the length.

Directions: **5** Circle the heavier one. Underline the lighter one. **6** Circle the one that holds more. Underline the one that holds less. **7** Write *1*, *2*, and *3* to order the items from the one that holds the least to the one that holds the most. **8** Circle the heaviest one. Underline the lightest one.

Name _____

Measure With a Ruler

1

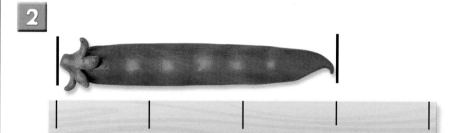

_____
- - - - - - - - - - - - -
about _____ inches

2

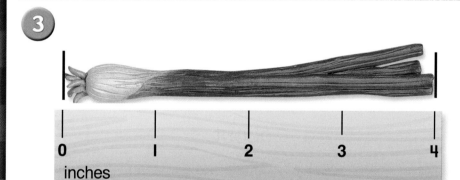

_____
- - - - - - - - - - - - -
about _____ inches

3

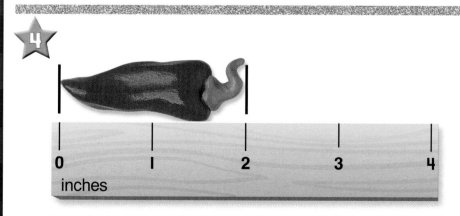

_____
- - - - - - - - - - - - -
about _____ inches

4

_____
- - - - - - - - - - - - -
about _____ inches

Directions 1–4 Find the length. Write the number of inches.

Name _____

1

2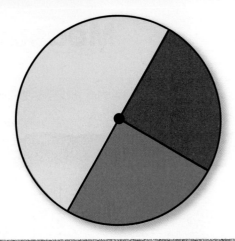

3

_____
- - - - - - - -
_____

_____
- - - - - - - -
_____

_____
- - - - - - - -
_____

4

about _____
- - - - - - - -

_____

5

1   3   _____
- - - - - - -
_____

7   _____
- - - - - - -
_____

11

Directions: **1** Circle the quarters. **2** Put an X on the color you are most likely to spin. **3** Write *1*, *2*, and *3* to show the order of events from first to last. **4** Use cubes to measure the length. Record the length. **5** Look for a pattern. Write the missing numbers.

HOUGHTON MIFFLIN MATH

UNIT 7

Addition and Subtraction

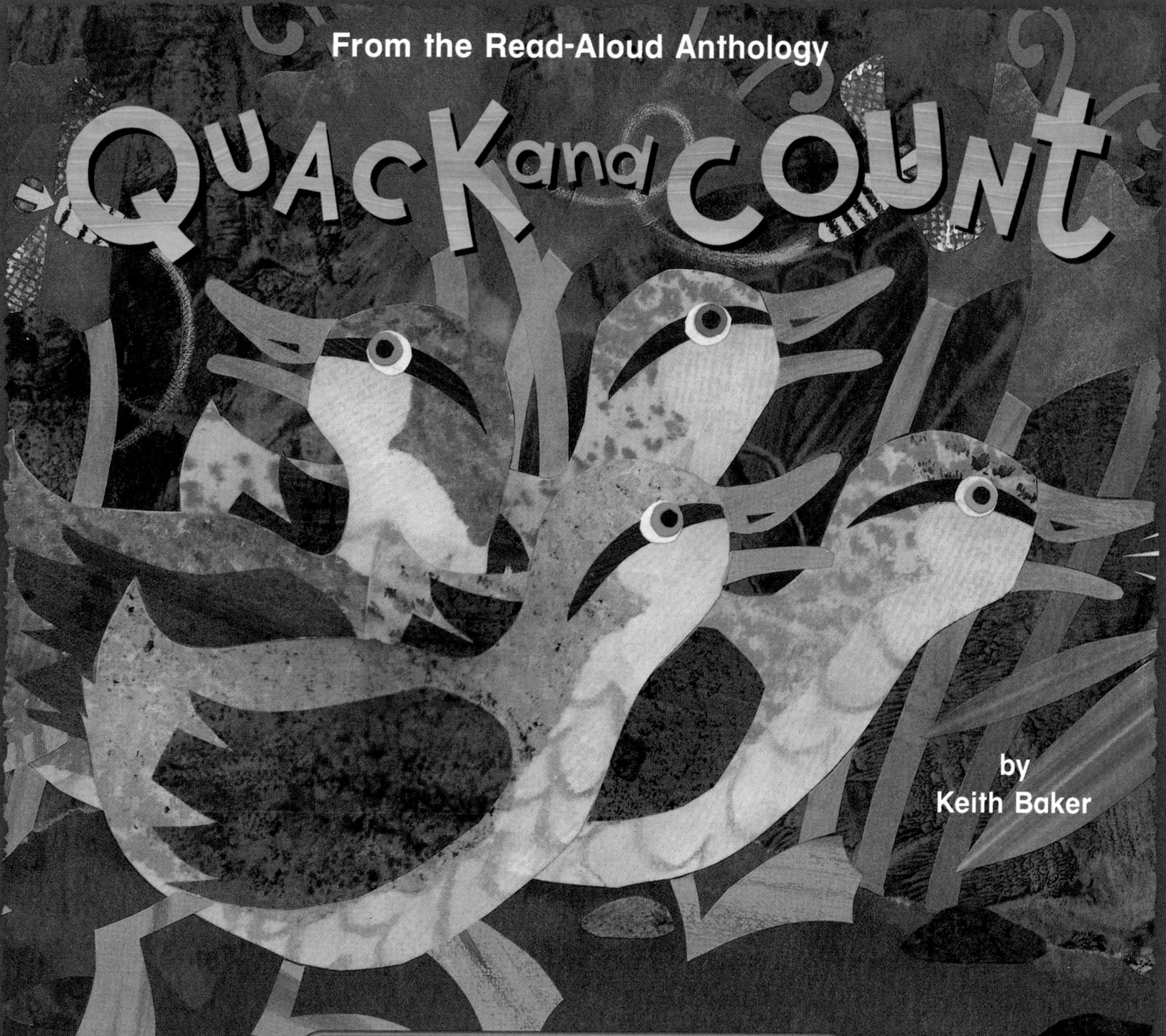

From the Read-Aloud Anthology
Quack and Count
by
Keith Baker

Access Prior Knowledge

This story will help you review

- Counting
- Names for numbers

Printed in the U.S.A.

ISBN: 0-618-33877-2

Vocabulary

add
Putting groups together to find the total or the sum.

6 ducks in all

subtract
Taking away to find the difference.

3 ducks are left

addition sentence
An equation such as

$$3 \quad + \quad 2 \quad = \quad 5$$

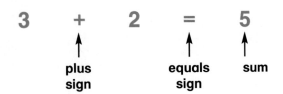

plus   equals   sum
sign   sign

subtraction sentence
An equation such as

$$7 \quad - \quad 1 \quad = \quad 6$$

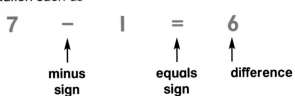

minus   equals   difference
sign   sign

Vocabulary Activities

- Help your child recognize addition and subtraction situations. (5 people and 1 joins them; 6 in all. Have 5 crackers. Eat 2; 3 crackers are left.)

- Encourage your child to tell addition and subtraction stories, using objects such as pennies or dry beans. Have your child say the number sentence.

Visit *Education Place* **at** **eduplace.com/parents/mw/** **for** *e•*WordGame, *e•*Glossary **and more.**

Literature to Read Together

- **Splash!**
by Ann Jonas
(Mulberry Books, 1997)

- **More Bugs? Less Bugs?**
by Don L. Curry
(Capstone, 2000)

- **Catch That Goat!**
by Polly Alakija
(Barefoot Books, 2002)

Addition

Directions Put one cube on top of each turtle. Write the number. Move some cubes to the log and the others to the rock. Draw the cubes. Write the numbers. Compare your drawing to others in the class.

244

Name_____

1

2

3

4

Directions 1–4 Tell a story about how the picture shows adding one. Write how many in all.

Chapter 13

245

_____

- - - - - - - - - - - - -

_____

_____

- - - - - - - - - - - - -

_____

_____

- - - - - - - - - - - - -

_____

_____

- - - - - - - - - - - - -

_____

Directions 1–4 Tell a story about how the picture shows adding one. Write how many in all.

At Home Help your child model adding 1 to numbers 0 through 9. For example, use 3 spoons, add one more, and have your child tell how many spoons there are altogether.

Name ______________________

Add 2 to Numbers 0–5

Hands-On

1

2 + 2 = 4

2

5 + 2 = ____

3

1 + 2 = ____

Directions 1–3 Show each number with counters. Draw. Write how many in all.

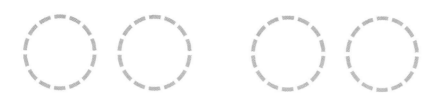

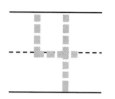

▲ 1

$$3 \quad + \quad 2 \quad = \quad \underline{\hspace{2cm}}$$

2

$$0 \quad + \quad 2 \quad = \quad \underline{\hspace{2cm}}$$

3

$$4 \quad + \quad 2 \quad = \quad \underline{\hspace{2cm}}$$

Directions 1–3 Show each number with counters. Draw. Write how many in all.

At Home Let your child use pennies or other small items to show you how to add 5 and 2, 2 and 2, and 1 and 2. Have your child tell you how many in all.

248

Add 2 to Numbers 6–8

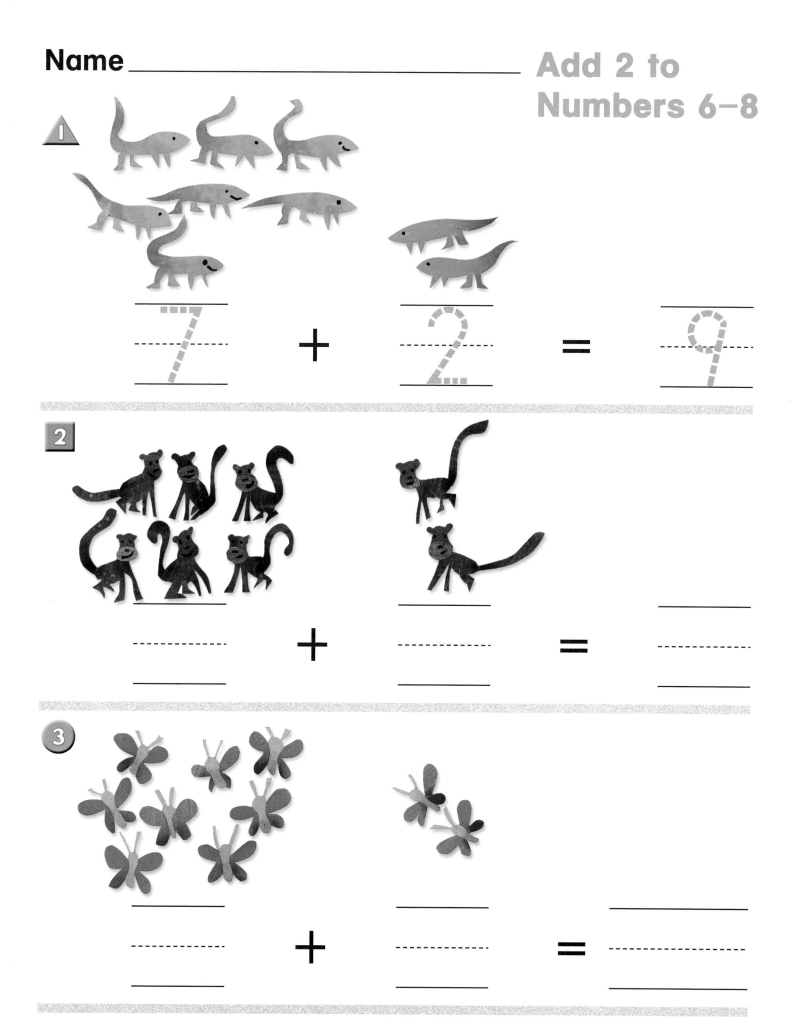

△ 1

$$7 \quad + \quad 2 \quad = \quad 9$$

2

$$\underline{\hspace{2cm}} \quad + \quad \underline{\hspace{2cm}} \quad = \quad \underline{\hspace{2cm}}$$

3

$$\underline{\hspace{2cm}} \quad + \quad \underline{\hspace{2cm}} \quad = \quad \underline{\hspace{2cm}}$$

Directions 1–3 Write the number in each group. Add. Write the sum.

1

——— ——— ———

- - - - - - - + - - - - - - - = - - - - - - -

——— ——— ———

2

——— ——— ———

- - - - - - - + - - - - - - - = - - - - - - -

——— ——— ———

3 Algebra Readiness ▶ Patterns

———

1	+	2	=	- - - - - - -
2	+	2	=	- - - - - - -
3	+	2	=	- - - - - - -
—	+	2	=	- - - - - - -

Directions 1–2 Write the number in each group. Add. Write the sum. **3** Look for a pattern. Complete each number sentence.

At Home Have your child draw dots or simple shapes to show adding 8 and 2. Then help your child record the number sentence 8 + 2 = 10.

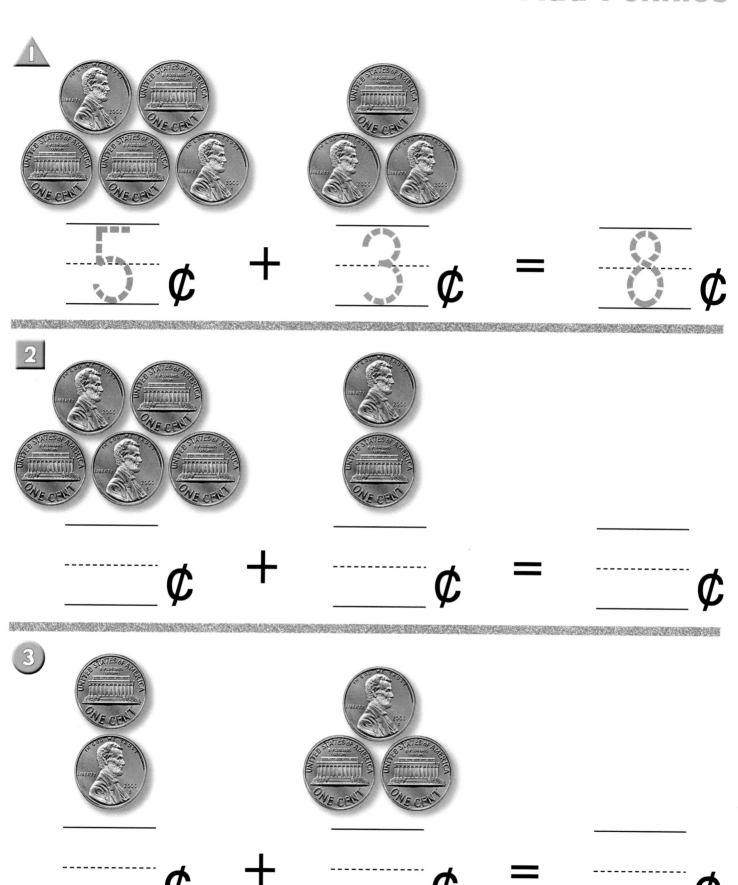

⚠ 1

_5_ ¢ + _3_ ¢ = _8_ ¢

2

____ ¢ + ____ ¢ = ____ ¢

3

____ ¢ + ____ ¢ = ____ ¢

Directions 1–3 Write the number in each group. Add. Write the sum.

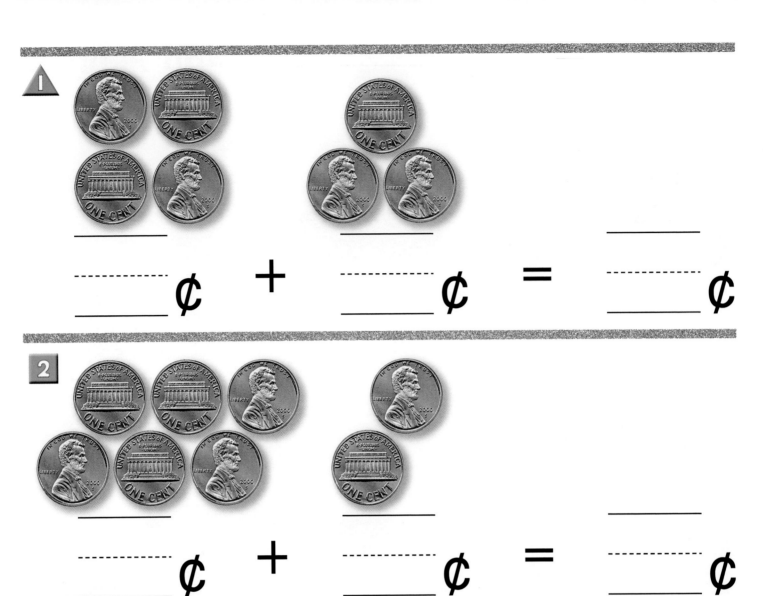

1

_____
_____ ¢ + _____ ¢ = _____ ¢

2

_____
_____ ¢ + _____ ¢ = _____ ¢

3

_____
_____
_____

4

_____ + _____ = _____
_____   _____   _____

Directions 1–2 Write the number in each group. Add. Write the sum. 3 Write how many in all. 4 Write the number in each group. Add. Write the sum.

At Home Provide your child with pennies. Have him or her model facts, such as 4 + 3, 7 + 3, and 8 + 2, and tell the sum for each fact.

252

Name _____

△ 1

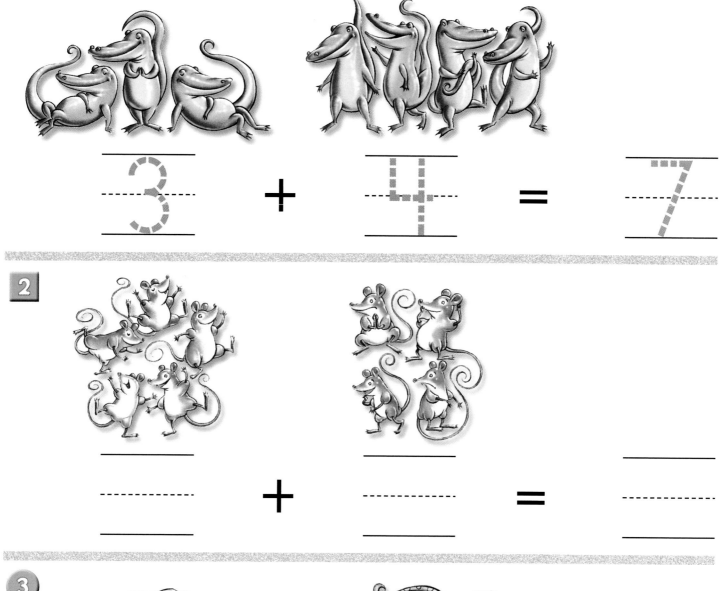

3 + 4 = 7

2

___ + ___ = ___

3

___ + ___ = ___

Directions 1-3 Write the number in each group. Add. Write the sum.

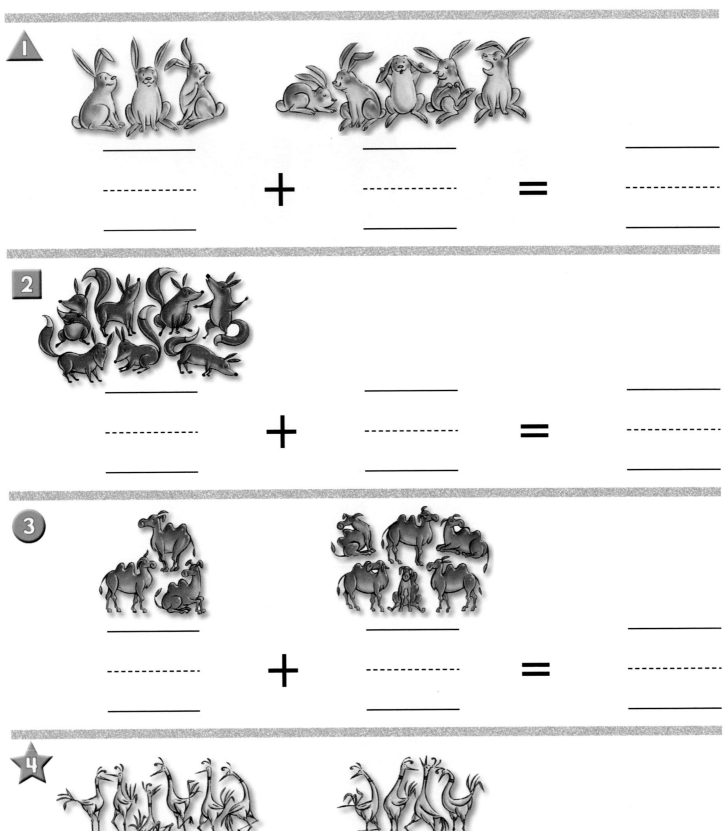

1

_____   +   _____   =   _____

2

_____   +   _____   =   _____

3

_____   +   _____   =   _____

4

_____   +   _____   =   _____

Directions 1–4 Write the number in each group. Add.
Write the sum.

At Home Help your child tell addition stories and
write the accompanying addition sentence. For
example: We have 3 boys and 2 girls in the family.
3 + 2 = 5 people.

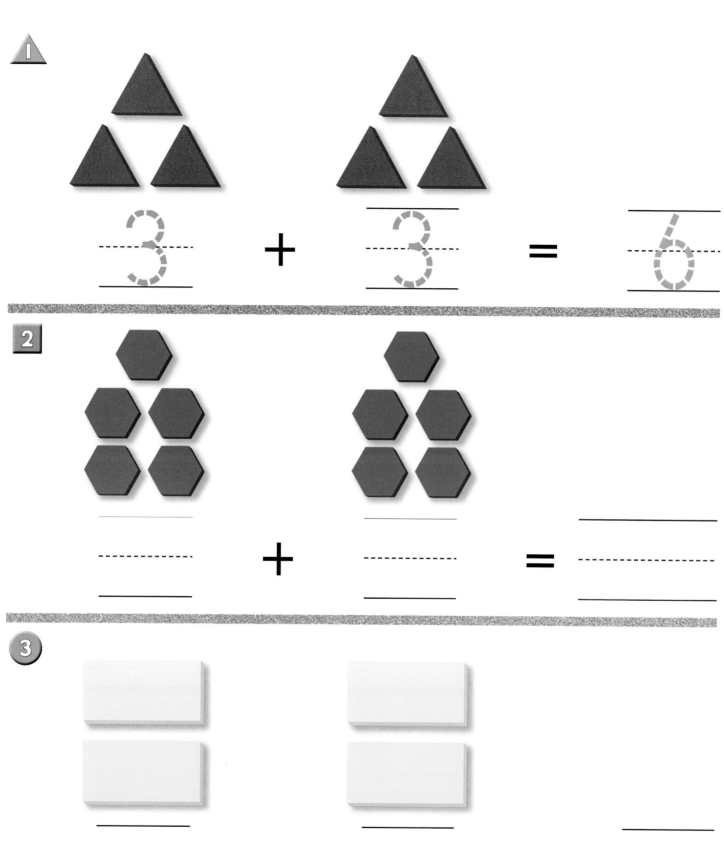

1   3 + 3 = 6

2   ___ + ___ = ___

3   ___ + ___ = ___

Directions 1–3 Write the number in each group. Add. Write the sum.

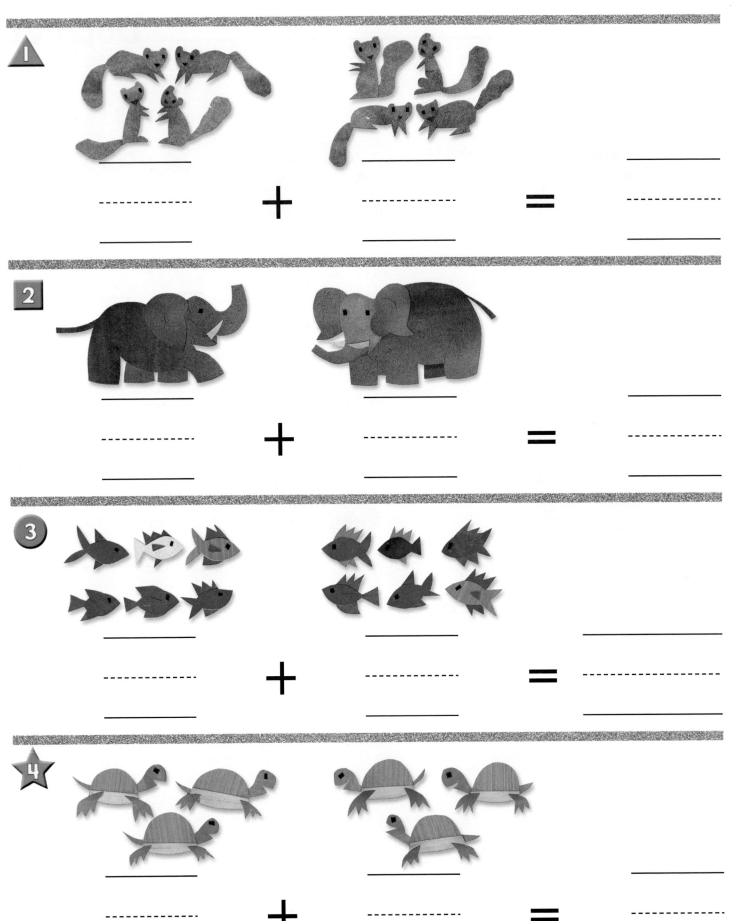

1 _____ + _____ = _____

2 _____ + _____ = _____

3 _____ + _____ = _____

4 _____ + _____ = _____

Directions 1–4 Write the number in each group. Add. Write the sum.

At Home Give your child pennies or other small items. Have him or her show you some addition doubles such as 2 + 2 and 5 + 5.

256

Draw a
Picture

Problem
Solving

1

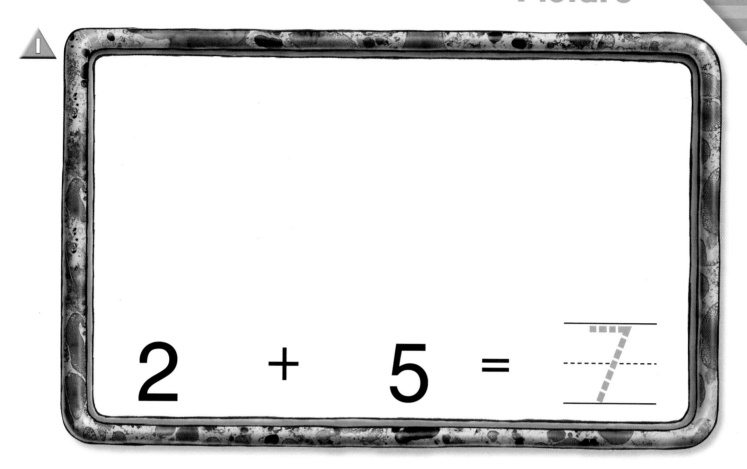

2 + 5 = 7

2

4 + 4 =

Directions 1–2 Draw a picture to match the fact. Add. Write the sum.

1

$$4 \quad + \quad 5 \quad = \quad \underline{\hspace{2cm}}$$

2

$$6 \quad + \quad 1 \quad = \quad \underline{\hspace{2cm}}$$

Directions 1–2 Draw a picture to match the fact. Add. Write the sum.

At Home Have your child tell stories about the pictures he or she has drawn. Have your child explain how he or she found the answer.

Feeding Time at the ZOO

This take-home book will help you review concepts you learned in Chapter 13.

1

Tony feeds the monkeys.

How many monkeys are eating?

_____ _____ _____

----------- **+** ----------- **=** -----------

_____ _____ _____

3

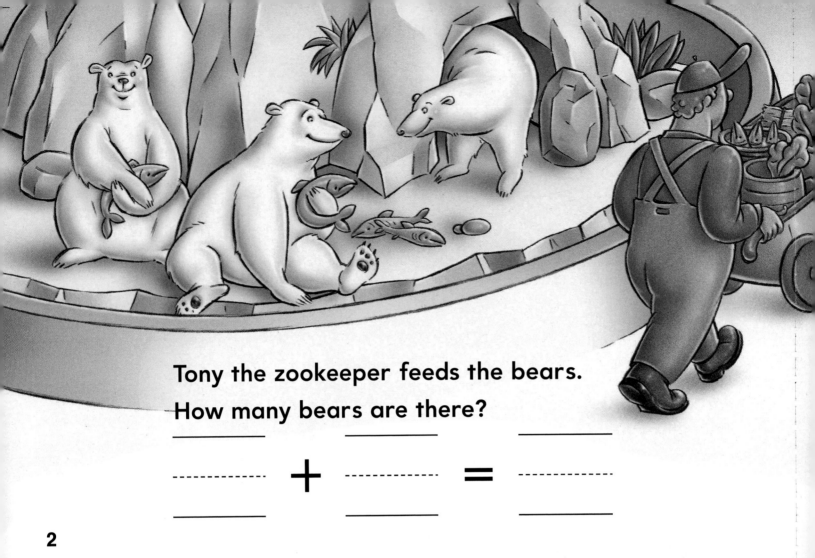

Tony the zookeeper feeds the bears.
How many bears are there?

_____ _____ _____

- - - - - - - + - - - - - - - = - - - - - - -

_____ _____ _____

2

Tony feeds the zebras.
How many zebras does Tony feed?

_____ _____ _____

- - - - - - - + - - - - - - - = - - - - - - -

_____ _____ _____

4

Tony feeds the seals.

How many seals are there?

_____   _____   _____

_ _ _ _ _ _   **+**   _ _ _ _ _   **=**   _ _ _ _ _

_____   _____   _____

Tony feeds the giraffes.

How many giraffes are eating?

_____   _____   _____

_ _ _ _ _ _   **+**   _ _ _ _ _   **=**   _ _ _ _ _

_____   _____   _____

Tony feeds the birds.

How many birds are there?

_____ + _____ = _____

6

We feed the goats.

How many cents do we have together?

_____ ¢ + _____ ¢ = _____ ¢

8

Name_____

_____
- - - - - - - - - -
_____

_____   _____   _____

- - - - - - - - - - **+** - - - - - - - - - - **=** - - - - - - - - - -

_____   _____   _____

_____   _____   _____

- - - - - - - - **¢** **+** - - - - - - - - **¢** **=** - - - - - - - - **¢**
_____ _____ _____

6 + 3 = _____
                - - - - - - - -

Directions I Write how many in all. **2–3** Write the number in each group. Add. Write the sum.
4 Draw a picture to match the fact. Add. Write the sum.

Art
Connection

eduplace.com/kids/mw/

1

_____   +   _____   =   _____

2

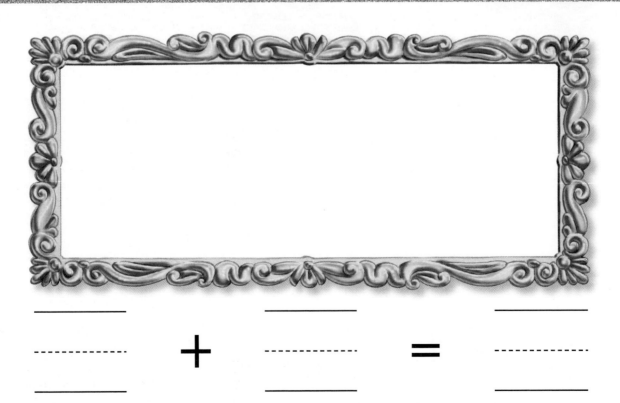

_____   +   _____   =   _____

Directions 1 Tell an addition story about the animals in the picture. Write the addition
sentence. 2 Draw your own. Tell a story. Write the addition sentence.

260

Subtraction

Directions Put a cube on each picture. Write the number in each row. Tell about the pattern you see.

262

Name _____

1

3

2

3

4

Directions 1–4 Count how many in all. Circle and cross out the one that is leaving.
Write how many are left.

1

_____
- - - - - - -
_____

2

_____
- - - - - - -
_____

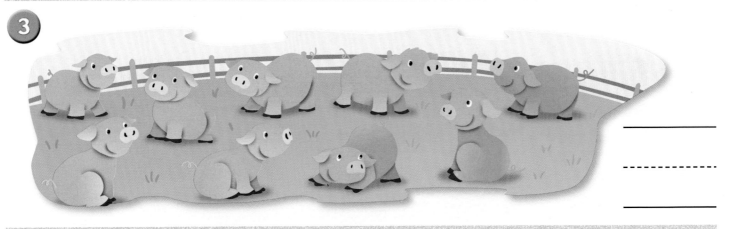

3

_____
- - - - - - -
_____

4

_____
- - - - - - -
_____

Directions 1–4 Count how many in all. Circle and cross out one animal. Write how many are left.

At Home Start with 10 pennies. Have your child remove one, and count the number that are left. Repeat the process until all the pennies are gone — zero are left!

Name _____

1

5 – 2 = 3

2

4 – 2 = _____

3

3 – 2 = _____

4

2 – 2 = _____

Directions 1–4 Show the first number with counters. Draw the counters. Circle and cross out a group of 2. Write how many are left.

Chapter 14   **265**

2 – 2 = _____

5 – 2 = _____

3

3 – 2 = _____

4 – 2 = _____

Directions 1–4 Show the first number with counters. Draw the counters. Circle and cross out a group of 2. Write how many are left.

At Home Give your child 5 small objects such as buttons or dry beans. Have him or her take away a group of 2 and tell how many are left. Repeat with 4, 3, and 2 objects, taking away a group of 2 each time.

Name _____

△ 1

- - -7- - -   **–**   - - -2- - -   =   - - -5- - -

2

_____   _____   _____

- - - - - - - -   **–**   - - - - - - - -   =   - - - - - - - -

_____   _____   _____

3

_____   _____   _____

- - - - - - - -   **–**   - - - - - - - -   =   - - - - - - - -

_____   _____   _____

Directions 1–3 Write the number of animals in all. Use counters to model taking away two.
Circle and cross out two. Write the number you crossed out. Write the difference.

- - - - - - - - - - - $-$ - - - - - - - - - - $=$ - - - - - - - -

_____ _____ _____

 2

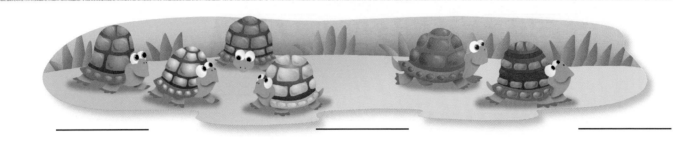

_____ _____ _____

- - - - - - - - - - - $-$ - - - - - - - - - - $=$ - - - - - - - -

_____ _____ _____

Algebra Readiness ▶ Functions

3

-1	
6	_____ - - - - - - _____
2	_____ - - - - - - _____
10	_____ - - - - - - _____

 4

-2	
4	_____ - - - - - - _____
8	_____ - - - - - - _____
9	_____ - - - - - - _____

Directions 1–2 Write the number of animals in all. Circle and cross out two. Write the number you crossed out. Write the difference. 3–4 Follow the rule to find each difference.

At Home Have your child show subtracting 2 from a group of 6, 7, 8, 9, or 10 small objects. Have your child tell you the number sentence.

Name _____

1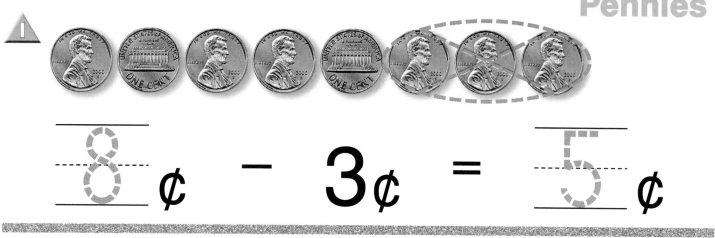

$$8¢ \; - \; 3¢ \; = \; 5¢$$

2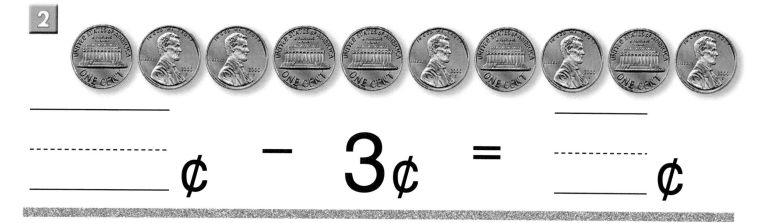

$$\underline{\hspace{3cm}}¢ \; - \; 3¢ \; = \; \underline{\hspace{3cm}}¢$$

3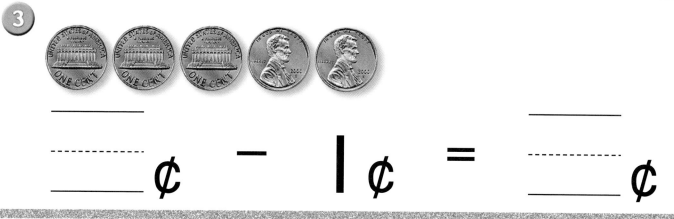

$$\underline{\hspace{3cm}}¢ \; - \; 1¢ \; = \; \underline{\hspace{3cm}}¢$$

4

$$\underline{\hspace{3cm}}¢ \; - \; 2¢ \; = \; \underline{\hspace{3cm}}¢$$

Directions 1–4 Count and write the number of pennies in all. Circle and cross out the number shown. Write how many are left.

1

_____ ¢ − **3**¢ = _____ ¢

2

_____ ¢ − **3**¢ = _____ ¢

3

_____

4

_____ − _____ = _____

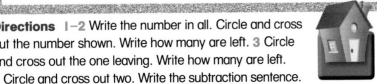

Directions 1–2 Write the number in all. Circle and cross out the number shown. Write how many are left. **3** Circle and cross out the one leaving. Write how many are left. 4 Circle and cross out two. Write the subtraction sentence.

At Home Provide your child with pennies. Have him or her model facts, such as 5 − 3, 8 − 3, and 6 − 3, and tell how many are left each time.

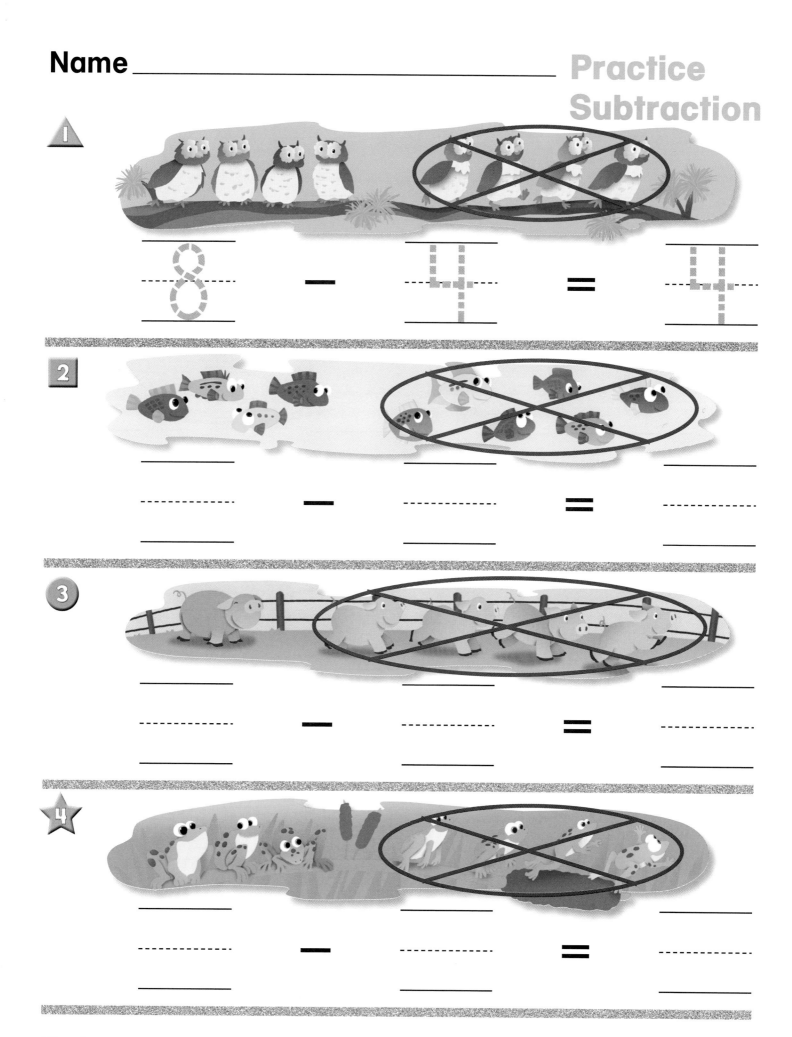

1

8   −   4   =   4

2

___   −   ___   =   ___

3

___   −   ___   =   ___

4

___   −   ___   =   ___

Directions 1–4 Write a subtraction sentence to match the picture.

1

_____   _____   _____

_ _ _ _ _ _ _ _   **—**   _ _ _ _ _ _ _ _   **=**   _ _ _ _ _ _ _

_____   _____   _____

2

_____   _____   _____

_ _ _ _ _ _ _ _   **—**   _ _ _ _ _ _ _ _   **=**   _ _ _ _ _ _ _

_____   _____   _____

3

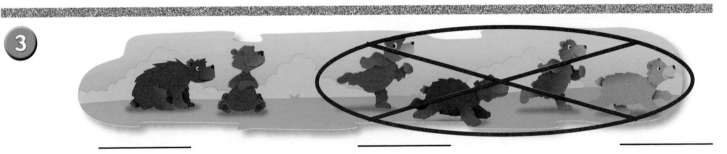

_____   _____   _____

_ _ _ _ _ _ _ _   **—**   _ _ _ _ _ _ _ _   **=**   _ _ _ _ _ _ _

_____   _____   _____

_____   _____   _____

_ _ _ _ _ _ _ _   **—**   _ _ _ _ _ _ _ _   **=**   _ _ _ _ _ _ _

_____   _____   _____

Directions 1–4 Write a subtraction sentence to match the picture.

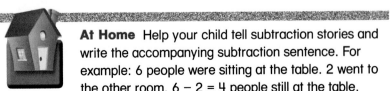

At Home Help your child tell subtraction stories and write the accompanying subtraction sentence. For example: 6 people were sitting at the table. 2 went to the other room. 6 − 2 = 4 people still at the table.

Name _____

Problem Solving

⚠ 1

2 3 = 5

2

7 ◯ 3 = ____

____

3

5 ◯ 4 = ____

____

Directions 1–3 Tell a story to match the picture. Decide if it shows addition or subtraction.
Write a plus or minus sign in the circle. Write the answer.

△1

6 ◯ 4 = _____

2

4 ◯ 6 = _____

3

9 ◯ 3 = _____

Directions 1–3 Tell a story to match the picture. Decide if it shows addition or subtraction. Write a plus or minus sign in the circle. Write the answer.

At Home Have your child tell you how he or she knew whether to add or subtract for each picture.

274

AWAY THEY GO!

This take-home book will help you review concepts you learned in Chapter 14.

1

One baby bunny hops away.
How many bunnies stay to play?

☐ − ☐ = ☐

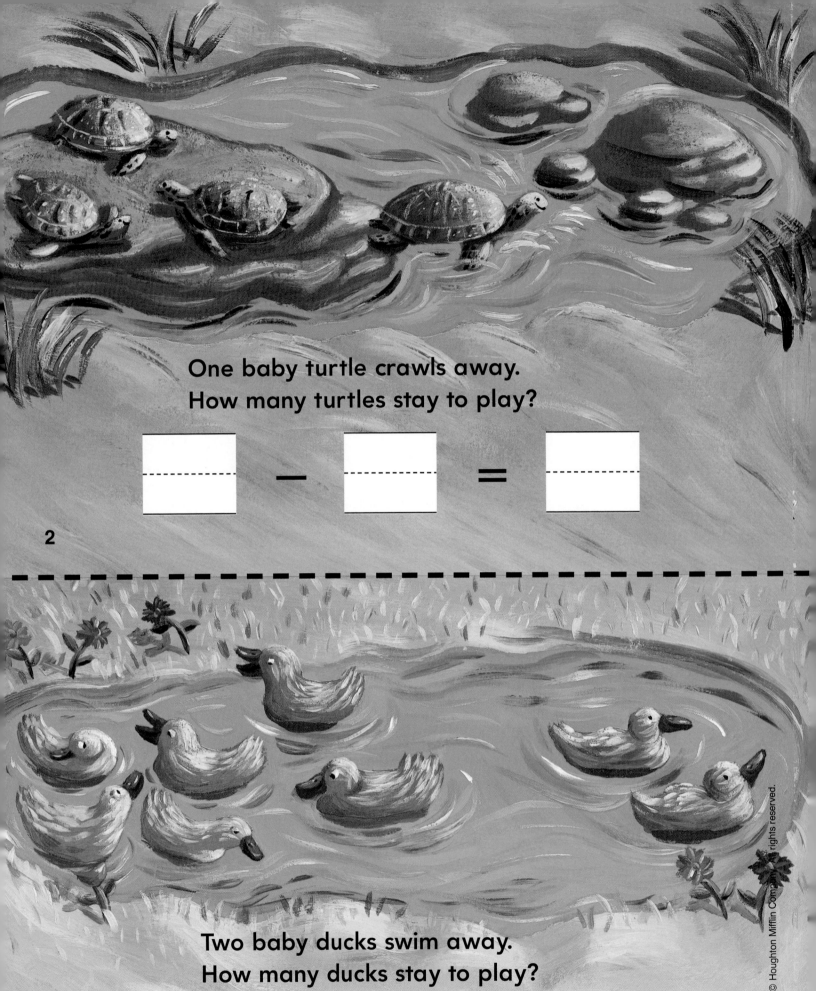

One baby turtle crawls away.
How many turtles stay to play?

☐ – ☐ = ☐

2

Two baby ducks swim away.
How many ducks stay to play?

☐ – ☐ = ☐

4

Two baby birds fly away.
How many birds stay to play?

☐ − ☐ = ☐

Three baby skunks walk away.
How many skunks stay to play?

☐ − ☐ = ☐

Two baby deer run away.
How many deer stay to play?

☐ – ☐ = ☐

6

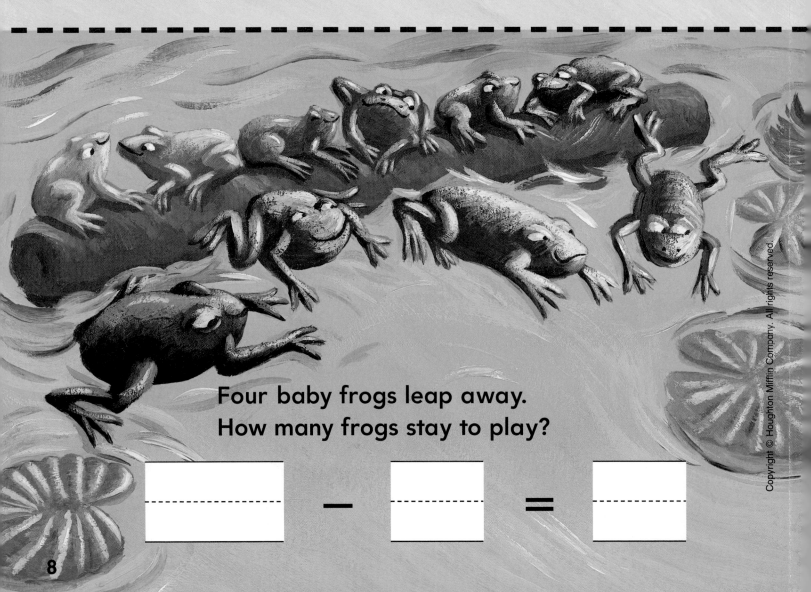

Four baby frogs leap away.
How many frogs stay to play?

☐ – ☐ = ☐

8

Name _____

1

_____

- - - - - - - -

_____

2

$$7 \quad - \quad 2 \quad =$$

_____

- - - - - - - -

_____

3

____ ¢ $-$ ____ ¢ $=$ ____ ¢

4

$$6 \quad \bigcirc \quad 3 \quad =$$

_____

- - - - - - - -

_____

Directions 1 Circle and cross out the one that is leaving. Write how many are left. 2 Draw balls to show the first number. Circle and cross out a group of two. Write how many are left. 3 Write a subtraction sentence to match the picture. 4 Decide if the picture shows addition or subtraction. Write a plus or minus sign in the circle. Write the answer.

Chapter 14

Add or Subtract 1

What You Need

How to Play 1 Take turns with a partner. 2 Roll the number cube and move that number of spaces. 3 Count the dots. Add or subtract 1. Tell your number sentence. 4 Play until a player reaches Finish.

Name _____

1

_____

- - - - - - - - - - -

_____

2

_____   **+**   _____   **=**   _____

- - - - - - - -   - - - - - - - -   - - - - - - - -

_____   _____   _____

3

_____ ¢   **+**   _____ ¢   **=**   _____ ¢

- - - - - - -   - - - - - - -   - - - - - - - - -

_____ ¢   _____ ¢   _____ ¢

4 ⭐

$$5 \quad + \quad 4 \quad = $$

_____

- - - - - - - -

_____

Directions I Write how many in all. **2–3** Write the number in each group. Add. Write the sum.
4 Draw a picture to match the fact. Add. Write the sum.

5

_____

- - - - - - - - - - -

_____

6

5 – 2 =

_____

- - - - - - - - -

_____

7

_____

- - - - - - - ¢

–

_____

- - - - - - - ¢

=

_____

- - - - - - - ¢

8

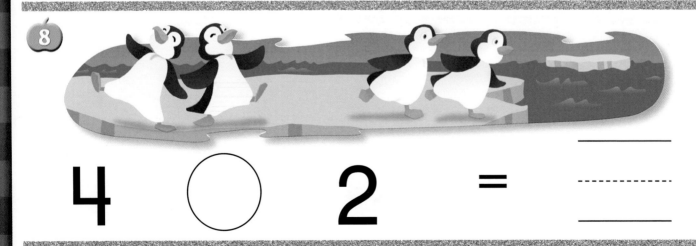

4 ◯ 2 =

_____

- - - - - - - - -

_____

Directions 5 Circle and cross out the one that is leaving. Write how many are left. **6** Draw balls
to show the first number. Circle and cross out a group of two. Write how many are left. **7** Write a
subtraction sentence to match the pennies. **8** Decide if the picture shows addition or subtraction.
Write a plus or minus sign in the circle. Write the answer.

278

Missing Addends

1

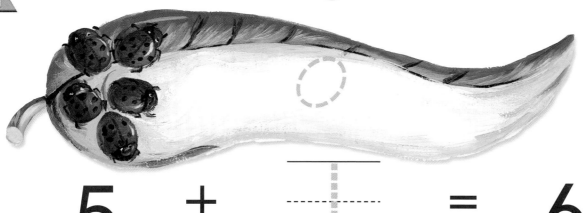

5   +   _____   =   6

2

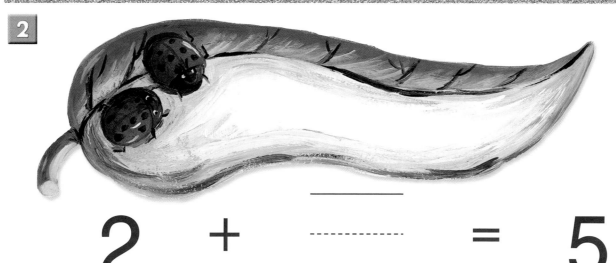

2   +   _____   =   5

3

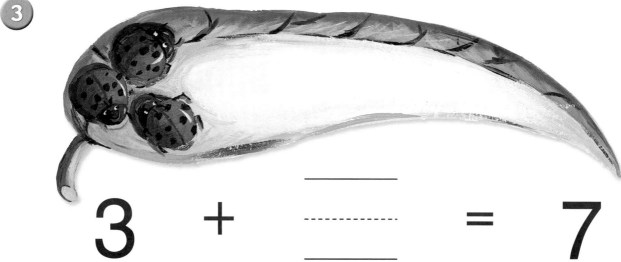

3   +   _____   =   7

Directions 1–3 Count the ladybugs. Draw more to make the sum. Write the missing number to complete the number sentence.

 1

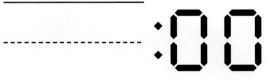
:00

2

¢

3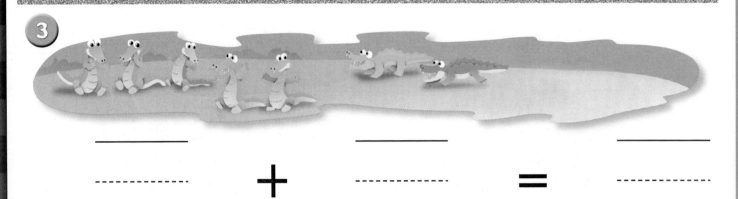

_____   _____   _____

_____ + _____ = _____

4

5

Directions 1 Write the time shown. 2 Write the number of cents. 3 Write the number in each group. Add. Write the sum. 4 Circle the heavier one. Underline the lighter one. 5 Circle the fourth one. Underline the second one.

Greater Numbers

From the Read-Aloud Anthology

Counting Our Way to Maine

by Maggie Smith

Access Prior Knowledge
This story will help you review
- Oral counting to 20
- Matching one to one

MATH at Home

Dear Family,

We are starting a new unit called Greater Numbers. In Chapter 15, we will read, write, and order numbers 10-20. In Chapter 16, we will read, write, and order numbers 20-31.

Love, _____

Vocabulary

teen numbers
Numbers between 10 and 20.

| **11** | **12** | **13** | **14** | **15** |
| eleven | twelve | thirteen | fourteen | fifteen |

| **16** | **17** | **18** | **19** |
| sixteen | seventeen | eighteen | nineteen |

ten-frame
A chart to show groups of ten.

10   **20**

30

count on
To start at one number and count by ones from there.

10   **11 12**

Vocabulary Activities

- Provide your child with 25 small objects and drawings of 3 ten-frames. Have your child place the objects in the ten-frames and count. Point out that there are two groups of 10 and a partial group.

- Give your child 13 objects. Have your child make a group of ten and count on from ten to find the number.

Visit *Education Place* **at eduplace.com/parents/mw/** for *e* • WordGame, *e* • Glossary **and more.**

Literature to Read Together

- **Bears at the Beach: Counting 10 to 20** by Niki Yektai (*Millbrook Press, 1996*)

- **The Icky Bug Counting Book** by Jerry Pallotta (*Charlesbridge, 1992*)

- **When Sheep Cannot Sleep: The Counting Book** by Satoshi Kitamura (*Farrar, Straus & Giroux, 1986*)

282

Numbers 10-20

Fewer than 10

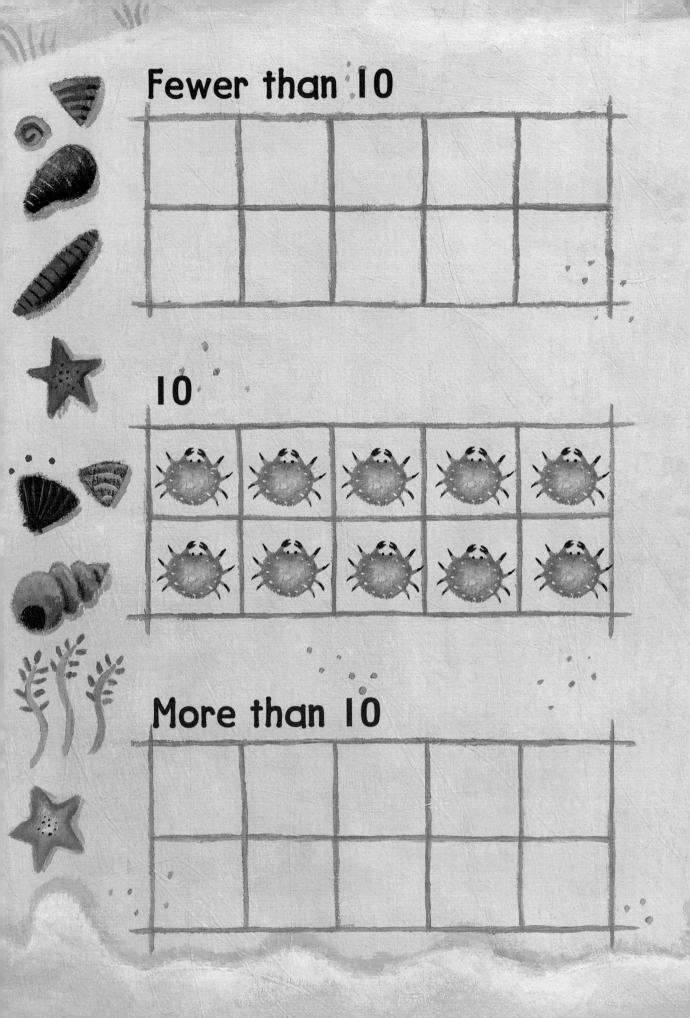

10

More than 10

Directions Put a cube on each crab. Count and tell the number. Place fewer than 10 cubes above the crabs. Count. Draw the cubes. Place more than 10 cubes below the crabs. Count. Draw the cubes.

284

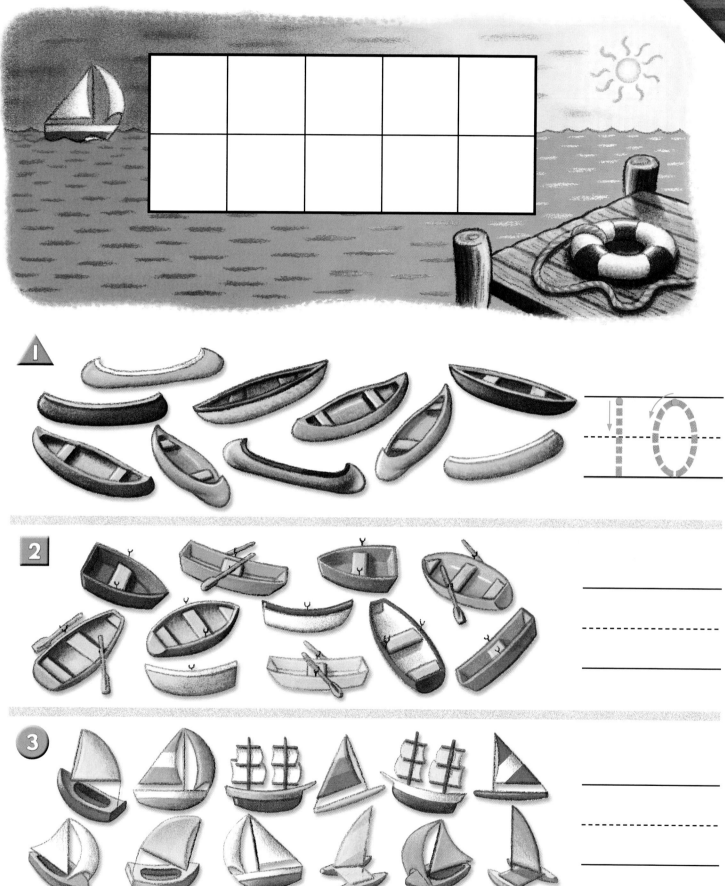

Directions 1–3 Place a counter on each item. Move the counters to the ten-frame.
Count the filled ten-frame as 10 and then count the extras. Write the number.

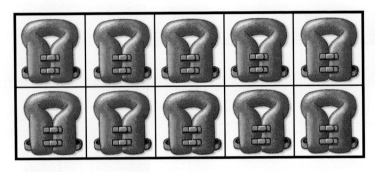 

_____
- - - - - - - - - - - - - - - - -
_____

2

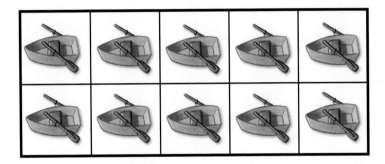

_____
- - - - - - - - - - - - - - - - -
_____

3

_____
- - - - - - - - - - - - - - - - -
_____

⭐ 4

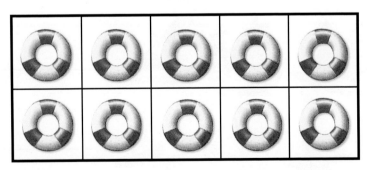

_____
- - - - - - - - - - - - - - - - -
_____

Directions 1–4 Count the filled ten-frame as 10 and count on. Write the number.

At Home Let your child count groups of 10, 11, and 12 small objects and practice writing each number.

1

2

3

Directions 1–2 Place a counter on each item. Move the counters to the ten frame. Count the filled ten-frame as 10 and then count on the extras. Write the number. **3** Write each number.

_____

- - - - - - - - - - - - - - - - - - - -

_____

Problem Solving ▶ Number Sense

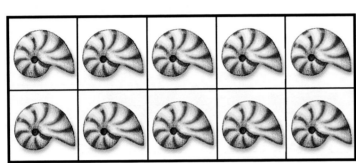

Directions 1-2 Count the filled ten-frame as 10 and count on. Write the number. **3** Circle the set that is close to 5. **4** Circle the set that is close to 13.

At Home Have your child make groups of 13 and 14 items using pennies or dry cereal. Have your child show you that each has 10 and some more. For example, 13 is 10 and 3 more.

288

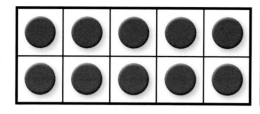

15

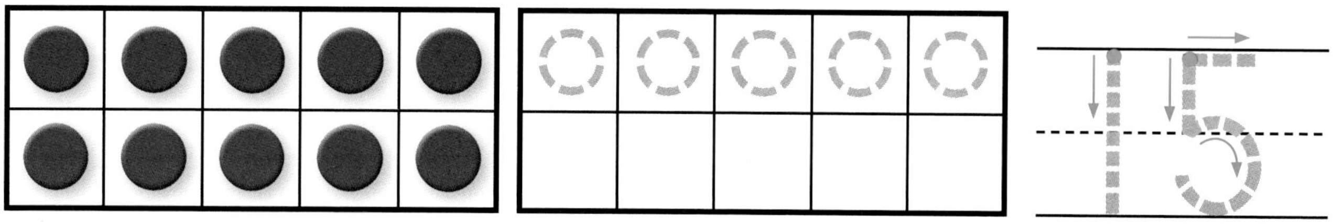

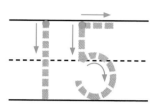

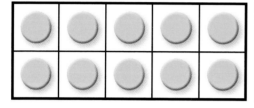

16

_____
- - - - - - - - - - - - - - -
_____

3

15

_____
- - - - - - - - - - - - - - -
_____

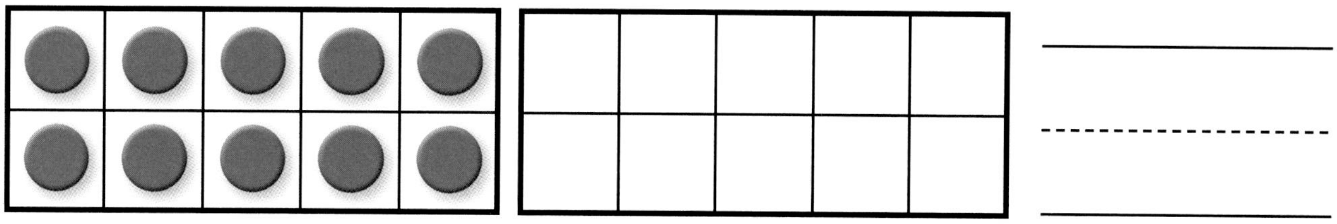

4

16

_____
- - - - - - - - - - - - - - -
_____

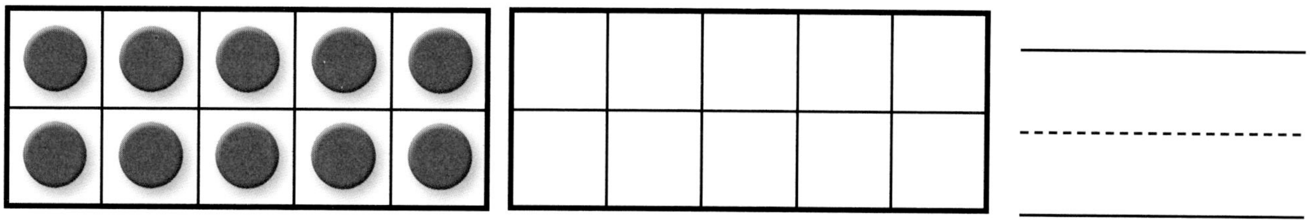

Directions 1-4 Count and draw more circles to make the number shown.
Write the number.

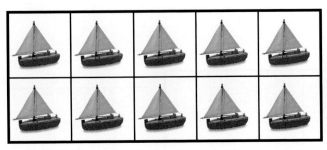 

14

15

16

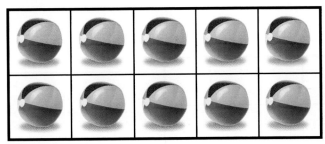 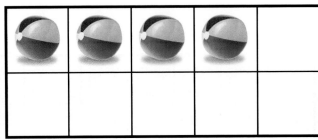

14

15

16

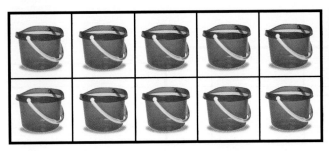 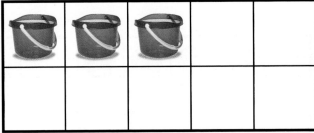

13

14

15

13

14

15

Directions 1–4 Count the items. Circle the number.

At Home Let your child read some of the numbers shown on these pages. Have your child practice writing the numbers 10 through 16.

290

Name _____

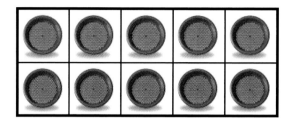  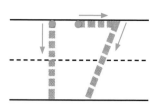

2

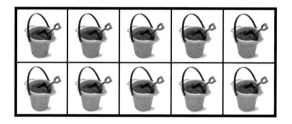 

3

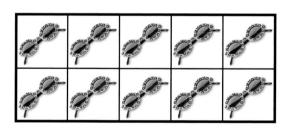 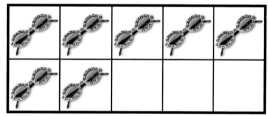

4

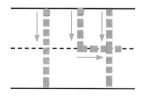 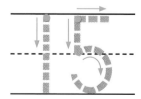 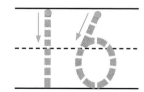 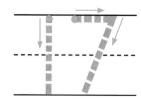 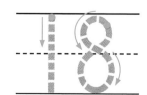

Directions 1–3 Count the filled ten-frame as 10 and count on. Write the number.
4 Write each number.

17

18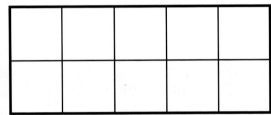

③ ④

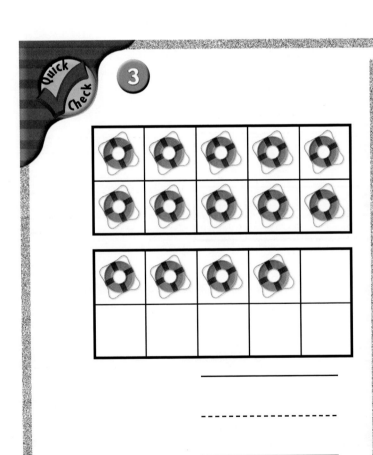

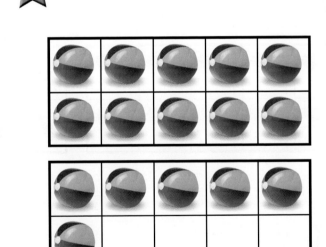

_____

- - - - - - - - - - - - - - -

_____

_____

- - - - - - - - - - - - - - -

_____

Directions 1–2 Count the items. Draw more to make the number shown. **3–4** Write the number.

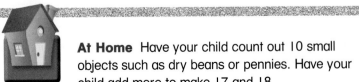

At Home Have your child count out 10 small objects such as dry beans or pennies. Have your child add more to make 17 and 18.

Name _____

  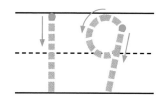

2

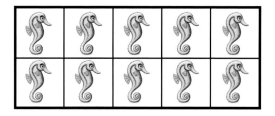 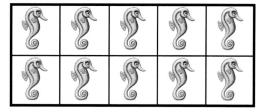 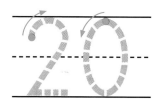

3

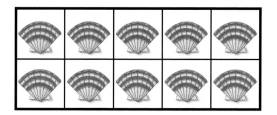 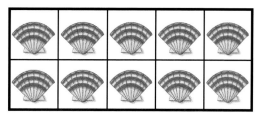

_____
- - - - - - - - - - - - - - - - -
_____

_____
- - - - - - - - - - - - - - - - -
_____

Directions 1–4 Count the filled ten-frames by tens and count on. Write the number.

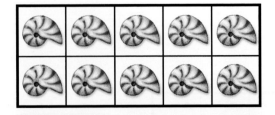

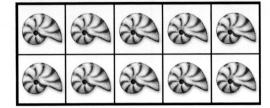

18   19   (20)

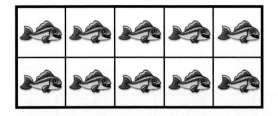

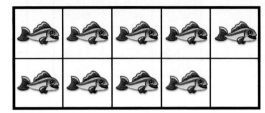

18   19   20

18   19   20

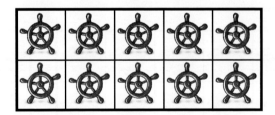

18   19   20

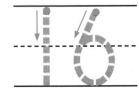 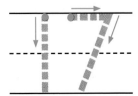 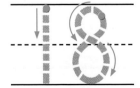 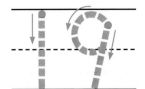 

Directions 1–4 Count the items. Circle the number.
5 Write each number.

At Home Have your child count out 20 small objects, such as paper clips, and show you that 20 is two groups of 10.

294

Order Numbers 10–20

Directions Count the filled ten-frame as 10 and count on. Write each number.

10 11 12 13 14 15 16 17 18 19 20

10 _11_ 12 _13_ 14

2

13 ____ 15 ____ 17

3

16 ____ 18 ____ 20

Directions 1–3 Write the missing numbers.

At Home Write the numbers 10 through 20 on small pieces of paper and mix them up. Have your child put the pieces in order and then point to and say each number.

Name_____ Dimes and Pennies

   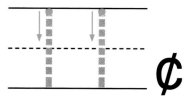 ¢

---

2   ¢

---

3       ¢

---

4   ¢

Directions 1–4 Point to the dime and say "ten cents." Point to each penny as you count on to find the number of cents in all. Write the number of cents.

1

_____
- - - - - - - - - - - -
_____ ¢

2

_____
- - - - - - - - - - - -
_____ ¢

3

_____
- - - - - - - - - - - -
_____ ¢

4

_____
- - - - - - - - - - - -
_____ ¢

5

_____
- - - - - - - - - - - -
_____ ¢

Directions 1–5 Point to the dime and say "ten cents." Point to each penny as you count on to find the number of cents in all. Write the number of cents.

At Home Let your child use one dime and nine pennies to show you amounts of money from 10¢ through 19¢.

298

Name _____

**Guess
and Check**

Problem
Solving

Guess

Check
- - - - - - - - - - - - - - - -

more than 10
less than 10

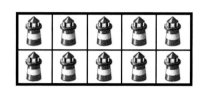 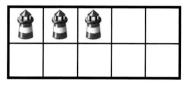

2

Guess

Check
- - - - - - - - - - - - - - - -

more than 10
less than 10

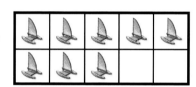 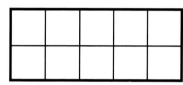

Guess

Check
- - - - - - - - - - - - - - - -

more than 10
less than 10

4

Guess

Check
- - - - - - - - - - - - - - - -

more than 10
less than 10

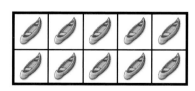 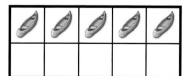

Directions 1–4 Guess whether the picture shows less than 10 or more than 10. Circle your guess. Count to check your answer. Write the number.

Chapter 15

299

Guess

Check

more than 15
less than 15

 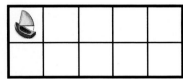

_____

- - - - - - - - - -

_____

Guess

Check

more than 15
less than 15

 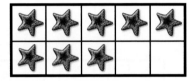

_____

- - - - - - - - - -

_____

Guess

Check

more than 15
less than 15

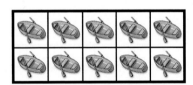 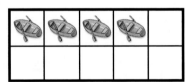

_____

- - - - - - - - - -

_____

Guess

Check

more than 15
less than 15

_____

- - - - - - - - - -

_____

Directions 1–4 Guess whether the picture shows less than 15 or more than 15. Circle your guess. Count to check your answer. Write the number.

At Home Have your child explain how he or she made each estimate (guess). Then have your child explain how the numbers match the pictures.

Counting Sea Treasures

This take-home book will help you review concepts you learned in Chapter 15.

1

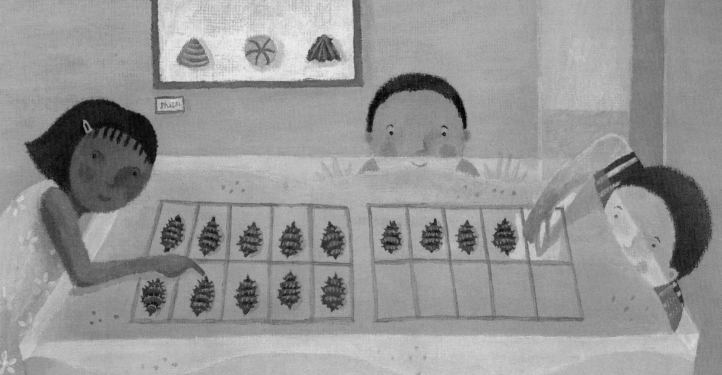

Some shells are rough.

How many are rough?

3

Some shells are smooth.
How many are smooth?

2

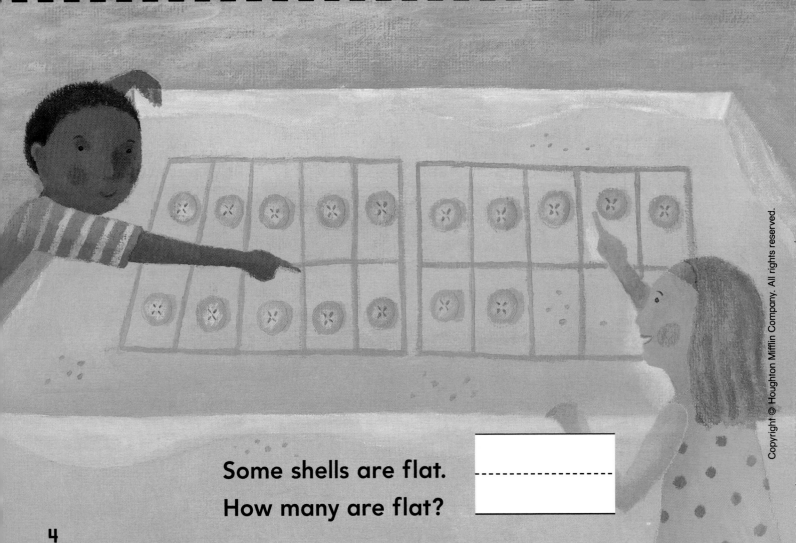

Some shells are flat.
How many are flat?

4

Some shells are round.
How many are round?

Sea horses are curvy.
How many are curvy?

Sea stars are pointy.
How many are pointy?

6

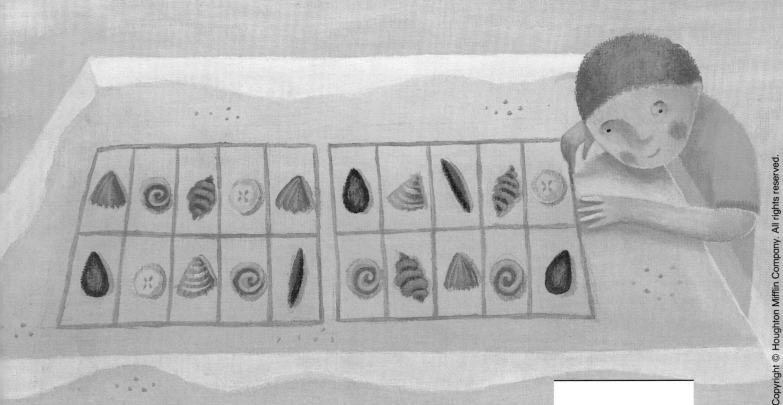

Shells come in lots of colors, too!
How many shells do you see?

8

Name _____

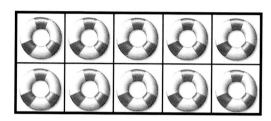 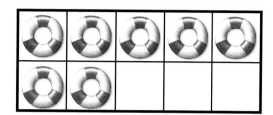

_____
- - - - - - - - - - - - - - -
_____

2

15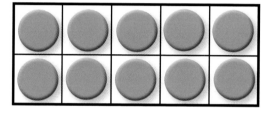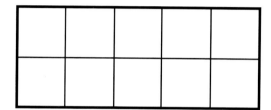

3

15 _____ 17 _____ 19
- - - - - - - - -   - - - - - - - - -
_____   _____

4

Guess

more than 10

less than 10

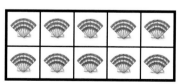

Check
_____
- - - - - - - - - - - - -
_____

Directions 1 Count. Write the number. 2 Count. Draw more circles to make the number shown. 3 Write the missing numbers. 4 Circle your guess. Count to check your answer. Write the number.

Chapter 15

301

1

_____

\- \- \- \- \- \- \- \- \- \-

_____

2

_____

\- \- \- \- \- \- \- \- \- \-

_____

3

more than 20   less than 20

Directions Talk about the Fourth of July celebration. **1** Count the number of flags. Write the number.
2 Count the number of stripes on a flag. Write the number. **3** Guess whether there are less than 20 or
more than 20 stars on the large flag. Count to check. Circle the answer.

Numbers Greater Than 20

_____

- - - - - - - - - - - - - - - - - - - -

_____

_____   _____

- - - - - - - - - - - - - - - -   - - - - - - - - - - - - - - - -

_____   _____

Directions Place a counter on each fish. Count. Write the number. Move the counters to each fish bowl so that each has the same number. Write the numbers. Draw.

304

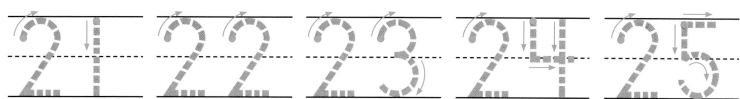

2

21

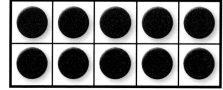

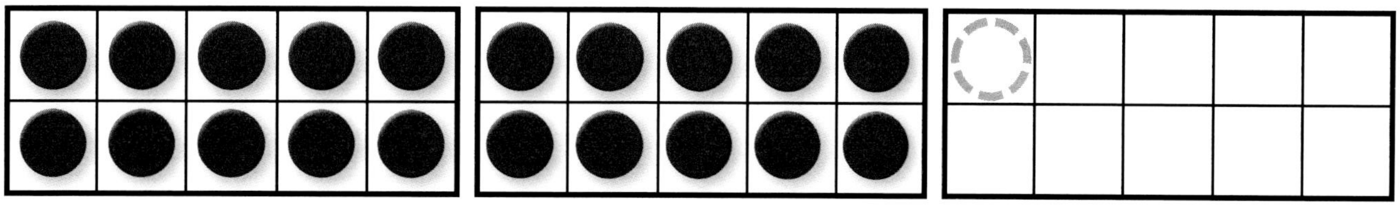

3

22

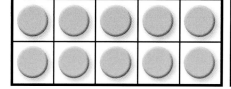

4

23

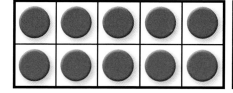

5

24

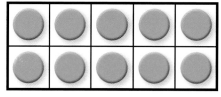

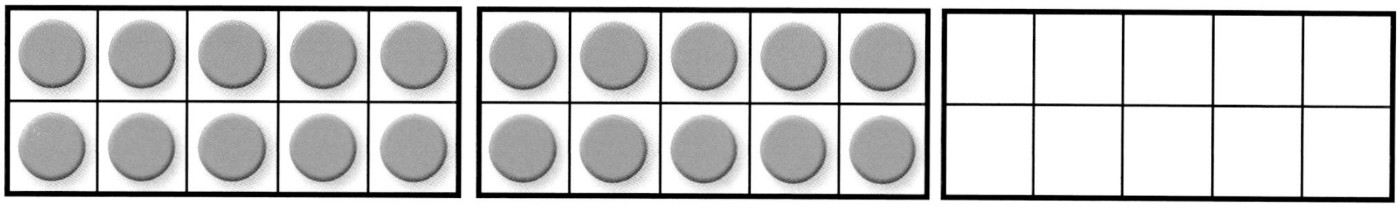

Directions | Write each number. 2-5 Count. Draw more circles to make the number shown.

1

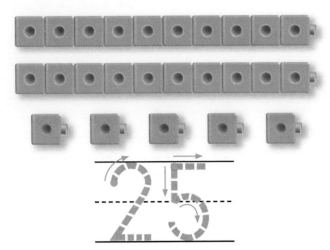

2

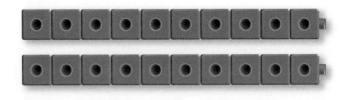

_____

- - - - - - - - - - - - - - - - - -

_____

3

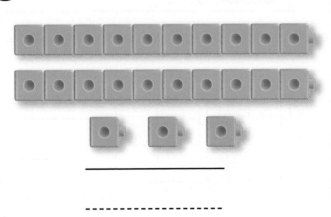

_____

- - - - - - - - - - - - - - - - - -

_____

4

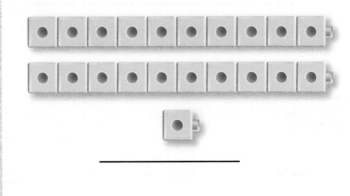

_____

- - - - - - - - - - - - - - - - - -

_____

5

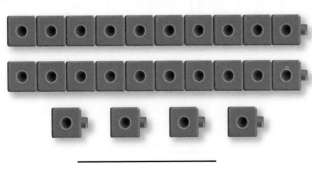

_____

- - - - - - - - - - - - - - - - - -

_____

6

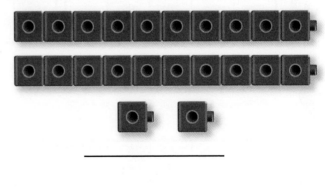

_____

- - - - - - - - - - - - - - - - - -

_____

Directions 1–6 Count the cube trains by tens and then count on. Write the number.

At Home Have your child count out 25 small objects such as dry cereal. Let your child arrange them in two groups of ten and five more. Repeat with other numbers 21 through 24.

  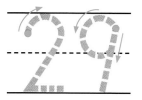 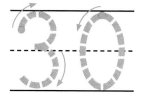

2

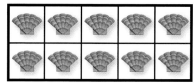  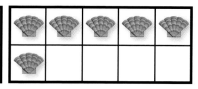

3

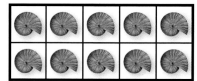 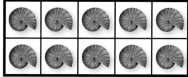 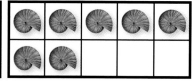

4

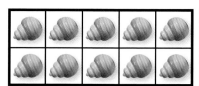 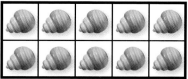 

5

  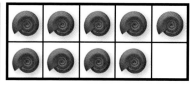

Directions I Write each number. 2–5 Count the filled ten-frames by tens and then count on.
Write the number.

1

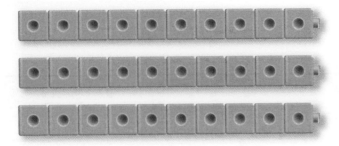

28   29   (30)

2

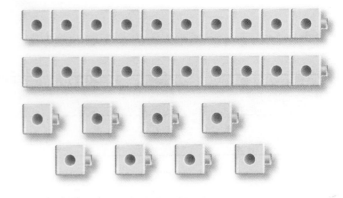

28   29   30

3

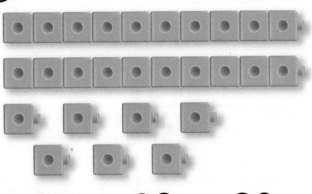

27   28   29

4

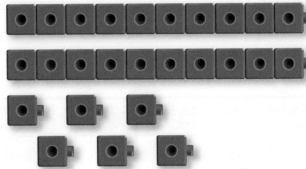

25   26   27

Problem Solving ▷ Number Sense

5

8   28

6

3   30

Directions 1–4 Count the cube trains by tens and then count on. Circle the number. 5–6 Circle the number that is close to the number of items shown.

At Home Have your child use small items such as pennies or dry beans to practice counting to 31. Have your child arrange the items in groups of ten and then count on.

Calendar: Using Numbers 1–31

July

Sunday	Monday	Tuesday	Wednesday	Thursday	Friday	Saturday
			1	2	3	4
5	6	7	8	9	10	11
12	13	14	15	16	17	18
19	20	21	22	23	24	25
26	27	28	29	30	31	

Directions Follow the teacher's directions to circle the dates.

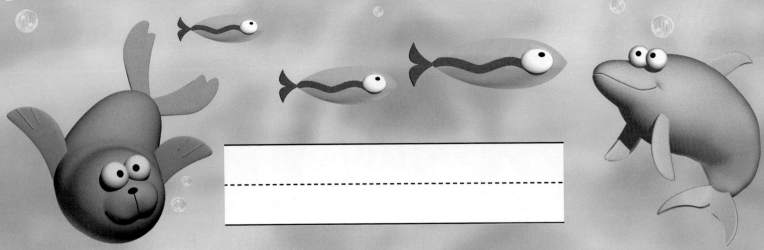

Sunday	Monday	Tuesday	Wednesday	Thursday	Friday	Saturday

Directions Make a calendar for the current month. Write the name of the month and the dates.

At Home Have your child point to the days of the week and the dates of all the Saturdays. Then have your child read several dates to you.

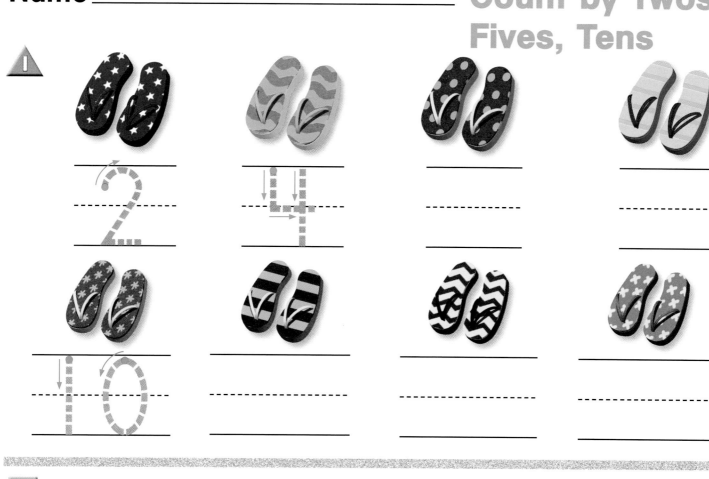

1

2

4

10

2

5

10

3

10

Directions 1 Count by twos. Write the numbers. 2 Count by fives. Write the numbers.
3 Count by tens. Write the numbers.

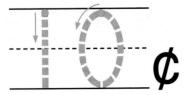 ¢   ¢   ¢

2

 ¢   ¢   ¢   ¢

3

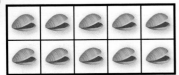 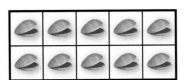 

4

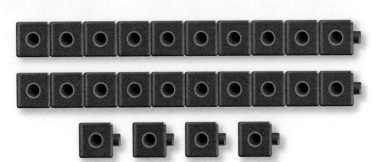

Directions I Count by tens. Write the cents. 2 Count by fives. Write the cents. 3–4 Count by tens and then count on. Write the number.

At Home Encourage your child to count aloud by twos, fives, and tens.

312

Use a Pattern

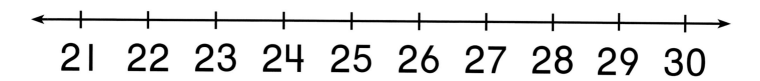

21 22 23 24 25 26 27 28 29 30

1

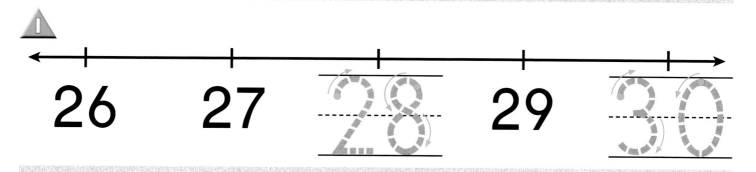

26   27   28   29   30

2

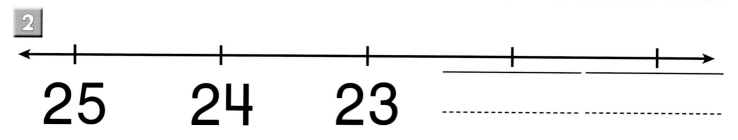

25   24   23   ____   ____

3

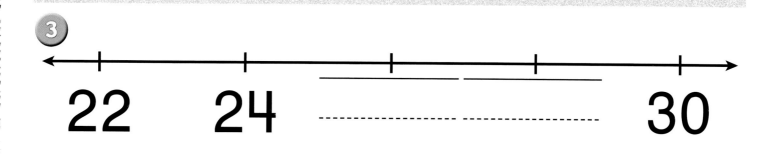

22   24   ____   ____   30

4

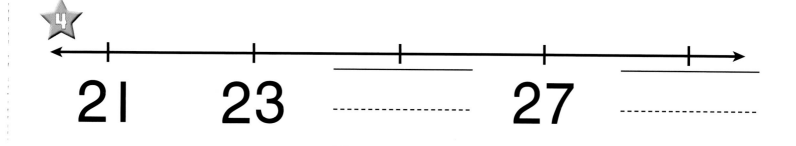

21   23   ____   27   ____

Directions 1–4 Look for a pattern. Write the missing numbers.
Use the number line to help.

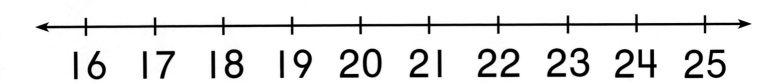

16 17 18 19 20 21 22 23 24 25

1

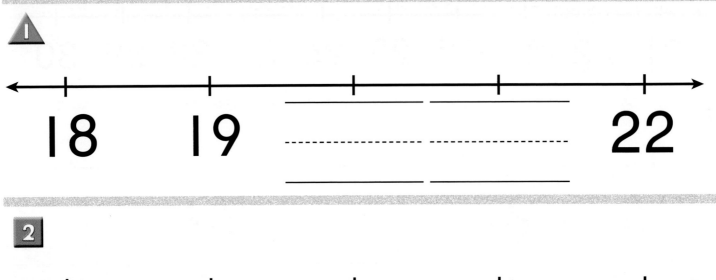

18   19   _____   _____   **22**

2

20   19   18   _____   _____

3

16   _____   20   _____   **24**

4

17   19   _____   **23**   _____

Directions 1–4 Look for a pattern. Write the missing numbers. Use the number line to help.

At Home Let your child explain several of the patterns and how he or she decided what the missing numbers were.

314

BEAR'S BEACH PARTY

This take-home book will help you review concepts you learned in Chapter 16.

I

I invited lots of friends. _____

How many are coming? _____

3

I am having a beach party today!

What is the date?

2

Dad blows up beach balls.

How many do you see?

4

Mom pours some drinks. ----------------------

How many cups do you see? _____

_____

Grandpa hands out hats. ----------------------

How many do you see?

Grandma makes some snacks.   ---------------------

How many do you see?   _____

6

Everyone gets a balloon!   _____

Count the balloons by twos, fives, or tens.   ---------------------

8

Name _____

1

23   24   25

2

27   28   29

3

25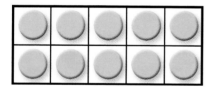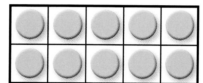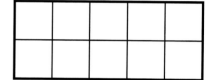

4

_____   _____

_____   **28   29**   ------------   **31**

5

_____   _____

25   24   ------------   ------------   **21**

Directions 1–2 Count the cube trains by tens and then count on. Circle the number. 3 Count.
Draw more dots to make the number shown. 4 Write the missing numbers. 5 Look for a pattern.
Write the missing numbers.

Chapter 16

315

Swim to 31

What You Need

Start

1 2 3 4 5 6 7 8 9 10 11 12 13 14 15 16 17 18 19 20 21 22 23 24 25 26 27 28 29 30 31

Finish

How to Play | Take turns with a partner. 2 Roll the number cube and move that number of spaces. 3 Read the number on the space. If you land on 10, 20, or 30, roll again. 4 Play until a player reaches or passes 31.

316

Name _____

14  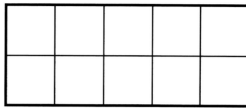 _____

2

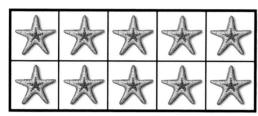 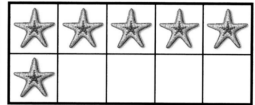 _____

3

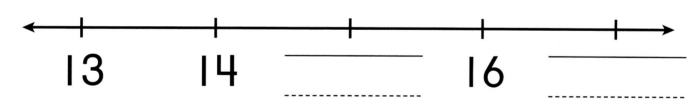

13   14   _____   16   _____

⭐

Guess   Check
                                                         _____
more than 15       _____
less than 15

Directions 1 Count. Draw more dots to make the number shown. Write the number. 2 Count.
Write the number. 3 Write the missing numbers. 4 Circle your guess. Count to check your answer.
Write the number.

5

28
29
30

6

20
25
30

7

28

8

_____   _____

21 22 _____ 24 _____ 26

9

_____   _____

20 22 _____   28

Directions 5–6 Count the cube trains by tens and then count on. Circle the number. 7 Count.
Draw more dots to make the number shown. 8 Write the missing numbers. 9 Look for a pattern.
Write the missing numbers.

318

Hundred Chart

1	2	3	4	5	6	7	8	9	10
11	12	13	14	15	16	17	18	19	20
21	22	23	24	25	26	27	28	29	30
31	32	33	34	35	36	37	38	39	40
41	42	43	44	45	46	47	48	49	50
51	52	53	54	55	56	57	58	59	60
61	62	63	64	65	66	67	68	69	70
71	72	73	74	75	76	77	78	79	80
81	82	83	84	85	86	87	88	89	90
91	92	93	94	95	96	97	98	99	100

Directions 1 Color in yellow all the numbers in the last column. Count by tens. 2 Put a blue x on all the numbers that end with a 5 or 0. Count by fives. 3 Circle in red every other number starting with 2. Count by twos.

Name _____

Cumulative Review

2

3

_____   _____   _____

- - - - - - - - -   **+**   - - - - - - - - -   **=**   - - - - - - - - -

_____   _____   _____

4

_____   _____   _____

- - - - - - - - -   **—**   - - - - - - - - -   **=**   - - - - - - - - -

_____   _____   _____

5
_____   _____   _____

- - - - - - - - -   - - - - - - - - -   - - - - - - - - -

18 19 _____ _____ **22** _____

Directions 1 Circle the one that shows equal parts. 2 Circle the one that holds more. Underline the one that holds less. 3 Write the number in each group. Add. Write the sum. 4 Count and write the number in all. Count and write the number in the crossed-out group. Write the difference. 5 Write the missing numbers.

Name_____

WEEKLY (WR) READER®
Activity Almanac

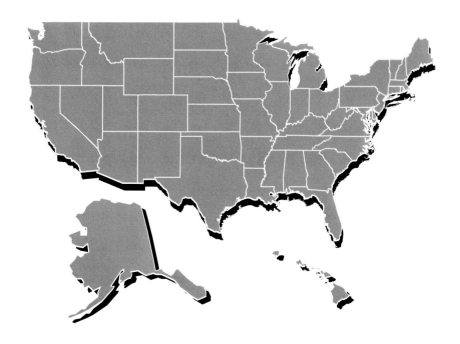

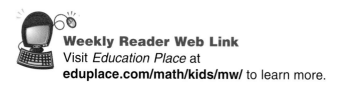

Weekly Reader Web Link
Visit *Education Place* at
eduplace.com/math/kids/mw/ to learn more.

Weekly Reader Photography Credits: 322–3 (Mockingbird) © D. Robert & Lorri Franz/CORBIS. (Cardinal) © Gary W. Carter/CORBIS. (Western Meadowlark) © Darrell Gulin/Stone/Getty Images. **Weekly Reader Illustration Credits:** 324–5 Ronnie Rooney. 326–7 Marcy Ramsey. 328–9 Duff Orlemann. 330–1 Michelle Dorenkamp.

CANADA

Washington

Oregon

North Dakota

Minnesota

Montana

Idaho

South Dakota

Wisconsin

Wyoming

Missouri River

Iowa

Nevada

Utah

Nebraska

Illinois

California

Colorado

Kansas

Missouri

Arizona

Oklahoma

Arkansas

Mississippi River

New Mexico

Mississip

Louisian

Texas

Rio Grande

MEXICO

T-

M

Yukon River

CANADA

Alaska

Juneau

Honolulu

Hawaii

Note: Alaska and Hawaii are not in position and are not drawn to scale.

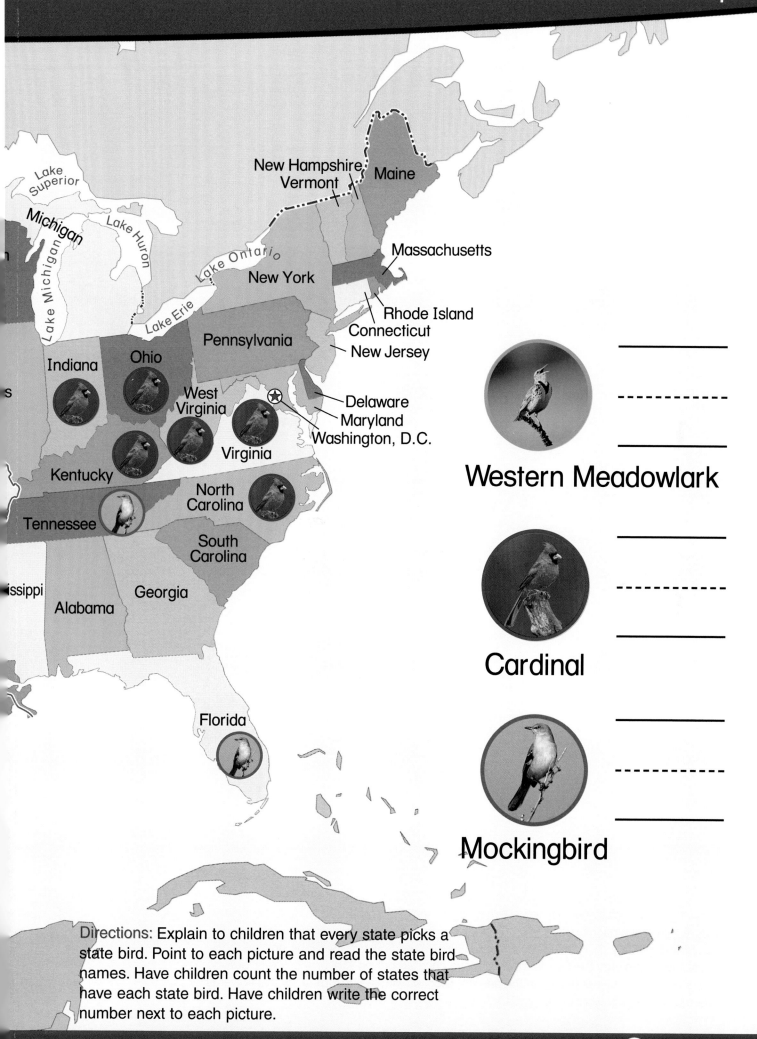

Western Meadowlark

Cardinal

Mockingbird

Directions: Explain to children that every state picks a state bird. Point to each picture and read the state bird names. Have children count the number of states that have each state bird. Have children write the correct number next to each picture.

How Does Your Garden Grow?

Directions: Tell children that New Jersey is called the "Garden State." All the flowers pictured on these pages grow in New Jersey. **1.** Have children circle the flowers that are outside the garden. **2.** Have children draw a line from a flower outside the garden to the flower that completes the bottom row. **3.** Have children put an X over the flower outside the garden that does not belong in the garden. Discuss with the children how this flower is different from the flowers in the garden.

Directions: 1. Have children count the number in each group of flowers and write the numeral. **2.** Have children circle the group of flowers they like best. Then have children find another group of flowers with the same number of flowers in it. **3.** Have children circle that group of flowers and draw a line between the two groups that are circled.

Frames and Games

Directions: Tell children that the Potawatomi people lived in Michigan more than 200 years ago. Potawatomi clothing had geometric or flower designs. These designs are still made today. **1.** Discuss with children the blue diamonds, red rectangles, and yellow triangles in the picture frame. **2.** Have children identify the geometric shapes in the design. **3.** Have children continue the pattern by coloring the rest of the frame with the same colors. **4.** Have children create a picture within the frame using only geometric shapes.

Directions: Explain that Native Americans used trees to make canoes, toys, and other things. Native American girls played a game with dolls made from bunches of pine needles cut straight across the bottom. They bounced the dolls on a tray to see how long they could stay up. **1.** Have children count the pine trees and write the numeral on the line. **2.** Have them count the canoes and write the numeral. **3.** Have them count the girls and write the numeral. **4.** Have children draw a picture using items in groups of 6–12. Suggest they use pine cones, needle dolls, and so on.

Around and Around in the Park

Directions: Ask children to tell what they see and do in a park. Tell them that some parks, like Richland Park in Mansfield, Ohio, have carousels, or merry-go-rounds. **1.** Have children circle the picture that shows the carousel in the morning and put an X on the picture that shows the carousel at night. **2.** Have children draw a picture of themselves in a park in the daytime. Then have them draw themselves at home at nighttime.

Directions: Tell children that there are carved and painted wooden horses Mand other animals on the carousel. Some are large and some are small. Ask where riders can sit on a carousel. **1.** Direct attention to the three carousel horses. Have children circle the biggest horse and put an X on the smallest horse. **2.** Direct children's attention to the bench seat with the grown-up and child. Have children circle the water bottle that holds more. Have them put an X on the bottle that holds less.

Tiny Turtles and Friends

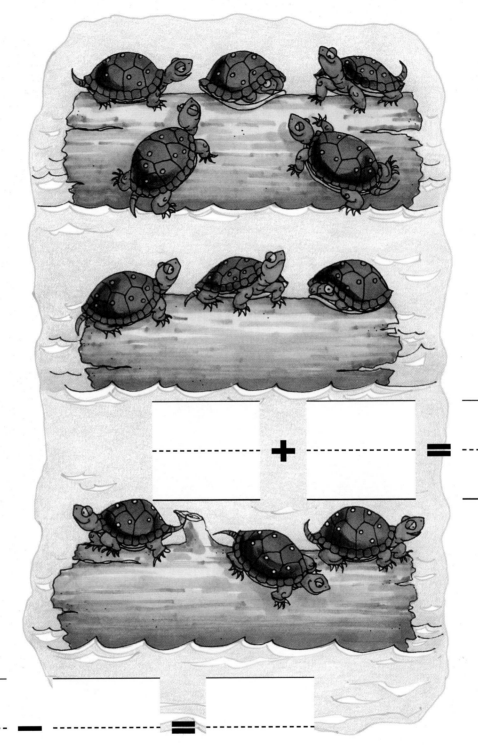

_____ + _____ = _____

_____ − _____ = _____

Directions: Tell children that tiny spotted turtles live in wet areas of West Virginia.
1. Have children look at the top two logs. Then have them write the number of turtles on each log in the addition sentence. **2.** Have them add and write the sum. **3.** Have children count the frogs on the bottom log. **4.** Ask them to cross out the turtles that are going away. Note: children may see one, two, or three turtles going away. **5.** Have them write the numbers and subtract to find the difference.

Directions: Ask children what other small animals they see in wet areas. Tell them that the noisy wood frogs are even tinier than the spotted turtles. They lay their eggs in the early spring.
1. Have children look at the top two lily pads. Tell children that there are 10 frogs on each lily pad. Have them count by 10s to find how many in all. Have them write the total on the line.
2. Have children look at the bottom five lily pads. Tell children that there are 5 frogs on each lily pad. Have them count by 5s to find how many in all. Have them write the total on the line.

NCTM Standards for Grades Pre-K–2

Number and Operations Standards • Expectations	Houghton Mifflin Math Grade K Correlation*
Understand numbers, ways of representing numbers, relation-ships among numbers, and number systems	
• count with understanding and recognize "how many" in sets of objects;	• Ch. 3, pp. 45–50; Ch. 4, pp. 59–60, 65–68; Ch. 7, pp. 129–132; Ch. 8, pp. 151–152; Ch. 10, pp. 185–186, 193–194
• use multiple models to develop initial understandings of place value and the base-ten number system;	• Ch. 7, pp. 133–134, 137–140; Ch. 10, pp. 187–190; Ch. 15, pp. 285–288, 297–298
• develop understanding of the relative position and magnitude of whole numbers and of ordinal and cardinal numbers and their connections;	• Ch. 4, pp. 71–74; Ch. 7, pp. 135–136; Ch. 8, pp. 147–148; Ch. 9, pp. 169–170; Ch. 15, pp. 295–296; Ch. 16, pp. 309–310
• develop a sense of whole numbers and represent and use them in flexible ways, including relating, composing, and decomposing numbers;	• Ch. 8, pp. 145–146; Ch. 15, pp. 299–300; Ch. 16, pp. 305–308
• connect number words and numerals to the quantities they represent, using various physical models and representations;	• Ch. 4, pp. 61–64, 69–70; Ch. 7, pp. 125–128; Ch. 15, pp. 289–294
• understand and represent commonly used fractions, such as $\frac{1}{4}$, $\frac{1}{3}$, and $\frac{1}{2}$.	• Ch. 5, pp. 93–96
Understand meanings of operations and how they relate to one another	
• understand various meanings of addition and subtraction of whole numbers and the relationship between the two opera-tions;	• Ch. 13, pp. 247–248; Ch. 14, pp. 265–266, pp. 273–274
• understand the effects of adding and subtracting whole numbers;	• Ch. 13, pp. 247–248; Ch. 14, pp. 265–266
• understand situations that entail multiplication and division, such as equal groupings of objects and sharing equally.	• Ch. 5, pp. 97–98; Ch. 8, pp. 153–154
Compute fluently and make reasonable estimates	
• develop and use strategies for whole-number computations, with a focus on addition and subtraction;	• Ch. 13, pp. 245–246, 249–250, 255–256; Ch. 14, pp. 263–264, 267–268
• develop fluency with basic number combinations for addition and subtraction;	• Ch. 13, pp. 251–252; Ch. 14, pp. 269–270
• use a variety of methods and tools to compute, including objects, mental computation, estimation, paper and pencil, and calculators.	• Whole/Small group activities in class.

* For each lesson, the key content and process standards have been identified.

Algebra Standards • Expectations	Houghton Mifflin Math Grade K Correlation
Understand patterns, relations, and functions	
• sort, classify, and order objects by size, number, and other properties;	• Ch. 1, pp. 5–18; Ch. 8, pp. 149–150; Ch. 10, pp. 191–192
• recognize, describe, and extend patterns such as sequences of sounds and shapes or simple numeric patterns and translate from one representation to another;	• Ch. 2, pp. 29–30; Ch. 16, pp. 311–314
• analyze how both repeating and growing patterns are generated.	• Ch. 2, pp. 31–34
Represent and analyze mathematical situations and structures using algebraic symbols	
• illustrate general principles and properties of operations, such as commutativity, using specific numbers;	• Ch. 13, pp. 253–254; Ch. 14, pp. 271–272
• use concrete, pictorial, and verbal representations to develop an understanding of invented and conventional symbolic notations.	• Ch. 13, pp. 253–254; Ch. 14, pp. 271–272
Use mathematical models to represent and understand quantitative relationships	
• model situations that involve the addition and subtraction of whole numbers, using objects, pictures, and symbols.	• Ch. 13, pp. 257–258, 267–268
Analyze change in various contexts	
• describe qualitative change, such as a student's growing taller;	• Whole/Small group instruction in class.
• describe quantitative change, such as a student's growing two inches in one year	• Whole/Small group instruction in class.
Geometry Standards • Expectations	Houghton Mifflin Math Grade K Correlation
Analyze characteristics and properties of two- and three-dimensional geometric shapes and develop mathematical arguments about geometric relationships	
• recognize, name, build, draw, compare, and sort two- and three-dimensional shapes;	• Ch. 5, pp. 85–88, 107–108
• describe attributes and parts of two- and three-dimensional shapes;	• Ch. 6, pp. 105–106, 109–110
• investigate and predict the results of putting together and taking apart two- and three-dimensional shapes.	• Ch. 6, pp. 111–112
Specify locations and describe spatial relationships using coordinate geometry and other representational systems	
• describe, name, and interpret relative positions in space and apply ideas about relative position;	• Ch. 2, pp. 23–28
• describe, name, and interpret direction and distance in navigating space and apply ideas about direction and distance;	• Unit 3, p. 119
• find and name locations with simple relationships such as "near to" and in coordinate systems such as maps.	• Covered in upper grades.

Geometry Standards (continued) • Expectations	Houghton Mifflin Math Grade K Correlation*
Apply transformations and use symmetry to analyze mathematical situations	
• recognize and apply slides, flips, and turns;	• Ch. 5, pp. 89–90
• recognize and create shapes that have symmetry.	• Ch. 5, pp. 91–92
Use visualization, spatial reasoning, and geometric modeling to solve problems	
• create mental images of geometric shapes using spatial memory and spatial visualization;	• Covered in upper grades.
• recognize and represent shapes from different perspectives;	• Ch. 5, pp. 89–90
• relate ideas in geometry to ideas in number and measurement;	• Ch. 6, pp. 113–114
• recognize geometric shapes and structures in the environment and specify their location.	• Whole/Small group instruction in class.
Measurement Standards • Expectations	Houghton Mifflin Math Grade K Correlation
Understand measurable attributes of objects and the units, systems, and processes of measurement	
• recognize the attributes of length, volume, weight, area, and time;	• Ch. 9, pp. 165–166; Ch. 11, pp. 205–208; Ch. 12, pp. 219–222, 225–228
• compare and order objects according to these attributes;	• Ch. 9, pp. 167–168, 173–180; Ch. 11, pp. 205–208; Ch. 12, pp. 219–222, 225–228
• understand how to measure using nonstandard and standard units;	• Ch. 12, pp. 211–212, 223–224, 229–230
• select an appropriate unit and tool for the attribute being measured.	• Ch. 12, pp. 231–232
Apply appropriate techniques, tools, and formulas to determine measurements	
• measure with multiple copies of units of the same size, such as paper clips laid end to end;	• Ch. 11, pp. 209–210, 223–224
• use repetition of a single unit to measure something larger than the unit, for instance, measuring the length of a room with a single meterstick;	• Ch. 12, pp. 213–214
• use tools to measure;	• Ch. 9, pp. 169–170, 175–176; Ch. 12, pp. 223–224; Unit 6, p. 239
• develop common referents for measures to make comparison and estimates.	• Ch. 12, pp. 233–234
Data Analysis and Probability Standards • Expectations	Houghton Mifflin Math Grade K Correlation
Formulate questions that can be addressed with data and collect, organize, and display relevant data to answer them	
• pose questions and gather data about themselves and their surroundings;	• Ch. 3, pp. 53–54
• sort and classify objects according to their attributes and organize data about the objects;	• Ch. 3, pp. 51–52

* For each lesson, the key content and process standards have been identified.

Data Analysis and Probability Standards (continued) • Expectations	Houghton Mifflin Math Grade K Correlation
• represent data using concrete objects, pictures, and graphs	• Ch. 3, pp. 51–52
Select and use appropriate statistical methods to analyze data	
• describe parts of the data and the set of data as a whole to determine what the data show.	• Covered in upper grades.
Develop and evaluate inferences and predictions that are based on data	
• discuss events related to students' experiences as likely or unlikely.	• Ch. 5, pp. 99–100; Ch. 9, pp. 171–172
Understand and apply basic concepts of probability	

Problem Solving Standards	Houghton Mifflin Math Grade K Correlation
• build new mathematical knowledge through problem solving;	• See **Problem-Solving Application** lessons, such as Ch. 2, pp. 33–34; Ch. 5, pp. 97–98; Ch. 7, pp. 135–136
• solve problems that arise in mathematics and in other contexts;	• See Science, Social Studies, and Art Connections at the end of chapters 1, 3, 5, 7, 9, 11, 13, and 15
• apply and adapt a variety of appropriate strategies to solve problems;	• See **Problem-Solving Strategy** lessons, such as Ch. 4, pp. 113–114, Ch. 8, pp. 153–154, Ch. 13, pp. 257–258
• monitor and reflect on the process of mathematical problem solving.	• Covered in upper grades.

Reasoning and Proof Standards	Houghton Mifflin Math Grade K Correlation
• recognize reasoning and proof as fundamental aspects of mathematics;	• Ch. 2, pp. 29–34; Ch. 7, pp. 135–136; Ch. 8, p. 152; Ch. 13, p. 250; Ch. 14, pp. 268, 273–274
• make and investigate mathematical conjectures;	• Ch. 5, pp. 99–100; Ch. 11, pp. 211–212; Ch. 12, pp. 223–224, 229–230; Ch. 8, pp. 299–300
• develop and evaluate mathematical arguments and proofs;	• Covered in upper grades.
• select and use various types of reasoning and methods of proof.	• Ch. 1, pp. 12, 17–18; Ch. 2, p. 26; Ch. 4, pp. 71–72; Ch. 5, p. 92; Ch. 6, p. 112; Ch. 7, pp. 140–141; Ch. 9, p. 174; Ch. 12, pp. 233–234

Communication Standards	Houghton Mifflin Math Grade K Correlation
• organize and consolidate their mathematical thinking through communication;	• See **At Home** in each lesson.
• communicate their mathematical thinking coherently and clearly to peers, teachers, and others;	• Whole/Small group instruction in class.
• analyze and evaluate the mathematical thinking and strategies of others;	• Whole/Small group instruction in class.
• use the language of mathematics to express mathematical ideas precisely.	• Ch. 1, pp. 15–18; Ch. 3, pp. 51–54

Connections Standards	Houghton Mifflin Math Grade K Correlation*
• recognize and use connections among mathematical ideas;	• Ch. 6, pp. 109–110, 113–114; Unit 3, p. 119; Ch. 7, pp. 135–136; Unit 4, p. 159; Unit 7, p. 279; Unit 8, p. 319
• understand how mathematical ideas interconnect and build on one another to produce a coherent whole;	• Covered in upper grades.
• recognize and apply mathematics in contexts outside of mathematics.	• Ch. 1, p. 20; Ch. 3, p. 56; Ch. 5, p. 102; Ch. 7, p. 142; Ch. 11, p. 216; Ch. 13, p. 260; Ch. 15, p. 302
Representation Standards	Houghton Mifflin Math Grade K Correlation
• create and use representations to organize, record, and communicate mathematical ideas;	• Ch. 3, pp. 51–54; Unit 2, p. 79; Ch. 6, pp. 113–114
• select, apply, and translate among mathematical representations to solve problems;	• Ch. 8, p. 147; Ch. 15, pp. 295–296; Ch. 16, pp. 305–306, 313–314
• use representations to model and interpret physical, social, and mathematical phenomena.	• Covered in upper grades.

* For each lesson, the key content and process standards have been identified.

Workmat 1

Multi-Purpose Mat

Double Ten-Frame

Workmat 6

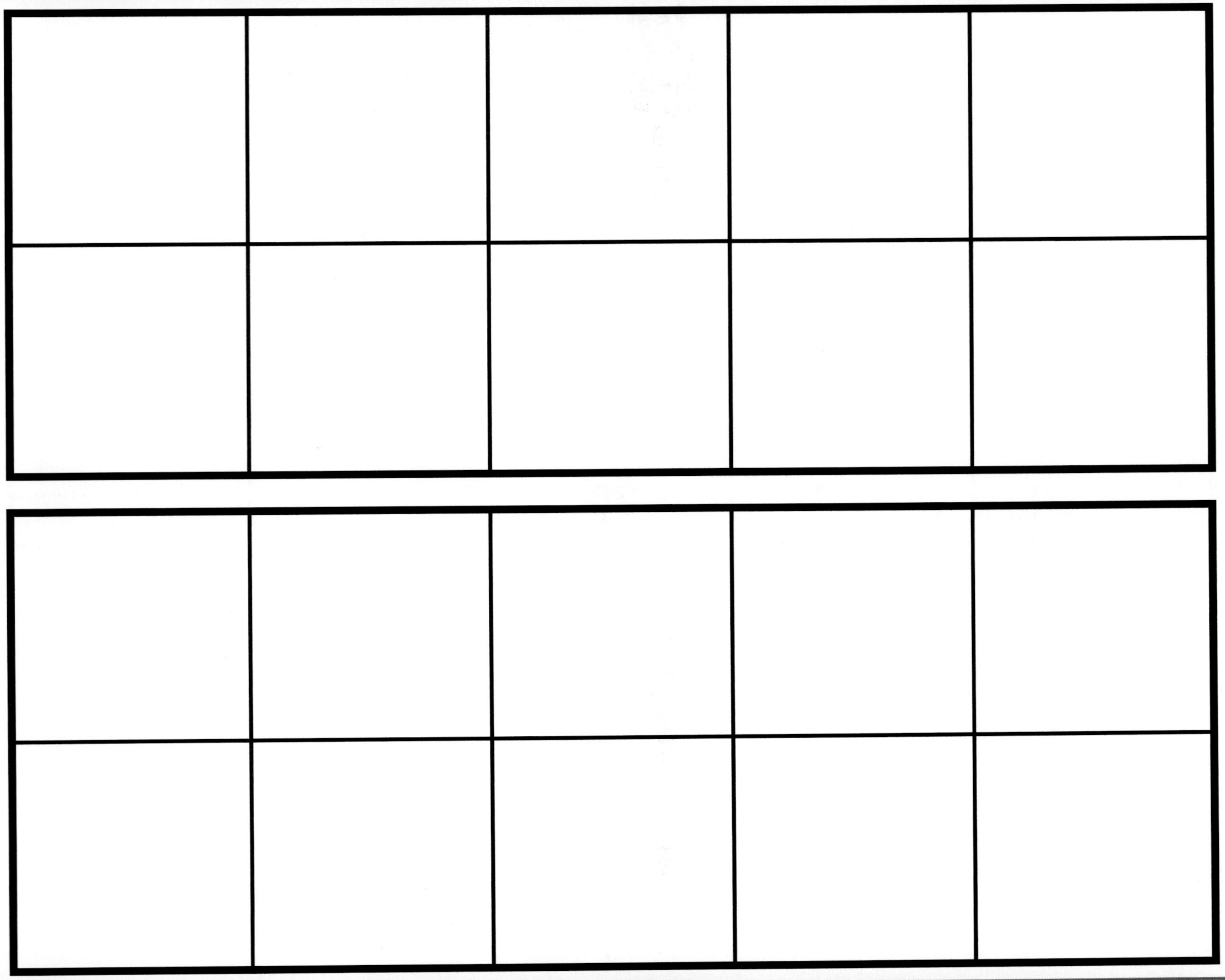

Whole

Part

Part

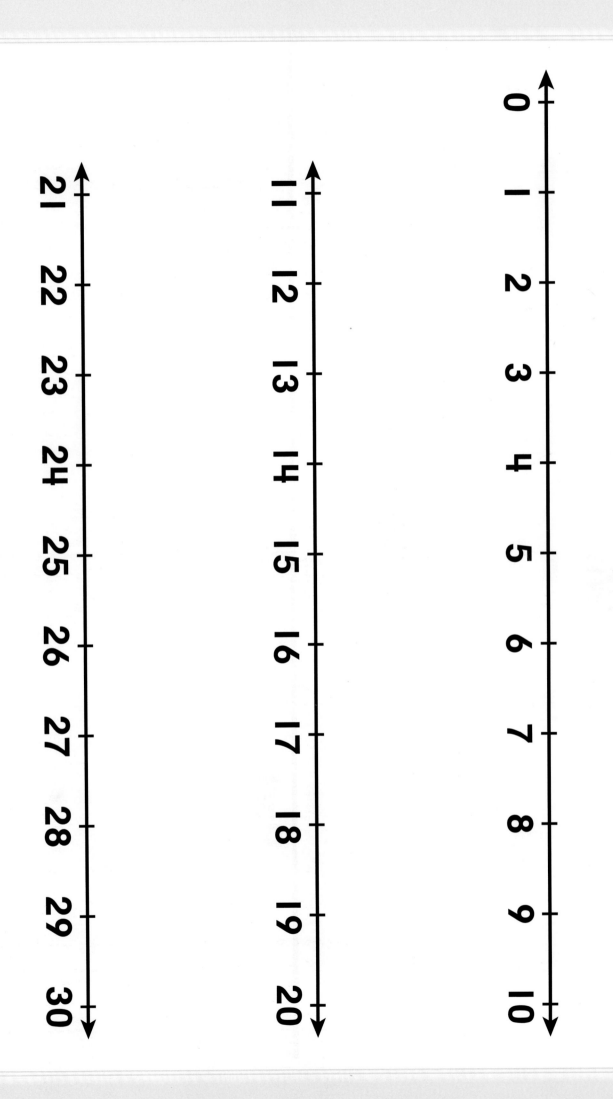